Here's to Friends!
This story could have been
about you too. Childhoods!
We all had 'em! So here's a
peek into a kids' thoughts.
Enjoy,
Tom Thornburgh
jtomthornburgh@gmail.com

No Tomfoolery

Growing Up Country
in the 1940s

James Thomas Thornburgh

ISBN: 1499341849
ISBN 13: 9781499341843
Library of Congress Control Number: 2014908410
CreateSpace Independent Publishing Platform
North Charleston, South Carolina

DEDICATION

To Mom and Dad and my three sisters Sue, Kathy, and Mary Beth. To all my family and kids Will, Amy, Beth, and Melanie who cheered me along the way. And to all my other friends of all sizes, shapes, and colors in the whole world who keep helping me and anyone else interested in growing up. And to all the ones I haven't even met yet. A special thanks to all the wonderful people with whom I've worked together over the years and who have courageously shared pieces of their life's journeys with me. Everyone's the greatest book inside! Then to Gabe, my close, traveling grandson and sidekick who kick-started this story trip. And to all the grandkids, Gabe, Simone, Leah, Ella and Maya who listen to their inside voices and tell you exactly like it is. Then especially to my little granddaughter Leah who is a hero for autism, teaching us trust, compassion, and humility, who never gives up and someday will be telling us in her very own words her very own thoughts also.

ACKNOWLEDGMENTS

The story's been there all this time. Just wasn't in the right mood or didn't take the time to do it. As years get along now, I've finally given in to a little more day dreaming and reminiscing. I only interviewed myself and that's probably enough right there. Mom and Dad were real solid support and comfort during my growing years and always urged me to not mumble and express myself, so I sure didn't want to let them down. My three sisters Sue, Kathy and Mary Beth were also deeply kind and caring and continue to keep an eye on me even now. And I certainly want to give thanks to those three outstanding elementary teachers in that little country school who stood over me and taught me in spite of myself. With their help I actually learned how to make the words going into this book. No more dangling participles for me! And a special thanks to all my grade school friends and all the adult characters, especially Farmer Carroll, who sparked my imagination and taught me all the important stuff that school couldn't. These people were a rich source for my gaining a fuller sense of the many and various personalities that exist out there. Special thanks also goes to the Bruster, Bruce Beckwith, my trusted buddy who in the first grade began sharing my story, then laughed through some of the recent drafts with me and refreshed my mind on many early experiences.

Bumbling along at a low tech level myself, special thanks goes to my son Will and his loving wife Aliza for setting up this computer machinery giving me confidence to begin this two-finger typing project. Then Kyle and Julia helped further this computer stuff beyond any of my understanding. And another special thanks to Jason Smith, another one of those wizard-types, for kindly sitting with me and patiently scanning all these old photos and captions into the manuscript. I also want to give a special tribute to James Hendry for thoughtfully sharing his publishing experience with his spellbinding book *A China Story*. He then introduced me to Nicole Lezin who kindly steered me toward CreateSpace who all have been totally responsive and patient with me in creating this book from my story. Bruce and I also appreciate Connie and Ron Hamilton for taking such good care of us during our recent trek back home to reminisce and check things out. And Jack and Karen Miller for giving us such good advice and precious photos.

Of course I might not have ventured on if it hadn't been for this trusted and thoughtful army of early readers who endured my early drafts with their keen eyes and generous feedback letting me know there was some hope for this project. They're all totally worth knowing and here they are! Marty Schram, Bud and Marge Pray, Allen Hutter, Susan and Jim Manley, Andrew Carpenter, Mary Donahue, Cynthia Rosenwald, Brian Levine, Lydia and Paul Vernaglia, Deedra and Larry Radanovic, Dick and Carol Gross, Sheila Weiss, Ann Tartaglia, Ann and Steve Werner, Linda and Dick Riegelman, Joel Chinitz, Cathy Wood, Gina Jackson and Sherry Stevenson. That's a whole flock of folks, but it proves nothing's done alone. It's possible I just may have another friend or two out there.

I want to give a special heartfelt thanks to my dear wife Gail who put up with her share of my crankiness and held my hand through this story again. Simply with her presence she affirmed once again that my actually growing up, finding her and listening more is every bit worthwhile. And of course the kids; Will, Amy, Beth and Melanie for the glimpses into where I'd been before as a child and cheerfully keeping this creation moving ahead. And a huge applause to all my grandchildren, and any other kids hanging around, who also give me much joy and a genuine peek into those early childhood years. So here's a special hug to Gabe, Leah, Simone, Ella and Maya! Thanks Gabe for not getting too bored with my tales, igniting the spark to get this thing going and squeezing this story out of me. Thanks to my loving teenage granddaughter Simone with her keen intuition and thoughtful insight for giving this grandpa such kind understanding and reassurance. Thanks to my five year old granddaughter Ella for being the sparkle she is, full of curiosity, enthusiasm and surprises lovingly inviting much reflection on my own early childhood. Thanks to my toddler granddaughter Maya every inch the cuddler and charmer letting Grandpa know in no uncertain way what a joy it is to be alive. And a special love to my special granddaughter Leah, for whom words cannot express enough, for allowing us all to become totally aware of how tremendously lucky we are to speak out our inner voices as she works so hard to find more and more ways to share hers! I'm a lucky man and can't thank them all enough! But Mom's rule is "Don't say can't!" so I'll just have to try.

TABLE OF CONTENTS

INTRODUCTION

Now, where did this story about a little kid growing up during and after World War II in the '40s and early '50s come from? Going back, I used to regale my all-ears grandson Gabe with tall tales from my childhood. That got him in heaps of trouble with his teacher while he retold them to his whole class. There were ardent discussions between Gabe and the teacher about "fact or fiction." Well, tall tales aren't exactly lying! Just stretching the honest Truth. I might have stretched 'em a little too far. Anyhow, that's what his teacher nailed him for. Some quick repair work over the phone helped out, and Gabe's a tough survivor, so he said, "Gramps, you gotta write those things down!". So it's all his fault! He made me do it. You learn a lot from kids if you listen. That's when I got my little Steno pad out and started jotting things down.

Well, before you know, these jottings piled up more and more, and I couldn't stop. I began having a real, involved conversation with myself, like a four-year-old kid, long years ago, talking right straight to me, and then me, a seventy-three-year-old grandpa, talking right back again. Really getting into it! As both of us listened to each other seventy years apart now, that conversation drifted and dragged me right back into those early childhood years of the '40s during the war and early '50s making my way through those early growing-up years. Once is enough! But my goodness, I was living it again! Yesterday seemed like today. I'm much better at remembering experiences than I am names. This all recalled a specific time and place but also the adventure of growing up that runs around inside all of us no matter where we hail from in the world or what all our circumstances are. Just part of being alive!

Things I recall really seemed crucial as a kid and surely were. On a global scale, things can look pretty small; however, for me as a kid, this inner world of thoughts was enormous and just about everything. It was all my own world, with others coming in and out. I guess that chunk of my life back then had simpler and cleaner edges to work with. Looking back, those confusing things are probably more visible now. The whole world can't see it, but for every single little kid, it must seem like a mountain full. So I guess if you multiply one kid's inner voice a few billion times or more, then you have the whole world with kids truly speaking a simple, uncluttered, direct, and candid Truth! Unless, of course, they're pulling your leg a little. Those tricky little guys!

It's a little like a newborn, tiny, tree root ball—shoots not all spread out or tangled up yet. Just a few roots squiggling around for direction, coming and going, and shying away from the easy, soft soil, but feeling their way around clay and sharp rocks to grab a good hold and keep from getting all twisted up inside. Kind of like cooking from scratch to see what kind of cookies you might come up with. Not too much flour and fat but just the right amount of sugar. Lots! Raw dough's the best! Not fully baked yet! I tried to make a cake without eggs once. Heavy as a brick! Hey! You try things out, and then you know! Making choices and taking chances. Lots of incredible surprises! There's a longing for something more every day. Most times though, things just seem to happen! It's a matter of digging and discovering.

In a world of simple innocence, kids get a whole load of meaningful things done. Not just talked about! Just figure it out and do something about it. May not be so simple for them, but kids can cut through bucketfuls of man-made clutter that grown-ups pile high. Kids may spot things we can't.

Many of us find crime dramas and mysteries riveting to watch and read; however, there's nothing more thrilling for this old guy than the twists and turns in the mysterious plot of a child's early growing-up years. That's before they get all scrubbed and trimmed up really nice and neat, and canned up airtight Mason-jar style. There may be a yearning to hang onto those innocent childhood years, but we know from this side, permanence doesn't exist. So losing it but taking along whatever we can is part of the deal!

The professors proclaim it's best to only write about what you know. I guess in this case, that would be me. So that's my new assignment here in this grandpa's new school room. Writing about an early me and my adventures there! Not just a school lesson but a little bit or two about life also. This story might have a plot, but it's hard to know where it's going, so just enjoy the voice!

Since those doggone kids are candid to the core, makes sense to listen really closely, because those four-year-olds can only talk within their given age. Things can seem all mixed-up for you, but that's the way untethered little kids think. Stuff just freely pops into their heads, so everything's not all in its proper place for you here. No complex structures or high elaborations exist yet, so things can get a little disorganized, which begs us to fill in the gaps and not get too picky. See through kids' eyes how they're trying to keep their footing. Not too tight! Not too loose! It's the listener that really counts! Gabe stuck right in there and let me ramble on some. You can just hear these innocent little folks picking friends, making it through the grades, taking trails, and avoiding hazards. Their traveling trip through unmapped territory is to truly be themselves. It's all like takin' the back roads and not being quite sure where you're going.

Since this effort began with a few scattered thoughts for the grandkids, the question became what to share, how much to reveal, and how open to be. Since those guys are pretty frank with me, I decided no hiding here, and turnabout is fair play. I figured this was a chance for an open offering without hedging to tell it like it was! Why be shy!

Not sure just how anybody really makes it in life. Sometimes it looks easy, but no matter what your luck and where you're coming from, it's surely not. Lots of things get lost in life, but somehow you find yourself out there somewhere. Many are still trying. Easy to take a wrong turn! Ever crash a snow sled into a tree? Otherwise, you can slide til dark. In this haul, got to know when to push and when to pull!

Every kid's different, but playing hard almost anywhere leads to learning. Trying all sorts of stuff, kids learn by doing, looking, and listening to others, and most of all, to themselves. So here's how one little kid tried it. Me! Or it could have been about Bruster, Jackie, Dickie, Eddie, Rosie, Ruth Ann, or even you. Gotta see what fits! Try it out!

This story can be for anybody still growing. Anything goes! This story's not for the choosy or those already there but for anyone around who wants to travel alongside a little kid growing up in the '40s and early '50s to see what it was like.

This trip might recall plenty of tussles going on inside ourselves back then—lots of urgings and people pushing and pulling this way and that. Things that can twist you all around and take you smack out of the middle. Hey! Maybe that's why I'm letting you in on this. Might help you keep your balance and not fall off, especially when those old greedy ideas of wanting too much fill your head and can dump you right off your stool. It really doesn't matter whether you're driving the big draft horses or little goats or just trying like anything to sit still in a school desk or church pew, dreaming about all those delicious, sweet, tempting candy bars. Strange! Some good folks can really help you if you listen, and others can get you all messed up. It's no fun to be left out and all alone, so picking people is a big part of this story, too. Words are totally inadequate to describe the tight bonds we had. We just had 'em, but not yet all the perfect words to talk about 'em.

So that's some of my struggle. Grandchildren, being a little almost like real human beings, go through some of it, too. So it's a good idea to help give them a little leg up. Although we're all pretty much in the same boat, they've got a lot more complex things jostling them around now than we ever thought of back then. For some of us, things might have been simpler in 1944. For others, probably not. Depends on where you came from. There's a wide range of troubles and suffering out there in the world. Simpler for some might have been better, but that's a hard one to call. Only each and every kid can give you the answer on that. So this story is not an authorized instruction workbook that nobody listens to anyhow. This is no let's go potty manual for building early childhood skills, but may be just a little help for you to stay out of trouble along the way and see if good things happen. If you haven't grown up yet, this book might help you, even if you're an old-timer. We're never finished! Sometimes kids speak the Truth for all ages. Maybe you can just settle back and see how we come out on the other end. You might even call this more like a fightin' struggle going on inside than just a bedtime story.

Moving on to the country in 1947, things seemed freer. More imagination was used out there, thinking up all kinds of things. No copycatting and no city sidewalks to stick to. You had lots of choices whether you wanted 'em or not. Just trying this and that for better or worse. Didn't have to ask! Just did it! You had to use your kid wits. Got to pick who was good to hang around with and who wasn't. Could even choose trying to become famous if that was actually something you really wanted to go for. Of course, we thought we knew exactly how everything would turn out back then. Not so sure now! Some good and some not! Looks easy from here, but not so!

Well! I'm rattling on and doing most of the talking here, so it's about time to get a little sneak peak at a little kid from another bygone era that might even have some relevance today. Some of these reflections might be familiar to you. Even though Mom and Dad sure tried their best, my family and friends today are still after me to look a little wider and listen a little more. Of course, you don't know me yet, but that's OK, because I don't know most of you, either. So, since I'm becoming more human now and closer to arriving, let's get to it and see how it goes.

If you have any helpful tricks for me, just let me know. And if you have any extra help for my old friends Bruster and Jackie, they'll take it, too. Old friends like us aren't so picky anymore, and we'll share it all anyhow! Take advice from anywhere we can get it! With all the inside struggles going on, have to fight hard!

Remember! When you're telling this story as a little kid, you can't put in a whole lot of elaborate stuff or doctor it up all fancy! Has to be told to you like kids see it, and they just talk like they talk! Right in their age. Can't get too picturesque about all the characters, but you'll meet 'em all along the way. Now, the snapshots were taken with Dad's old Brownie box camera he gave me. Hope you have a good eye, because they're a little blurry. You'll note I spelled better as I went up the grades, and I'm proud of that.

Now, life starts with Mom and Dad, so let's drift down back there to tell you a little about them and the rest of my family. And living during World War II with my grandma and grandpa before we moved out to the country, I'd better let you know about them, too. Then, the others you'll just run into along the way out here in Fowlers Mills, Ohio.

Mom was born in Boston, and Dad in West Virginia. That's an unusual combination right from the start. I'll tell you about 'em first, 'cuz they're the ones who started it all. You'll know Mom right off, 'cuz she was 5' 9", and Dad was only 5' 7" on his tiptoes. That's a rarity there! Kind of a unique pair! Some said it wouldn't work.

They met as leaders in a New Hampshire kid's camp and just held on right close together after that. I never was quite sure who the real leader was. Both of 'em I guess. Two strong forces coming in different ways. Dad just told Mom back down there in West Virginia, "If you're going to say yes, be sittin' on Aunt Eve's front porch in the mornin', and we'll drive over to Louisa, Kentucky, to the justice of the peace!"

So there she was, all smiling and dressed up, sittin' pretty, and that's what they did in 1937. And the justice's wife gave them milk and cookies, celebrating the ceremony Methodist style. Not a drop of caffeine. No, sir! Yep! They sure knew how to party hardy, and they were happily stuck together for nearly sixty years. They even stuck solder on Mom's thin little old worn out eight dollar wedding band (bought on the fifty cents a month plan) just to make it last forever. What a nice, long, beautiful ride!

Mom was the one who really made you mind and made up most of the rules. She was tall and straight and not one of those little, jumpy, frilly, chatty types of moms. Didn't talk a lot, but when she did, you'd know it. Let you run all around the fields and hills all free, but when she said, "Be home at six for supper!" you'd better be there! She gave you that one long look that told you exactly what was on her mind. And nobody better mess with her kids, 'cuz she would take 'em on. Yep! Mom was a thinker inside and stuck to her guns. She'd rather think a whole day thoroughly on something and wait until the next day to let you know. She took a long look at things from all sides, and then, when she made up her mind, she knew it, and you did, too. She meant what she meant! That's why everything in here is the Truth. She was strong on the outside but soft as mushed bananas inside. She wasn't a little cheek squeezer but a hugger for real! When you got sleepy in the car, Mom put her arm around you and buried your head in her lap, so you could hear her heart beat. Yep! Mom was always there for you!

My Dad was a curious type who wandered and wondered all about. He was always "on watch," navy style. He was just one who couldn't go by a closed door without opening it up and peeking inside. He was always thinking on the outskirts and not so much in the center of things. Mom said his navy tattoo should have been Born to Roam. He had more friends and talked to more people he didn't even know in gas stations, down the hall, or anywhere else. He'd forget where he was until Mom told him. Dad was a gentle, playful sort of guy who sure knew how to look on the funny side of things. He didn't need any joke scripts all written out for him! He was funny even when he was sleeping and spittin' through his nose. One of those doggone sunny types.

Both of 'em would give you the shirts off their backs. Don't ask Mom, though, 'cuz she had some big ones underneath. Dad was shorter than Mom. It's supposed to be the other way around. But Dad had a huge chest; short, twenty-seven-inch legs; and enormous, thirty-four-inch-long arms that would reach out to everybody. That was Dad for you! Dad could get really misty eyed easily. Mom didn't much, but she sure could bust loose buckets of tears. I saw her a couple times! Dad was a real dreamer but dumb like a fox! He wasn't the spanker in the family. That was Mom's job! But you couldn't push Dad too far, or you'd really see that stubborn streak explode. Saw it happen once or twice!

Now, big sister Sue could be a little snarky and get in a tizzy with me at times, but she's always been the kind who likes everybody else, and they like her back. She never knew what an enemy was. She pretended to be a dim-wit like *My Friend Irma* on the radio, but she could make the meanest old sourpusses fall over laughing. She used to love acting funny and impersonating Johnnie Ray and singing "Cry." She was one of those good-looking tomboys awhile and later became everybody's prettiest top girlfriend. As a kid she had long pigtails and long legs and could really run; she scraped her knees a lot. Sue knew what was in my mind all the time, so I didn't even have to shout out loud for a cookie and milk. She had it right there for me! She was practicing up with me, 'cuz later on in life, she continued taking care of everybody there is, whether they needed it or not. You'll see a lot of her in action, 'cuz she and I were Mom's prewar babies.

Little sister Kathy, seven years my younger, was one of those extra-chatty toddlers, grabbing this and that and chattering all the time. One little ball of excitement! But boy, she had a mind of her own, which she never gave up, and watch out if she didn't get what she wanted! She still loves to play and giggle loud. Still quick and funny! I'd put her on my back with her little red cowboy hat on and run and snort her like a horse all over our little farm. Boy! Was I glad when she got toilet trained and stopped pulling my hair out. Kathy was stubborn to her stirrups, but what a hoot!

Mary Beth was ten years younger than me and came along in 1951. And I've got to tell you, she was the cutest little baby! She had only one-and-a-half years to get a little of that farm life into her before we moved on up to the county seat of Chardon in 1953. So she was more typical of that small-town type of girl and didn't have so much country in her! She was brought into the world on the last day of the year 1951, and she brought forth the joyous ringing of our New Year's bell, followed by the peal of Pearl Freeman's bell ringing out all over Fowlers Mills Valley. Back then our new baby Mary Beth mostly burped, spit up, and pooped, but she sure was cuddly! Little old ladies just couldn't keep their hands off her. I mean, how much can you really say about babies? They're just kind of there, waitin' to be fed. And that was my whole main family right there!

Now, starting this story, we were living with Grandpa and Grandma Wright in 1944 in Berea, Ohio, while Dad was off in the war. Grandpa was born in a farmhouse in upper New York state with a father who drank too much and never worked a whole lot and a little Dutch mom, Phoebe, who pushed Grandpa to make something of himself. Grandpa heard a calling one day to make the world a better place and became a Methodist minister to stamp out poverty, drunkenness, and just plain, wicked, old evil. Two older sisters, Ada and Ida, sent him on to college. Grandpa had a big stomach and saggy cheeks that fell down under his mouth, which all shook when he laughed. And boy! Could he laugh the loudest! And his white hair sitting on top of that big head was the shortest. Like a buzz cut. Of course, he was the one who'd bounce you up and down really hard on his knee and yell the loudest. That's until Grandma made him stop, so we didn't throw up on their oriental rug.

Grandma was tall, slender, and straight as an arrow. She kept a good lookout and was always interested in any ideas we had. She was practical and matter-of-fact. She kept all her pennies in a jar and little pieces of used soap in a wire basket to make soap suds. She wasn't so cuddly, though! The frigid weather where she grew up in Watertown, New York, does that to you. She knew our every step but didn't let on much. She loved barnyard cribbage and enjoyed a good laugh but always played her cards close to her chest. Every year we could expect an early Christmas present of pj's sent directly, all carefully gift-wrapped, from Spiegel's catalog. The size and fit were exact! Not exactly a toy but necessary indeed!

Now, Grandpa preached really loudly in a huge black robe to hide his belly and sounded so serious while I tried to sit still in the pew and crayon in my book. When we got back home from church, he'd take off that coat and tie, let his gold pocket-watch chain dangle down, and giggle away through his nose, mimicking the pious little old ladies in the front row. Then he'd roll up his sleeves to avoid getting greasy and yell, "Flossie! Are the mashed potatoes done?" Then, with a flourish, he would start carving up the roast beef or big bird with the sharpest of carving tools. His trusty whetstone was always right by his side to sharpen things up. He could wake the dead, he laughed so loud. But his most favorite time in life was wearing his old tennis shoes, torn pants, and a floppy old, sweaty hat and handkerchief on his head, playing a farmer scything, burning brush, or walking down the middle of a stream fishing for trout. Grandpa loved to do just what he wanted to. He even took me right smack out of school in fourth and fifth grades, so we could drive old Route 20 together up to New Hampshire to open up the old cottage there and burn more brush. He knew what was best for me! It was like he was a big kid again traveling, and I was his best friend! I lost myself up there on Hedgehog Hill for a whole day once, but when we found each other again, he stayed right by my side and never let me go. That's how close we were!

My West Virginia grandma was a little quiet. She just thought that nobody could do anything wrong. Never said a hateful word and took care of everybody even if she had to travel two hundred miles by bus. Around her, you always felt the most important. If you told her a story or showed her something you made, she always wrinkled up her nose, smiled, and said, "Oh precious!" She was tiny, but boy, she could really bustle all over the house. She moved five times as fast as my West Virginia grandpa. She loved poetry and Ralph Waldo Emerson, painted five watercolors hanging up today, and read lots of little newspaper clippings she saved forever. Grandma went to college in Charleston, West Virginia, and back to the Henderson Holler farm to school-teach all her brothers and sisters there. But she really spent her whole life taking care of people—old, sick, and little.

My grandpa in West Virginia wasn't the brush-burning type and never set the world on fire, but Fritzie was the sweetest old man. Like Grandma, he never said a nasty word in his life. In fact, he never really talked a lot. He was Grandma's right-hand man! Grandpa's job was being the Christmas package wrapper, and he saved tied-up balls of string to use forever. He took fast walks, but that's the only time he moved fast except when helping Grandma. All my aunts loved him, and we did, too. They said he was a true Southern gentleman and walked straight up like one, too. He usually had this sweet little smile hidden under his glasses.

So I've introduced you to my main family, and we'll have to go on from here. And later you'll meet some pretty girls who are a bit shy but so kindhearted, never angry, and just have a way with boys. And then there'll be some boys who really didn't mess up the rules, seemed to know where they were going, were easy on the teachers, and played it straight. Then others who never seemed to catch on to the rules or just couldn't keep up with them if they tried. And some just never got out of the city soon enough, and it's a shame they never quite caught on to the country life. But you'll see all kinds of kids. And of course, farms have farmers, so we sure had some of those. You'll meet 'em. I guess that's the point of reading the story! It sounds kind of interesting, so I might even read it myself. Remember, though, it's through a kid's eyes, so we can't get too fancy and high falutin' here! Have to take 'em as we see 'em!

And how about thanks to Mom and Dad for making me and to grandpas and grandmas for making them, and to all the other people for making everybody else. And thanks for the memory while I still have it. And here's to the boys of Munson Township and Fowlers Mills and to the girls, I guess, too, for making my life real! I might be getting there, but not sure how, considering all the trouble they put you through. And

Gabe! Please don't go ratting on me to your teacher! It's all the Truth, and if you don't believe me, just go ask Mom or Bruster. They never knew how to lie! Heck! We could have called this book *Bruster and Me*. We knew all the answers 'cept the ones we didn't. The rest of you now—just take a little trip back to World War II time with me, and see how it goes!

CHAPTER 1

WAR'S OVER

Hey! Listen to me! I'm four now! I gotta tell you something! The war's over! Harry bombed 'em! And I'm the first to know. Gotta tell Mom! Nobody knows it! Just me! Pots and pans are banging all over the street. Lots of noise and car horns beeping away. Everyone's shouting, "We won! We got 'em! No more Tojo! No more Hitler!" No more boom, boom, shooting games! This is exciting! Grandpa, that one with the little white hairs, is tossing and throwing me up in the sky. I'm getting dizzy and ready to throw up. Grandma's getting us lots of chocolate, red, and white ice cream all stuck together like our flag stripes. We get lots of ginger ale like when my tummy gets sick. Grandma got some Jell-O one time and made a pie. Mom says ice cream and apple pie are America. She says, "We do it for the war," but I like Grandma's raspberry pies better. I've gotta find Mom and tell her! The radio says it's August, 1945. Boy! It's hotter than birthday candles!

Boy! No more letters from Daddy telling me to be brave and take those scary showers, get my hair all wet with soap, and get all clean like the brave sailors do in the navy. Mom said I drowned when I was a baby, 'cuz I don't like my hair wet. And I can do it my own self anyhow! Daddy's really going to be proud of me. No more naps in this stupid crib! I can jump out of it, anyway. Not going to hear that plane flying around any more. Mom says, "It's protecting your father." He's on some island over there behind the Terminal Tower.

17 April 1945

Dear Tommy,

Tonight the big ship that Daddy is on passed by an island that was all prettily lighted by electric lights, and it looked so friendly way out here in the big ocean. It made me think of places like Berea and Shaker Heights when the sky is dark and the lights are turned on in the houses.

It is just about your bed time now, and I am smiling over something. You see, where I am it is tomorrow for you. Where you are is yesterday for me. I won't go into all that because you would just get mixed up and mother would have to take time out to explain it to you. When you get to be a big boy and go to school you will find out about things like that. No, I'll tell you what I'll do. When I get home I'll show you how it happens.

Mother tells me that you have been such a good boy. I'm so glad to hear that you don't break up your toys and things any more. Toys aren't so easy to get these days and I knew you will want to be a real good boy and take care of the nice things that people give to you. Later on you can get some new ones when those you have now are worn out.

Daddy just washed his hair under the shower a little while ago. It feels so good. I do it every chance I get so that I can keep nice and clean. Mother says that she has a little trouble with washing your hair. I was quite surprised because I thought you liked to let mother wash your hair. You must keep your hair nice and clean just like you keep your body nice and clean. Your hair will look better and will comb a lot easier too. I wish you would be a good boy and let mother wash it. I wash mine quite often. All the sailor boys and all the officers like to keep their heads clean. They don't mind the soap. They close their eyes real tight and breathe through their mouths when they wash their hair under the showers.

Well, son, Daddy will stop now and write a letter to Sue. She wrote me a fine letter not long ago. Why don't you write me one? I'd like to get one from you too.

Give mother and Sue a big kiss for me. Take good care of them while I'm away.

Lots of love,
Daddy

Daddy says I'm good I didn't break my toys, but I wasn't being too good getting my hair washed. He writed me a letter to tell me that.

22 APRIL 1945

DEAR TOMMY,

I HAVE JUST WRITTEN SUE A LETTER,
SO NOW I SHALL WRITE ONE TO YOU. I
WROTE YOU A LETTER NOT LONG AGO, BUT I
KNOW YOU HAVE NOT RECEIVED IT YET. IN
FACT, I THINK IT IS PROBABLY STILL IN
THE LITTLE POST OFFICE HERE ON THE SHIP.

I FORGOT TO TELL SUE IN HER LETTER
THAT I HAD A DREAM ABOUT HER LAST NIGHT,
BUT YOU CAN TELL HER FOR ME. IT WAS A
FUNNY DREAM ABOUT A JAP AIRPLANE AND
SUE AND I WERE TRYING TO GET AWAY FROM IT,

DO YOU STILL GO TO NURSERY SCHOOL?
IT MUST BE LOTS OF FUN, ISN'T IT? DO
YOU PLAY GAMES AND LISTEN TO STORIES?

TOMMY, ARE YOU BEING A GOOD BOY AND
ARE YOU KEEPING YOUR HAIR NICE AND CLEAN
LIKE I ASKED YOU TO IN A LETTER? OH,
I FORGOT. YOU HAVE NOT GOTTEN THE LETTER
YET. WELL, I AM GOING TO LOOK FOR A
LETTER FROM MOTHER ONE OF THESE DAYS
TELLING ME THAT YOU LIKE TO HAVE YOUR
HAIR WASHED AND KEPT NICE AND CLEAN. IT
WOULDN'T BE SO GOOD TO HAVE YOU GO AROUND
WITH DIRT IN YOUR HAIR.

DID THE EASTER BUNNY FIND YOU ALL
RIGHT ON EASTER MORNING? I DIDN'T SEE
ANY BUNNIES, BUT I DID SEE A GOAT CLIMBING
AROUND. I THINK IT WAS LOOKING FOR ITS
MAMA.

BYE BYE FOR THIS TIME, TOMMY.

LOTS OF LOVE,

Daddy

Daddy writed me another one to get my hair washed, but I can be a better boy. My Easter basket had my alive little chickie Purple Peep in it.

Gotta find Mom. Wow! There's Mom. Boy! She's excited! I've never seen her look like that. Mom's crying now. Hope she's not hurt! My job's taking care of her. She has a big smile and is hugging everybody in the house but mostly just me. Why's she crying? If you're happy, you don't cry.

She cried when I gave her all my toys for her birthday. Maybe she'll give 'em back to me. I don't like it when she cries. I feel bad. We all miss Daddy. I want to make her happy. Girls cry, but us boys don't! Not me and Grandpa!

I try to remember what Daddy looks like. I don't remember him, but one time I saw him in a white suit with a big hat and yellow metal things on his hat and coat. He looks like a policeman. There's his picture on Mom's bed. One time Mom let me say things to him on the telephone all the way to California. He said, "I miss you!" and I said, "Hi Daddy!" I want him to beat all the bad men up and come home and visit my family. I'll cook him lots of apples and help with his big suitcase.

Dad is off to war, but we're real happy.

See how excited we are.

I'm a sailor-suit boy.

That's Dad in the navy. Looks like a policeman.

I don't know if Sue misses him. My sister doesn't miss anybody. She just rides her new blue bike all the time. That's all she does in her snowsuit, too. Mom got it with big, fat tires from some big lady in the country for ten dollars. Mom said twenty moms wanted that bike. But Grandpa drived so fast to that lady's house, we got there first. Grandpa says they don't make bikes for children anymore in the war. They just make scrap metal. But Sue got a brand-new old one. She gets everything she wants! I wish I did. Grandpa says they only make big tanks and jeeps for soldiers from scrap. He knows everything about wars! He was there one time.

See how good Sue is to me, and my feet are up.

Mom's happy 'cuz she won't have to stick any more sewing pins into Aunt Gertie's *G* in Daddy's letters. He always writes, "How is Aunt Gertie?" And Mom puts it on top of a map to see where the pin sticks. You won't believe this, but one time it stuck right into Saipan and one time into Okinawa. That's right by California. One time it surprised Mom and me, 'cuz it stuck right into Seattle. That's another island. Made a big pinhole, and Mom laughed and shouted and cried all at the same time again. Only moms can do that. I just can't do all that at the same time, and I can do lots of things! I'm a big boy now, but I never saw that before! Grandma packs up Mom's brown leather suitcase with straps really fast, and Mom's so happy now!

Everybody's smiling now and happy. I'm not! Mom's not going to let us go on the train to Seattle to see Daddy. I miss Mom so much! She's never gone anywhere by herself. And it was me who bringed her all my toys for her birthday. Not Daddy! Mom said Sue would take care of me and ride me on the back of her bike. I don't like bikes anymore! They fall you off and get my boots caught in the spokes. Why didn't Daddy tell me he's in Seattle? Then we can all go! Grandpa says Daddy didn't have time, 'cuz his Caswell ship's screw broke off in the water, and the sailors drived it home fast to fix it in Seattle, so they could drive back and beat up all the bad men. Grandpa drived to the train with Mom inside and drived back only hisself in his purple Dodge.

I'm knowing screws and nails and hammers, 'cuz Grandpa lets me fix things that break. He lets me look in his toolbox if I'm good. I painted my tricycle all blue with a whole can of paint one time. I painted my face and hands blue, too, and my pants and all over the floor. I was a blue boy. LB made me a friend and made me do it! Then Grandpa says no tool box anymore. He said a cross word to me. But he can, 'cuz he's my grandpa! I can't! But Grandpa and I are good friends, 'cuz he gives me a penny for every little black hair I pull out of his head. He only wants the little white hairs. His hair is white, and his last name is Wright. That's funny! Sometimes they say Grandpa's hair is silver, but he wants it white. Grandpa says it makes him smarter! And Grandpa's so smart! He knows everything 'cuz he looks at his pocket watch all the time. He keeps the time. He knows when we're sposed to do things. He tells us the things we can't do. I can't be late or mess up his tool box. He makes us put everything back and makes us follow the rules. He says, "Tommy! Pick that up! Put that back!" If you don't, he says cross words. I don't like rules. I want to do it my own self. I don't know if I will ever be a good boy. I try, but I'm still being bad.

Grandpa loves to make fires and burn grass and trees. He has big arms and a big tummy that shakes a lot. He's a good eater, too, and he can cut up a turkey the best. Everybody wants to see Grandpa do that. Boy! He smiles a lot at me and the turkey, too. And he can really cook big chickens in a big black pot on the fire, too. Makes 'em look like soup. We love 'em and eat the gizzards with the gravel in it, too. That's how they did it on Grandpa's farm. Grandpa loves farms the best!

Grandpa gets cross with me, but he's my best friend. He has a best friend, too, Rabbi Silver, and his hair is silver, too, but black on top. That's funny! His hairs are big. Grandpa only has little ones. He's a preacher, too. That's why they're best friends. I don't call him Mr. Silver. I don't know what to call him. Grandpa calls him Abe. He calls Grandpa Louie. That's 'cuz that's his first name. They eat the same lunch every week behind the temples at Tasty Shop. His friend has one more name, too. It's Hillel. Nobody ever says that name before. Funny, 'cuz he doesn't have a name like Chuckie or Terry like my other friends. He has all four names in just one grown-up. Mom says Sue and Tommy, both our names, at the same time. But I'm Tommy! I wrote Daddy a letter one time all by myself. You can see it's from "YMMOT." That's me!

Told you I knew how to spell my name YMMOT.

See the letter all by yourself! See, I can write now. Sue said it's backward, and I can still run backward. She laughed at me and called me a dummy. But I'm not! Sue knows everything I don't know.

Rabbi Silver can talk Jewish. He picks me way up like a puppy, and I can touch his silver hair. He's nice! Grandpa says only Methodist things. Mom says I can learn Jewish if I want to, but I like his silver hair best. Lots of times Grandpa throws me up in the sky and tells me stories about his farm and his dog Jip when he was a little boy like me. Grandpa and me are the same! We both like farm and puppy stories! I like it when Grandpa bounces me up and down on his knee and sings a funny song.

Here comes, here comes Eddie Finnegan;
He grows whiskers on his chin again;
He's a nice man, Eddie Finnegan;
Let's us do it all again, again!

Boy! Sue and I take turns bouncing so high. Daddy writes Mom letters, too. Here's one, but I can't read it!

Kowloon, China
22 October 1945

Dearest Eck,

We arrived here this afternoon. It is a beautiful day. We are just off Hongkong in a very lovely harbor. Chinese families are coming out in their small boats to look at us and beg what they can from us. Things are appearing from sailors' sea bags which we didn't know they had. There was one boat with an old man and his three daughters. The daughters were quite pretty, so one sailor threw a pair of pink step-ins or panties down to them. I guess he got them from somebody back in the states. The prettiest and oldest of the girls looked as if she were coming out of her trousers anyway. She was cute and had a pretty smile.

There were fathers, mothers, and their little babies too. One woman had her baby strapped

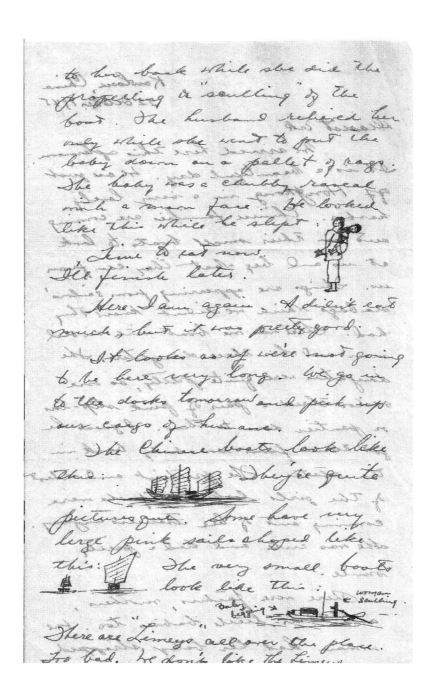

to her back while she did the
propelling a "sculling" of the
boat. The husband relieved her
only while she went to put the
baby down on a pallet of rags.
The baby was a chubby rascal
with a moon face. He looked
like this while he slept.

Time to eat now.
I'll finish later.

Here I am again. I didn't eat
much, but it was pretty good.

It looks as if we're not going
to be here very long. We go in
to the docks tomorrow and pick up
our cargo of hives and

The Chinese boats look like
this: They're quite
picturesque. Some have very
large pink sails shaped like
this: The very small boats
look like this: woman
sculling.

There are Limeys all over the place.
Too bad. We don't like the Limeys.

② This certainly is a rugged country. The mountains and cliffs down by the sea. I'd skate to have to fight a war here. No wonder were being used as a ferry boat.

The climate seems fine, so far. Today was cool and bright. From my port hole I have this view:

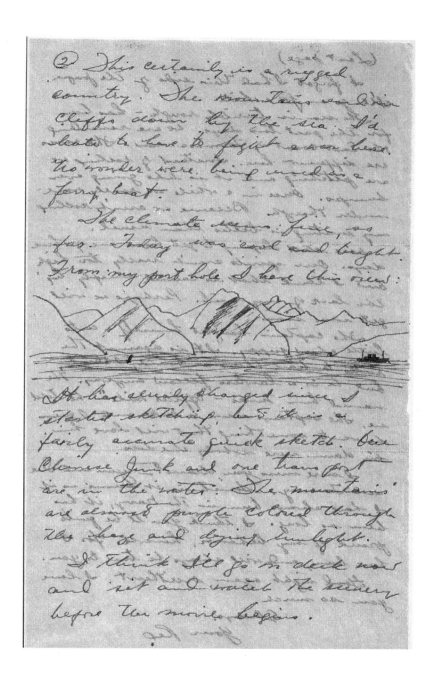

It has already changed since I started sketching, but it is a fairly accurate quick sketch. One Chinese Junk and one transport are in the water. The mountains are almost purple colored through the haze and dying sunlight.

I think I'll go on deck now and sit and watch the scenery before the movie begins.

(Last page)

I forgot I had this side of the page. I'll go on for a while.

The sea is terribly rough — has been for the past two days. We are rounding the East coast of Formosa now. The waves are different here. Instead of rolling we are pitching and it is like going over bumps. Once in a while we really roll under though. Because we aren't rolling my writing is better than usual.

We're still hoping to get home one of these days. Our spirits aren't really too high but I think that is caused chiefly by the lack of any mail. Perhaps we will get some soon.

The captain bought himself a cute little chow puppy. It is against the rules to have them on board, I think, but he is a lawless fellow anyway. He named him Mike — "Officer Mike" he told me. The captain's name is Mike and I guess he wants something that will love him. Sure damn sure nobody else does.

I sure miss you, dearest — you and Sue and Tommy. Sometimes it seems as if I have always been in the Navy, it has been so long. I think you'll be quite proud of my behavior, however, for I have been, and will always be true to you.

Good night again, sweetheart. I love you so much.

　　　　Always,
　　　　　Your Red

Love letters from Dad to Mom. See how they missed each other in the last words.

So Daddy's coming home to visit our family now, and I have to say good-bye to Grandpa. Daddy's going to take us far away, and we won't have to play that dumb song, "Sentimental Journey," again and again and again, on that scratchy old Victrola any more. Mom loves that song, but it makes her cry. I want to break that record so she won't cry. Mom says, "That's our special song." I don't know who "our" is, but it better not be my song! I don't like it! All Sue and I sing is that Pinocchio record all the time and skip around the basement. We skip real slow when the Victrola almost goes off and stops.

Mom says we all helped beat the Japanese at home. My job was to break that little hard red bubble in the white margarine and push it inside to make it yellow butter just like the sailors eat. Mom says it's dye. My thumbs hurt, but I don't cry. I'm too big. It's more fun than going to ask people next door for scrap metal. I'm just helping Daddy win the war! Mom says I'm a soldier at home. My thumbs get tired. It's a lot more fun to pound Grandpa's nuts on the basement floor with a hammer, 'cept those walnuts can stain. And I don't like to play trucks in that sandbox. That's where the cats go to the bathroom, and it smells really funny. You can't let those other little children play in it at all!

See how I'm getting away from that cat box smell in Berea.

Boy! Daddy really surprised us! This big man came right through the front door. It looked like him in his picture. I think it was him. He had on his navy shirt and pants and his policeman's hat. He had a big, white bag and a big, blue navy chest and a big, wood gun inside an old itchy blanket some old Japanese man gave him. The man was in a cave and gave the gun to Daddy to bring home to me. That man was so nice to give me a present like that. He said, "Take this present home to your little boy!" So Daddy did.

Japanese flag Daddy got from the war.

When Daddy opened the navy trunk, it was like Christmas. Lots of presents! Little dolls with strings that danced, little cups with old Japanese people faces, two fans, little umbrellas, two counting things with little balls on them that made lots of noise when you threw them around the floor, and pretty pj's for my mom. Mom's face got red. She smiled so big. She gave Daddy a big hug, too. So hard I think she hurt him, but he didn't cry. He's like me, 'cept he's a big navy boy, and I'm going to be, too. He has lots of muscles inside him. Mom never hugged me that hard. It's so much fun to get Daddy home to visit our family! I don't know where his bedroom's going to be, but we'll get one for him! He can sleep in mine if he wants!

They talk about him all the time, but I never saw him alive before. Mom smiles more now and doesn't stay in her room so much. Sometimes Mom says I have to go to my room to think about it. When I'm good again, I come out. I don't really think about it! I just play with blocks and Lincoln Logs and put Teddy Bear with his one eye to sleep. His other one got pulled out, so he just shuts it.

31

Daddy's home now, and we can really go everywhere and get lots of surprises. I surprise Daddy and pretend I'm sleeping, but I'm really not. We fool each other a lot. Boy! He's fun to play with. He plays more fun than LB does!

When I grow up, I'm going to wear Daddy's navy uniform and be in a war with him. Sue can't 'cuz she's a girl. But Daddy says they had girls in the war they called Navy WAVES, and they would wave at all the navy boys to make them feel better about not going home. But Mom says, "No more wars! That's the last one!" I'm not happy about that. When I get five, I really want to get a real cap pistol and shoot and play war and have lots more fun. Now I won't have any more war fun! So Mom put Daddy's navy uniform in the closet, and he put on pants and shirts like me. He gave me his blue navy helmet to play with. I can sit and rock in it. Now we just have to do other things and sit around and talk. Pretty boring!

Kind of funny! The four of us are all together now, going everywhere the same. Just four of us. I'm four now, and my sister is seven, and Mom and Dad are older than us. I wasn't home when Sue was born, 'cuz she's older than me. I don't know where we're going to go now, but we can think of something. We always do!

◆

One day Grandpa took us for a Sunday drive in his Dodge car. Grandma said it didn't need a horn to get out of the way, 'cuz it says "Dodge" in front. Isn't that funny? Grandma's even getting funny! He drived us to a bus, and we got in, and a man with Dad's Navy hat drived a long time to Orange. That's funny, too. Like something you eat. Everything's funny now! Dad's funniest! He makes lots of jokes. Us boys are funny. Girls don't say jokes!

Us boys are the same, so Dad and I sit in one seat, and Mom and Sue sit right in front of us. Sue won't let me see out the window, though. She eats more than me and is too tall and has big pigtails. I'll cut them off so Dad can see out, too. But I'm having so much fun, I can't talk about it too much.

The bus stops driving at some old store, and we wave to the bus driver and walk all the way to our new lot in Orange. All four of us walk together. I don't know where we're going, but it sure is fun! Only us and no Grandpa and Grandma to make us behave. Boy! It's a long walk, but Sue and I play in the woods while Mom makes us baloney sandwiches from that store—one slice of baloney and two pieces of bread. One top and one bottom! Bears like baloney 'cuz it smells like it. Daddy sits down to smoke a cigarette. That's something all the navy boys learn in the war. Smoke keeps the bears away! We jump over the creek and trees and stuff, and then Mom and Dad say, "It's time to walk back again!" So we walk back down the hill, and every time a car comes by, Dad grabs my hand and holds it tight.

I ask Mom, "Why don't we have a car?"

Mom says, "Daddy is going to be a teacher again," and I know teachers don't have cars. They ride buses and walk on the road like soldiers.

It's hot and dusty, but we finally get to that store again. Dad buyed us a bottle of Dad's Old Fashioned Root Beer and a bottle of Vernors Ginger Ale. I can taste that root beer all day long. First time I ever drinked it, and I love it! Why did Dad have to give some money to that man and not give us the bottle his own self, 'cuz his name's on it?

One time Mom gave me a cross look. Mom doesn't have to say any words, 'cuz the way she looks at you can make you feel bad. Dad kept wanting to hold my hand every time a car comes down the road. He says it's 'cuz we boys walk together. But I just tell him, "I don't take orders from you! I take orders from my mom!" He looks so sad! The way Mom looks at me makes me want to cry. Daddy looks so sad, but he gives me the biggest hug, and I sure like that. His face is scratchy, and Mom smells better, like soap. Better than Dad, but I don't care. I don't know where we're going to go, but I know some place fun. I'm so happy Daddy's part of our family now and didn't go to somebody else's. We talked about him a lot, and now he's right here. So now we can take care of him and make him feel better, 'cuz he was on that Caswell boat too long. And Daddy's so funny, too. We laugh and laugh, and that makes your tummy feel good.

He says, "Be really quiet because the corn has ears!" Boy! I can split my sides laughing so much! He loves cow jokes. He says "Cows lying down on the ground out there is ground beef, and those other cows are out standing in their field!" I don't know what he's talking about, but the Grandma who can't laugh, sure laughs more now, too. And her sides don't even hurt anymore. I know all the houses can hear us, we laugh so loud. We can't stop it. Mom always says, "Don't say 'can't,'" but we just can't. We're having lots of fun now!

Well! We never got a house on that Orange lot, 'cuz Mom says teachers don't build new houses. In the bus, I see people living in basements with no tops on them yet. Mom says they're waiting for more money. I think it's fun to live in the basement. But you know Mom won't let Sue and me live there, 'cuz there's no place to brush our teeth. And Mom says teachers teach children how to read and write and tell them stories. They don't know how to fix bathtubs and windows, so we're going to have to get a house from Grandpa's friend in Cleveland Heights to stay in. Then we'll get our very own house. I hope I get a farm just like Grandpa and a dog named Jip. I really like farm and aminal stories!

◆

Well, it's a really long time to stay inside this house! I'm only going to tell you just some of the terrible things here, 'cuz I really don't want to know they all happened. Well! First they make you go to kiddygarden at Boolevard School. I thought when you get born, you get your teacher picked for you. But that's their job, 'cuz teachers are already there. They're just sposed to make you be good and learn things like Dad does. But they do things to you and make you stay in one place and sit on your bottom all day long. And that's really dumb! And that mean old teacher makes me help a girl take off her snowsuit 'cuz I tripped her. That teacher doesn't know I don't like that girl, anyhow, 'cuz she has curly hair, and she cries like a girl, too. I can't help it if she walks too close to me. Can't she see I'm here first! She's not sposed to come in that door anyhow.

Those big first graders get to be in the playground all the time. They never have to stay inside. I really wanted to be in that first-graders boys' club, but you have to give them your candy bar from my lunchbox, so I didn't stay in that club very long. I'll give them your candy but not mine! They said it was dues for doing something. They didn't let Terry and me do anything with them anyhow!

One time the third graders let me stand out in some dirt they called right field, but I just standed out there while they ran up and down, hitting balls and stuff. I don't know what this game is, but I stayed out there a long time. It's so boring, and after the whole day, the bell rang to go back inside. The next time outside, I just ran around the whole schoolyard all the time, just jumping and yelling. That's lots more fun!

Inside our kiddygarden room, I feel real sad every time Jay stands in the corner and cries. He never talks! He only cries and has an old brown sweater with holes in it. Then that meanie old teacher shooshes us all up and puts her big arm all around Jay and really hugs him. She sits with him while we sit real quiet and color our books. Mom said he's so sad 'cuz he lives in the Hebrew Children's Home and is an orphan in the war. I don't know when his mom and dad are coming back. Mom gives me some of my clothes and candy to give to him. I don't think he ever says any words. He just cries!

Kiddygarden! That's me, third row, second from the right. You can tell Jay in the brown sweater at the end from the the Hebrew Orphan's Home and I are not happy! That's why I'm next to him and take care of him.

The only nice man in that whole school is somebody's Uncle Bill who helps us cross the street to school in the morning. He has a police hat, smiles, says lots of funny things, pats me on the head, and says, "Bet school's going great, huh, kid?" Well! I bet I never told him the Truth about that horrible school! They should push that dumb school down! But I really like Uncle Bill, 'specially when they let us out of that mean school to go home. He's my onliest uncle in Cleveland.

I'm getting into more trouble. Mom sometimes says that's my middle name. Nobody ever calls me my first name anyhow. All I am is my middle name Tommy. I like to hide behind the garage, and nobody ever finds me. And I chase baby birds and stuff. I know Mom doesn't like that. But I'm being a better boy. I'm trying really hard and am showing off to my best friend Terry. I was Superman with a mask on my eyes and fell all the way down the stairs and bumped my knee. I wanted Terry to want me to be his best friend, too.

In two weeks Mom saw little red marks going up my leg and my forehead and says I'm hot. I see lots of airplanes and horns blowing. Mom says, "There aren't any airplanes up there."

Only I see 'em, 'cuz I'm special, just like my West Virginia grandma says! Boy! I was seeing fairies up in the sky and talking funny, too. Dad carried me to the bus really fast. The bus drived so fast right to Doctor Beulah Wells's door who wants to weigh me, but I'm not going to step up on the scale, 'cuz I know she shots you in the bottom if you do! You just can't tell what doctors are going to do to you anymore! They can hurt you! Then she got real scaredy and yelled, "blood poisoning!" real loud. That didn't sound good. She got some bald man and his little girl really fast right out of the waiting room to drive Dad and me to the hospital fast. That Doctor Wells can really yell! She probably yelled all the time in school, too.

You remember Dad didn't have a car yet, 'cuz he's a teacher. I don't remember everything, but all the people were standing around in a bed looking for something. Then they jumped on me and poked a big needle right smack in my bottom. I wished that needle was still lost.

They said, "This is good for you. Will make you feel better! Just in time!" Who are they joking? I wasn't being a bad boy! A spanking feels a lot better. They should have told me about that first shot, 'cuz I'm already five. Boy! I jumped so hard, I bent the needle. I showed them, and they never forgot it! And then to make me madder, those meanies gave me fifty more shots taking turns on my bottom for ten days. They said, "That will make you feel a lot better! Penicillin is so good for you!" I don't think so!

The nurses tried to be nice to me, and one really pretty one gave me a big kiss on my cheek. I'll never forget that! She was so pretty. But everyone was talking about those white blood soldiers fighting those red blood soldiers or germs. I don't know how many germs you have in your bottom, but I have more than twenty, and I can count good, too. So give me all the penicillin you got! Yep! I'm no crybaby! Dad was a soldier, too, and was teaching me how to fight like him. I'll show 'em! Yep! Dad and I are fighters! One crybaby in the corner crib, Howie, screams too much.

"Gookie, gookie, I want a gookie!" I'll give him a gookie right in the mouth! That'll shut it! He should be big like me and stop wearing diapers and being a baby!

Now, this is kind of embarassing, so I won't tell you all of it. But one time a mean nurse with big, black glasses on came in with a big rubber bag and a little hose and went right to work and tried to give me an enema. That's a big hospital word they say a lot. They said the fever was blocking me up.

You learn a lot of important stuff in these hospitals. And everybody always makes a big line every morning after breakfast just so they can see my bottom. Sometimes I think they eat all my toast and jam up, too. They always had some old doctor man with some shiny thing hanging in his ears and around his neck and some big boys in short white coats following him. Everybody wanted to peek!

"Here, take a look at this!" But those doctors just know everything what's wrong with you.

That doctor said I have a "crummy tummy."

And all the other boys in the line say, "You're right, sir! That's exactly what this patient exhibits!"

Boy! They are so smart! And I know that's what I have, too. And the old doctor man was so happy, he just smiled a lot. That makes my crummy tummy feel a lot better, too!

Well! Back to this enema thing. She just puts this big hose right up my bottom and just sits there smiling. She shouldn't do that, so I'll show her. I sure did! I'm not going to give in and go wee-wee, or like some of them call it, tinkle. Nope! Not just 'cuz she wants me to. But I finally got tired of holding it and gave up and wee-wee'd all over her. Boy! Did she jump around and get mad!

She yelled, "Stop that urine!" I yelled back "You're in. Not me. I want to get out!" Then she shouted "Stop it. Don't, you're an eight," or some other big wee-wee hospital word that sounds like that. I'm so mad at her. I yelled back in my big voice, "No! I'm not eight, I'm only five!" I guess she was talking these big hospital words if you get older, but I'm only five! She's so dumb! Then she yelled at me, "You're in trouble! Urine all over!" I yelled "No! You're in trouble and you're in all over!" I was mad and not saying good things! She said I'm drinking too much, so I'm never ever going to be drinking again. I wished she'd stop saying those *you're in* words. They're not nice.

I was so happy to have an older boy in the bed next to me, and we talked a lot. He was really nice and thought I was seven or eight. I told him he should be the nurse. They made me stay there ten days, and my bottom got so sore, like full of pins. At last they let me get out of that horrible place, and I'm never going back!

They said I could go home in a wheelchair, but I said, "No thank you!" I walk right out all by my own self! I hate that place! It smells funny, too, like somebody's bathroom. And everybody smiles at me, like they're so glad I got sick. I miss all the presents Mom and Dad brought every day, little toys and stuff. One time my temperature was too high, and Mom and Dad couldn't see me, 'cuz I was being bad. But that day they got me a little green farm tractor to play with in my sheets.

Well! Fall's almost here, and I'm really busy helping Mom do the washboard and coloring my books and stuff. One time I found a little baby blue jay jumping around in the back yard and wanted to catch him.

Mom said, "You put salt on his tail."

I shaked the whole saltshaker on him, but he was jumping so much I couldn't catch him. It was scary and made me jump. And then I saw Mom and Dad in the kitchen window hiding and laughing. Sometimes moms and dads trick you. They don't tell you the Truth! Why don't they just come outside and help me? This is my very first time to catch a bird with salt. I sure learn a lot from them! They know so much, and I never find out why they're so smart. They know more things than my sister Sue, and she always tells me she knows more than me. Some people just know everything when they get born.

But I know one thing. Sometimes it's not hard to fool someone. One time long ago, an old boy let Terry and me go inside his secret fort right down in the ground in Cain Park Hill. We found some matches. Wow! They were fun to light when us boys learned it. I burned a hole in my cousin David's new hand-me-down jacket. Just a tiny one! I didn't mean to, but Terry did. I'm a little scared now, 'cuz I really played with matches, and that's something you never do until you get married. Maybe I'll marry Terry, but I don't want to yet. I don't know how, but Mom saw that little teenie hole big as a quarter. I told her that big boy took my jacket and put a hole in it. That's what big boys do to little boys like me. I thought Mom and Dad believed me, but maybe not, 'cuz they sure talk a lot now about fires and matches. And how bad they are for little boys. Sue had to go out of the room, 'cuz she must have tattled on me. I never ever, never told anybody another lie!

But everything got bad again! I just hope I get my own house soon, so everything gets better. Well! Here's a terrible surprise! I got these funny red colors all over my back and face. They called it scarlet fever. *Scarlet* is a new color I'm knowing. I look so bad they won't even let me out of my bedroom. That's not a nice thing they do to little kids like us! The doctor came and stuck his flashlight and a big stick of wood down my mouth and made me say, "oooww!" He wants me to throw up, but I won't! He even puts a sign on our house telling everybody I was cornteened for two weeks. That's mean, too! I'll paint all those letters up with scarlet paint just to make him mad. What a mean doctor! Aren't any of them nice to little kids? Now Terry and all the kiddiegardners will know I have this. That's not funny!

This thing I did one time was pretty bad for me, too. I kissed a girl in my first grade, and Mrs. Ramsdel told everybody a big talk about germs. Every kid looked right at me. They didn't look happy, and I don't think they wanted a kiss from me. Boy! This is horrible! That girl is so pretty! I don't have to tell you her name. She's shy like me, too. She has curly hair and isn't really noisy like the other girls. She waved at me one time, and I planned a long time to kiss her smack on the lips. But that telling everybody made me not ever want to kiss a girl again. Those girls won't be a real friend like Terry. Somebody must have told on me. Girls don't know anything, anyhow, and be careful, 'cuz all these girls can give you germs, and then you get cornteened!

And old Mrs. Ramsdel was right. I have one of those horrible germs now and am locked up in my room. The only time I feel good is when my very sweetest old grandma from West Virginia, the one with the little round ball of hair stuck on top of her head, rode in a bus all the way from Huntington to our house just to take care of me. She takes care of everybody! Grandma is the only one who can't get scarlet fever, 'cuz she grew up on a farm in Tioga up Henderson Holler and rode her very own horse Dolly to school. She ate all her vegetables when she was little. One time Dad gave her one of those navy cigarettes, and everybody laughed, 'cuz that was her very first time. And she coughed and squished up her little nose like a little bunny, she was so happy. She always does that when she's happy. And she knows how to say, "Precious! Oh precious!" over and over. That's her favorite word! She is so cute, and that little grandma can take care of anybody, and she sure does! Sure as you're born!

That's Grandma! You can tell she always says "precious" a lot. And that's Grandpa! He belongs to Grandma. He stands up like a soldier.

I have a nice Aunt Bunny, but she doesn't wrinkle her nose like a bunny. Grandma wears the same old dress every day and never ever eats any food herself. She just cooks all the time! I'll tell you about that in a minute. And Grandma's rule is not the same as Mom's.

Grandma says, "Dessert before dinner is OK!" And Grandma has these cute, wrinkly bottoms on her arms that hang down and jiggle around. They looked like water wings, like Mom bought me one time, so I won't drown again. Grandma lets us tickle them, so she can squish her bunny nose up and giggle and say "precious" again. I wouldn't be alive and be her precious boy if it wasn't for Grandma!

———◆———

One time in spring, Dad drove us all the way down to Huntington to visit all the cousins. We were in the back seat, not even fighting the whole day, even though Sue didn't know how to sit on her own side yet. Boy! We were so excited when we finally saw the stern wheelers on the Ohio River with their coal barges and lights on at night! We saw every relative there is alive when we got there. There were more than one hundred cousins, I think. And everybody loves everybody and so did I. Boy! They kiss you and hug you hard and call everybody honey and all that stuff all the time. That's where I liked that kissing thing again. They all kiss on the mouth, too. That's like a real kiss! Old aunts have hairs on their mouths that scratch a little, but they don't hurt. They all talk funny, too, and that's so much fun.

Uncle George and Aunt Willa always give us a special candy bar from their store candy counter, and I counted every single bar for them. I'm always helping out down there! And Aunt Rose, with all this red, sweet-smelling stuff on her cheeks, always gives us a brand-new dollar bill. The one you can't fold up. And Aunt Eve always gives us something we never know what it is, but a thing you can always save in your trunk if you ever need whatever it is. One time when winter was all over, we finally figured out it's earmuffs that you just don't wear in summer!

And Uncle Hickie always shows me his finger stump that got cut off in a saw. He lets me look and look and touch it. That's so exciting to see, and I always ask him to tell me all about it. He tells me he just picked his cut-off finger up, wrapped it up in a hankie, and carried it all the way home, real carefully, to Aunt Nina to see. He was so careful that way all the time! He didn't do stuff too fast like me. That must have made Aunt Nina so happy! Maybe sometime I can get a stump just like Uncle Hickie! On the same hand, too!

**Uncle Hickie with only his finger stump and Aunt Nina
on Grandma's farm in Tioga, West Virginia.**

Now, and you might want to take a picture of this, at dinner time, Grandma comes out of her little back porch kitchen with—and if you can wait and be patient—I'll name all the dishes: succotash, fried chicken, potato salad, sweet beets, sweet peas, lots of sweets, carrots with butter and sugar, pot roast, biscuits and gravy, ice cream and pound cake, raspberry pie, baked beans, cabbage in fat, and shelly beans with lots of bacon grease drizzled all over 'em, and all that really good stuff that makes you strong! Grandma puts lots of sugar in everything she cooks. And lots of Crisco to make you more stronger. And plenty of those white navy beans so Dad won't forget the war.

And I eat everything on my plate clean and more, 'cuz Mom says, "This is real Southern cooking," and that's why it's so healthy for us. That's why I'm getting lots of muscles. Look at Daddy's muscles, and Grandma's his mom. You didn't know that, did you? Well, I'm telling you this to help you know what everything on the table is. Grandpa has muscles, too, 'cuz he had barbells when he was a cadet.

We always keep eating Grandma's one little more goodie bite til our tummies ache. I almost throw up sometimes, but I don't want to hurt Grandma's feelings. Boy! Grandpa is a good soldier! He eats and eats til he busts. Just like Grandma tells him to, and he only stops when she says he can. That way, he doesn't have any trouble or behave bad.

Grandma says, "Now, Fritzie! Eat all your vegetables!" and he sure does. Every one of them! But Grandma never sits down in a chair. She just carries food dishes around so fast all day long, just shaking her bottom and those water wings on her arms, 'cuz she's always bringing in more food. She never eats one time in her whole life. She calls it a labor of love! And at night old, old Great-grandma T sits on the front porch swing and sings "Little Blind Willie" and "Amazing Grace" so high that it makes everybody cry! Dad says, "That's real mountain singin'!"

Boy! She could sing so high even if she didn't know where she was.

44

Anyhow, if you forgotten all about me, I still have this scarlet fever thing! And my West Virginia grandma is still right here by my bed taking care of me. I'm scared Grandpa's all alone and won't eat his vegetables, but Mom said, "He'll be OK!" He's a big boy now! Grandma is the best taker carer of anybody! I just keep thinking about that all the time. I get my very own glass with lots of ginger ale anytime I want to. It's all mine. Nobody else can have it. Just me! So getting sick isn't really so bad! Maybe I can do it again!

And I even drew a picture of my kitty on the wall for her, and she said, "Lawzie me, Tommy! That's precious! You are a wonderful artist!" and she never washed it off. Boy! She gave me lots of squeezes and called me "honey" all the time. And Grandma always says "Bless your heart!", but she should bless my muscles, too. If you ever get scarlet fever, ask my grandma to sit down in one of those buses and come right on up to take care of you. She'll really make you feel so much better! And I never, ever was a bad boy with Grandma. If you ever draw a picture on Grandma's walls, she loves it. Like I told you, she never wipes it off. She just puts shellac on it so you can see it all the time. You should visit her house in Huntington and see all her walls. And Grandma loves poems. But like I'm telling you, make sure you tell everyone there to stay out of the kitchen! Only Grandma cooks in there!

The very first time I ever remember Grandma, she was taking care of Great-grandpa T who was named for me when I was born. He was the first, and I was the second. He was lying right in the middle of the living room in his bed right by the gas fireplace. It burned real hot with blue fire in the middle of summer to make it really hot and cozy for him. Grandpa lit it with matches, but he didn't play with them and burn holes, 'cuz he was older than me. And if it got too hot, we stuck our heads out the window to get our breaths. And Grandma sat right beside Great-grandpa T all the time, patting his head!

One time Great-grandpa T started telling me the story about a little boy hunting for a rabbit in a hole, and he never finished it. You couldn't tell his wrinkles from his smile. He fell right to sleep. I'm the only one that never heard all that boy and rabbit story, 'cuz I never saw him again.

And that's when I became the first, and then I think he became the second, James Thomas. Mom and Dad told me he was going to sleep for a long time, so I guess I'll never hear that story til he wakes up. He'll probably sleep til Christmas when Santa can see him again by the fireplace. And if they don't move his bed, he'll get to see Santa, too. That lucky Great-grandpa T! He was a farmer on the Frying Pan Farm and had a horse stable, and Grandma was little on that other farm in Tioga and rode that horse Dolly I told you about. So I guess I'm going to be a farmer, too, just like them. They called Great-grandpa T "Honest Tom," and I felt a little bad about that, 'cuz I already told a lie one time.

But 'cuz of Grandma, I was getting better with this scarlet fever thing. And I was getting awfully *boring*. That's a new word my sister Sue taught me. She was so smart, but sometimes she got really *snarky*. That's another big word she said. 'Cuz I always had to stay in my bed, she put her head inside the door and smiled at me and tied a new toy to a string on the fishing rod. I pulled it in just like a fisherman. I missed her, 'cuz she couldn't come inside the room, 'cuz of that dumb Cornteen sign. Sue was really nice to me. I shouldn't have said she was snarky. She really helped take good care of me lots, but she never called me "precious."

◆

I've been in this dumb room two weeks with Grandma and lots of toys, ginger ale, ice cream, and old Golden Books I don't want anymore. They knew that, 'cuz when I got all better, they let me get out of that smelly old room, and they burned everything up in a big fire. All my toys, pj's, sheets, and all my best books, like *The Little Engine That Could, Dumbo,* and *The Ugly Ducklings,* but I didn't care. I don't want those smelly old books with germs around here anymore, anyhow! I'll miss that *Billy Goat Gruff* one, 'cuz I really like him!

But one day Grandma got so excited! That ball on top of her head started bouncing up and down, and her little nose squished up. She said, "Let's look out the window!" Well! You're not going to believe this, but it's the Truth this time. We saw this old, gray '35 Plymouth car coming down the road and my dad driving it, sitting inside right up in the front seat. Not the back seat like me. He told me he bought this prettiest car for one hundred dollars, 'cuz he was a navy man. I know that's lots of pennies and nickels in the piggy bank, but I'm really excited. Now we're going to go all kinds of places. Now we can find a farm all our very own!

Anyhow, in two more days, I'm getting out of this dumb room. Mom promised me. I'm going to punch that doctor in the nose. He makes me so mad! Grandma is already packing her old leather suitcase with straps on it to ride that Greyhound (It's really a bus, not a doggie) all the way back to Huntington to make Grandpa eat some food again. It wasn't nice for Grandpa to be all alone, 'cuz he doesn't know what to do if Grandma's not there. I know he didn't even take a bath or eat his vegetables. Grandma's going to have to put more bacon grease on his shelly beans now, so he can get strong again. But Grandma talks to him on the telephone every Sunday, but only for three minutes! It costs too much! But she sends him a letter everyday with one George Washington stamp on it to tell him all about me and how good and brave I am. That only costs one penny. I'm learning a lot about counting money now. I get a dime every year in my Christmas stocking, and I have five now.

Well! Here I am sitting on the running board in our new car. Everybody says, "What a beautiful automobile!" but it looks like an old car to me. It has four doors that open and a cloth roof with cracks in it, but that doesn't matter. This is our very first car! Now, before Grandma could go home, Dad said she needs a ride in the country. So we all go, and Dad drives. Mom says Dad was born to roam! Boy! He loves to drive! He can drive fast backward like he can the other way. He's the best backer-up man and likes to look at things going different ways. But he's not backward like Sue called me one time. He is really good, and most the time he keeps his eyes open. He just learned that in the navy, driving the marines and tanks up the sand in the war. He didn't have a car yet, so he rode them up on navy ducks. That's funny, the marines riding ducks. You know something? I'll be driving just like him in about two years if I work hard.

But then it thundered and rained cats and dogs! Not just a little wee-wee! The roof leaked and leaked, and Grandma, Sue, and I got under a big, black umbrella in the back seat. Boy! We were lucky we brought one. We just giggled a lot and squooshed up under that umbrella, and Grandma made those funny bunny noses again. Boy! That's what you're sposed do in a rainstorm!

Well! Dad the old navy man says, "You have to take good care of your things," so they don't get broken or rusty. So Dad bought some tar, and we boys put all this gooey stuff all over the roof, and it never leaked again. We boys decided that gray wasn't our favorite color. We both like grass, lizards, little turtles, green peas, spinach, and everything that's green! When we get Chuckles candy, I pick the green one out first and let Dad have the yellow lemon one. Yep! We share everything the same! So dark-green paint's what we got, a big can of it and two brushes. Dad and I also like butterscotch ice cream the best. We just like everything the same. Like Mom says, two peas in a pod, and peas are green, too.

We boys painted that whole car green. I paint real good. Remember my tricycle? So I painted the really big stuff like the doors and fenders. Dad only painted around the little holes and the little, teenie stuff. Gosh! It was a beauty! And we called that new car the Green Hornet, of course! I started to call it our brand-new automobile! That's a big word, but now that new '35 Plymouth Green Hornet was like a whole family automobile. Now we can drive all over the country and really find our family farm. And we love that Green Hornet. We always carry two quarts of oil in the back seat to pour into her like a baby bottle when she gets dry. Feed her like a baby!

You know what? Dad and I are kind of the same. Yep! I'm more than half of him, even though I was only born out of half his tummy. Mom born me the other half. We even eat our ice cream in the same little rows, and we hold our spoons right down to the bottom, and not one bite is left. We can really scoop ice cream! And just like Dad, all I can think about is root beer and ice cream. Dad learned how to make root beer floats in the war, and that was one of his jobs, even though they didn't have ice cream there. Us kids ate it all up at home in America! Boy! That was a special treat!

Yeah! Dad and I are just the same! 'Cept he's a little taller than me, but we both roll our new, washed-up socks up in a little ball really nice like he did in the navy. I just did that for one year, but we both like same things, and we're both country and hill kinds of boys. Dad was a hill-billy when he was little with all his cousins in West Virginia. And Dad says they always have hillbilly parties. And that's why they call my aunt Willa Billy. And that's why Dad says one leg's shorter, 'cuz he always walked on crooked hills. And both my grandpas were country boys, too. It just runs in our family!

You should see Grandpa Wright. He can cut long grass in the field, grow razberries, burn big piles of branches with the biggest fire ever, and cook a whole chicken in a big pot over a big fire better than any-body else! I just told you a little bit before, 'cuz I didn't want to spoil your supper. Don't eat hackberries 'cuz they taste bad. But then he'd grab a cluckin' chicken and twist its neck around and take a hatchet and cut off his head. Just like that! Of course the chicken has to run around a little with no head on to show us he could still run fast, but then it gets a little tired and falls down and is really quiet. Then Grandpa pulls out all its feathers. It doesn't even hurt! You've got to pluck 'em. He even cooks the gizzards with that gravel in 'em. Boy! They were good! It wasn't store-bought, either. Grandpa did it all by himself. I mean, Grandpa could preach and stuff and had a big, brown, wood desk with a black pen in the college, but he really was a farmer, and he loved that the best of all!

One time I was seven, and Grandpa drove all of us in his big purple Dodge, and the radio said some guy named Harrison ran so fast they gave him a gold medal. Grandpa was so excited! He yelled and yelled, "Yea! Bones!" 'cuz he was in the same college with Grandpa. Grandpa called him Bones 'cuz he was skinny like me. Grandpa took us out to see Mr. Dillard run and jump over two pieces of wood right there on Beech Street, and Eddie Finnegan was right there in the road with him. Mom says I can't go in the street if Mr. Finnegan's not there. Boy! Grandpa yells and laughs so loud! Makes your ears hurt. He makes me laugh!

Well! I'm not sure how, but I got all better and wasn't sick any more. But we still had some problems. My sister Sue was showing off one time and rode down Cain Park Hill too fast and fell off that dumb blue bike. She broke her teeth and scraped her knees. She shouldn't be too big for her britches and should just ride a scooter like me. You have to be really careful like me! Riding a scooter, you always have one foot on the ground.

What a mess! But everything was all right, 'cuz it was so good it wasn't me. But Sue bleeds all over, so it's my job to walk her all the way home with that big bike and my scooter, too. That's a big job! I did feel so bad for her, though. Funny! Sue's bigger than me, but I had to help her instead of her taking care me. It was me who got the bottle of Merthiolate that we painted orange all over her knees that made her germs go away. I'm the biggest knower about germs 'cuz I had some one time. Boy! We sure have the troubles a lot!

Sue and me helping Kitty.

I'm tired and sit down back of the garage where Mom can't find me. I'm just thinking now I like our family the old way. Mom's happy now, but we have one more boy in our house. And where are we going to put his bedroom? And now Grandpa has to let me go. Bad things always happen to me and nobody else. They all pick on me. It's not fair! And we have to have that new Daddy boy. But he's funny, too. He makes me laugh like Grandpa, and he gives me hugs, so it's going to be OK. He's just like one more grandpa. He's got more years that me, but he and I are just alike. He makes me feel better when I'm sick and gave me a new car, so we can drive all over. And he can drive me away from that baddest school and that Orange place, 'cuz it has bears and no house. I guess Daddy knows how to make Mom and us all happy, so I guess that's pretty good. And now I'm Grandma's special boy, but I'm not ever getting sick again and no more shots. You know something? I guess I'm glad that war's over after all!

CHAPTER 2

OUR NEW FARM BEFORE WE MOVED

I hate waiting! I want our new farm, and I want to get away from all these old bad things. 'Cuz all these bad things are happening to me, I'm not being so good. Even some old alley cat, Dad says, "tomcat," and that's my name, bit a big piece out of my poor little Kitty's bottom. Poor little pussycat! We've got to get our own house and our own farm in the country, so this doesn't happen again! Look at what's happening to me! There's got to be something good! I'm just not a boy who's sposed to live in the city. I've got to be a country boy like my grandpas. It's way past time! Gotta be right away!

Guess what! Finally Mom and Dad find it! Here it is!

Our new farm.

Three and a half acres, pond and stream, a two-box stall barn, two big garden spaces, and a meadow with a hillside and some woods, all for eight thousand dollars just like the realer man said.

It has its own dam, too. There's also an old, eight-room house there, too, if you want it. I know my numbers up to one hundred, and that's a lot of money. Dad's a teacher, so I know my numbers are just right.

That's our New Year's bell.

Our new barn. Nobody knows everything inside. It's a special place!

See how close that cemetery is if we need it!

Sue and me in snowsuits. See right-of-way and back of mill.

Sue, me, and Kathy and bottom of a snowman and Partpart's house.

The next day, Dad drove us all out to the country at one time to see our new farm and a big hill and an old mill with a waterwheel that goes round and round. So right on the dirt road next to our farm up on the hill, there's a cemetery, which lots of people need today. Lots of dead people are up there, and that's where they stay all the time.

Sixty-four people live in Fowlers Mills. I counted all of 'em. They're all alive, but I won't tell you all their names, 'cuz there are too many, and I can't spell them all. But I'm a good counter. I can't spell too much yet, so I hope you can read this. Some of the names are funny, like Bert Partpart. That's like two names, like two parts in his name, and he has a wife, and he gave us the house. Dad says he is a realer steak man but has lots of sheep, too, so he's both. There are no sidewalks, so you can get lost out here. So I'll draw you a map you can tear out and put in your pocket.

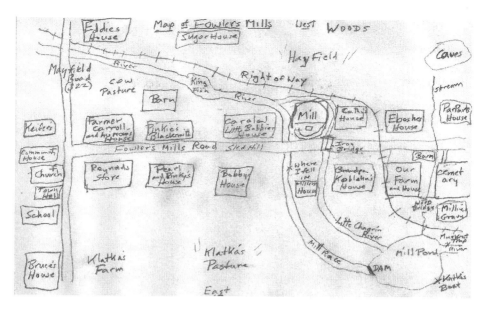

Map of Fowlers Mills.

At last I'm not like those other kids now. Now, I really am a farmer boy, and everybody will know me. I'll be the best boy! Everybody will see me and say, "That's the farmer boy!" I'm finally getting out of that city and going to the whole wide world where you can do anything you want to all the time. Nobody tells you what to do out here! Mom doesn't care! The war's over, and you do anything you want to now! You only have to follow Mom's rules.

Of course I've got to make my bed, feed Tippy that smelly Pard dog food out of a can, and go to school, sitting in front of a chalkboard with nothing on it most the time and a bunch of kids behind those desks. Tippy's Pard food smells so bad, you sure don't want a bite of that. Kitty food tastes a lot better. And with all the stuff we've got to do on a farm, we shouldn't have to go to school, too. I don't know why they make us. It's just too much!

Boy! I miss Mrs. Ramsdel with her limpy hip and short leg. She was so nice! She chose me the leader of the lunch line the last day I was at that dumb old school. I thought I was last, but she turned the line around and made me first. Gotta go the right way! Didn't make me like that school better, but she sent me lots of letters asking me if

I was OK. She really likes me, and I wanted to hug her again, but she really wanted me to go to the country. She just knows I am a country boy. And now she has to make all those bad kids in the city behave better, and I'm not even there to help her. She'll need help with those nasty kids!

But now we have a real farm barn and all those things right on our Fowlers Mills Road. We have two box stalls, one pond with water lilies, and one stream with one falling-down dam that goes way back to this big millpond, and our very own great blue heron that stands on long stick legs right there in the lily pads. And we have frogs that sit on the lily pads. We have one barn room up high they call a hayloft. We have one big dinner bell out back that you can hear ring all over Fowlers Mills and the valley and two big garden places. Of course, we have that cemetery next to us to play in and hide behind the stones and my new dog Tippy.

I'm so glad I have Tippy, 'cuz when we moved, the moving truck took my old Teddy Bear who didn't have any eyes anymore. Mom says he couldn't see anymore and got lost and went the wrong way. I guess that's what happens. I'm not sure. But Tippy is a real alive animal, so you can see what I mean about farms. You can really cuddle up, tickle her, and talk to her. She's not like old Teddy with his eyes and stuffing all falling out. Tippy didn't like cities, either, like me.

My wish had finally come true after all those so many years in the city. I couldn't stand it there! I didn't tell anyone that. I just made the best of it. It was so hard for me for so many years! Now, working out here in the country is like having fun. Life's fun! It's all good! Dad still has to teach, and thank goodness, he still loves driving a long way, so I do all the farming and barning. If I wasn't here, it would just be a big hayfield. That's all!

Since you're just knowing us, here's a little more what our farm looks like. There is a little brook running under our dirt road, with a little pool and a stream with lots of minnows going under some wood boards like a bridge over it. That's where a big, black snake sits in the sun a lot. The stream goes under the bridge, goes past some cattails by some muddy long grass and turtles we never go near, then into the pond, and then falls over the dam. Splash! There are so many names for all these things, but it's all the same water in lots of places. It's almost the same thing 'cuz you can drop a twig in it and watch it go all the way under the bridge and try to catch it. Sometimes lots of names are the same thing, so it doesn't really matter what you call it, just so you know what it is! We mostly just call it our pond. There's a big tree by the pond. We don't know what to call it, but that's where our owl sits at night and blinks his eyes so he can see everything. It's one of those tall quiet trees that stands there like a soldier, keeps an eye on us and lets the stream bubble around behind it.

And here's something! We even have a stone hitching post with an iron ring on top for horses in our backyard, under a big maple tree with a tire swing on a big limb. And there's a path you can run down to our dirt road really fast. On the road you can walk or run right down to the mill or to the pasture across the road or up the big hill to the store, the church, or our new, two-room school. That's if you really want to go there. To get to that school you gotta go uphill both ways. Then you gotta cross big Mayfield road, one of those roads where you gotta look both ways. But you can start going everywhere you want down our path. It really doesn't matter where! You just run.

Dad even showed me how to haul the garbage in a wheelbarrow over the creek bridge to bury it. Boy! I had a lot of work to do, but I knew I could take good care of Mom and Sue on our new farm. There are so many things to get done, you really don't have time to play games or even read a book. The only time you want to play Monopoly or Parcheesie is when you need a little time off and pretend you're sick so you don't have to go to school. You have to rest up. So you just stay in bed and play the game on both sides. I always win, 'cuz a dice always falls off that board when I move my leg, and sometimes I don't think buying Park Place is right, or that other pretend person isn't smart like me and makes some dumb moves. You really can't just work all the time! You gotta rest up!

But first you gotta get to know these new kids. I'm shy, so I have to think about this a long time. Bobby lives down by the mill, and his mom makes the best cookies. I think he eats lots of 'em, 'cuz he's a little chubby, and I'm pretty skinny. But he giggles a lot and knows everything about climbing all over the feed mill and all the feed bags in the feed-bag room, 'cuz his mom and dad own the mill. And he can walk on stones, 'cuz his feet are tough and don't hurt like mine do. Sometime I want tougher feet and do that. Bobby is a year smaller than me and has a little brother Georgie.

Then there is another Tommy who has my same name. They even make my name for all the Indian things like tommy hawk and tom-tom which has it two times. And Tommy guns. Gosh! How does everybody know me so much? Tommy lives beside the *millrace* (more farm words I'm learning). He's shy like me and has a little brother who doesn't say anything. His dad is the miller man who pulls up the four boards that make the millrace water go over the waterwheel. Boy! That shakes the whole mill and makes so much noise! The big men say lots of bad words when the wheel's going around, but you don't hear 'em so good.

And then there's Carol who has a father Heine. And she has one mom, too. Her mom just stays in the kitchen and never leaves and yells "Heine" a lot. Heine doesn't do anything but sit in his undershirt and undershorts in this big, dirty chair and drink beer and eat baloney sandwiches all the time, 'cuz he works so hard in Cleveland. Only men work! Moms stay at home.

Heine has a big tummy, a big chair, and a big bottom or *hinie*, so that's why they call him that. But he has a tiny, not hiny, 7-inch Philco television with buttons on the bottom like a radio with a picture in it and a thing with water in it that makes the picture look bigger so you can see all the exciting cowboy movies on it. That's all Hinie does. He loves to see the bad guys and posses run round and round. They never go anywhere. Just round and round. Hinie doesn't look like a cowboy in his undershorts that look like Dad's navy shorts and an undershirt with no arms on it with lots of hair under the arms. There are no cowboys in Fowlers Mills, but there are lots of cows around I'll tell you more about later.

There is so much you have to learn in Fowlers Mills. Carol lives in a little white house next to the mill on the other side, and she's so pretty and one year older than me and has a little brother, too, Bobby. Everybody has a littler brother but me.

Cathy lives with her mom and dad with white hair in the millhouse right next to the mill on that other side. It's a pretty, old white house, and Cathy has real pretty freckles and red hair. She is so pretty and is going to be Sue's best friend. Sue's new friend can help look after me, too, if she wants to. Cathy has a real Irish Setter who has pretty, shiny, red hair, too. Red hair is in their family except for her mom and dad. They have white hair just like their house and are really nice. Cathy's house was built real long ago by Hiram Fowler, and all the other people in Fowlers Mills are really old like Mom and Dad.

Betsy is our new puppy Tippy's mama. Tippy doesn't have a father, but Mom says, "She has a little collie in her, too," 'cuz she has a little white tip on her tail. This is a real good question for you! Can you guess why we gave Tippy that name? That's how my dad teaches kids in his school. He asks lots of questions. Tippy is the best dog in Fowlers Mills. Mom says Tippy is a little mixed-up with two kinds of dogs in her, but that's what makes her so strong and not get sick. That's funny! I get a little mixed-up sometimes, too and I'm strong and never get sick. I'm glad I'm not mixed-up all the time though. She runs all over the fields chasing rabbits or Partpart's sheep. She loves being free on a farm like me, and she and I are a lot alike. We always know what we both are thinking, and boy, can she dogfight! She can beat up all the other dogs, so watch out! They just put their heads down, their tails between their legs, and run away and hide. I want to fight like Tippy. If Tippy wasn't with me, I wouldn't be so brave like I am now. Sometimes she runs away, but she always comes running back to me to get petted. She just moans and purrs and loves to be petted and have those sticky burrs pulled out of her hair. It's hard to tell a burr from the fur, but she doesn't cry a bit when we pull 'em out. She doesn't run around like a chicken getting plucked. If you ever go inside somebody's house to play, Tippy just sits outside the door and waits right there for you. That's what kind of dog she is. I tell you! She is the BEST ever!

Tippy. Told you she was the best!

I just love being with Tippy all the time. Sometimes she even sneaks off and runs all the way up to our Amish neighbor's house. The Millers should live right next to the mill and be the millers, 'cuz Miller is their name. Now, when Tippy sneaks up to their house, she chases the chickens. That makes chickens want to lay more eggs, but Johnny's mom runs out with a broom and yells some words I don't even know what they are at Tippy. She and Tippy just have to become better friends. People say Johnny and Saloma's mom only talks German talk. Tippy loves to bark and chase their horse and buggy when it comes down the dirt road. Boy! She makes their horse go faster. Johnny's big brother Andy loves to race Tippy in his buggy. Boy! Tippy can really bite at the wheels going fast!

I'm so glad I have my sister Sue. Sue didn't get help growing up, 'cuz I wasn't born yet to help her. But if Cathy's dog Betsy didn't make Tippy for us, I don't think we'd have our farm. No, sireee! Growing up, I saw lots of aminals like Ferdinand the Bull and the ugly ducklings in picture books, but now I am going to live with real, live aminals. Ones you can really pet and feed and play with and talk to. Now I think you know all about the whole valley, hillside, and farm I'm going to be living in. That's where I'll be. Right there if you need me!

It's fun to drive out in the Green Hornet and visit our new farm. I'm all by myself under a tree at the barn and pond. Leaves are falling down, and I get to thinking again. Hope this old barn doesn't fall down. Now we're going to have our own house at last and won't have to be in Grandpa's friend's house anymore. I'm shy, but Cathy's really nice and meeted all the new kids to me and Sue. Her mom made her do that. All us new kids will be in the same two schoolrooms, so I hope they like me, and I can be friends. They're not all the same, but I know I can run faster than Bobby. I'll miss Mrs. Ramsdel, but we finally get to go to the country and do anything we want to. We know every kid already, so we better like each other anyhow. You don't know that until you move there. I thought it was just going to be a cow, a horse, a barn, some chickens, a dog, and some hayfield. Wow! It sure surprised me. There's a lot more there when you go see it! I like sitting under this tree!

CHAPTER 3

OUR NEW HOUSE

On Christmas vacation the moving truck came and took all our old stuff out to our new Fowlers Mills house. And like Mom said, "Are your car doors locked? Off we go!" Those men worked so hard, we gave them a bottle of Coca Cola and some sugar cookies. All our cookies have lots of sugar. Boy! Those men must have really liked it, 'cuz they gave us a whole calendar for all year 1947 saying Edsell's Moving Company on it and a thermometer. The kind so you know how cold it is. Not the behind kind! We got to hang our new calendar up "cuz it had three days left to New Year's. They were so nice to give us that. Those men really liked us! It was so cold and snowy and blowy, so there's no polio in our new house just like Mom said. Mom always knows how to not get us sick. And it's lots better our new house doesn't have heat upstairs. No germs that way!

I still don't have Grandpa's old Kodak box camera Dad promised me, so I'll have to tell you what everything looks like. I know! Like Mom says, "A picture's worth a thousand words!"

When you come and visit, I'll give you this map I just drawed you so you don't get lost. And I can take you all around, 'cuz we don't have little, tiny yards or sidewalks or houses all right next to each other like they have in the city. It's not the same. And when I grow up and get a camera, I'll show you everything. It's like you're right there. And I'm learning lots of new words, like *millrace*, *manure*, *stanchions*, *litters*, *night crawlers*, and stuff like that. Stuff you don't learn in the city! And I almost forgot *sows*, 'cuz the Eboshes across the road have lots of pigs!

Our dirt road was awfully dirty except when Mr. Hazen and his son Gale, that's a boy, put lots of oil on it from a truck or shoveled ashes all over it in the winter by the mill. That's the best hill for sledding, except when he puts cinders all over it. That's 'cuz they want to make the sleds go slow. We tie all our sleds together with rope to make them go faster. It sure works! Like a train! You can go all the way past the mill to the little iron bridge.

Everything happens just right here on Fowlers Mills Road! It goes from the big Mayfield Road on the top of the hill where the school, church, general store, community house, and Farmer Carroll's farmhouse and barn are. And to go there you gotta go uphill both ways. To get back home, you go all the way past the millrace and the mill, over the iron bridge in the valley, and all the way up another smaller hill straight to our house, which has to be over 150 years old. Whew! That's a long way, and I'm out of breath! And now you know why you need a map to find everything!

Our old mill. Didn't take this picture but found these old ones in the mill. It still looks like that 'cept we got a '35 Plymouth. That's where I almost went over the falls.

Milo Fowler built our new house, and he was Hiram's brother who lived down by the mill in Cathy's old house, and he built the mill, too. That's Hiram! These brothers get mixed up. Those Fowler brothers didn't really have to run too far to see each other. Just down the road! Mom says one part of the house is 100 years old, and the other part is 150 years old. There's that Partpart thing again. And they're all mixed up, too. I never know why Milo didn't just build his house all at the same time. I never know what part I'm in. Is it the 150-years-old part or the 100-year-old part? To me, anyhow, it's just the same old, big, old, brand-new house part. I don't know why Mom keeps saying 100, and Dad keeps saying 150 years. Mom just likes new things, and Dad doesn't ever throw away his baby toys. I think grown-ups should just say one thing, though, and tell the Truth! Don't you think so? One hundred years is not the same as 150 years. But there are better things to talk about than these grown-ups fibbing around like that. We have lots to do!

See the front porch. Bet you can't tell which part is over 150 years old. That's the right-of-way old railroad behind.

On the hillside next to our house, there's a cemetery that has one Revolution soldier in it. He's been there a long time, so I don't know what he looks like. Cemeteries aren't much good for anything except putting people in the ground, but you can have lots of fun up there playing hide-go-seek. It's best to hide behind an old-people stone, 'cuz they can find you easy if you try to hide behind a little-kid or baby stone. My best stone is the a big one they put the whole family in at the same time. That's a winner every time like Dad says! You know what? They should make a cemetery next to everybody's house. Then nobody would have to walk very far be in there!

The Eboshes live across the road in a one-room, old schoolhouse, and now it's a people house, and that's exactly why we have my new school with two rooms, 'cuz there are so many kids now, and there are going to be eight in my first grade, and the Eboshes have lots of pigs that squeal all the time to let you know where they are, and 'cuz they like their pigs so much, they never forget to slop 'em, so they can grow to be big porkers, and all these words are just too long, 'cuz I forget where I even started them. That's enough pig talk!

When you get grown-up, you always know where to start and when you get all through something. Now remember, if this is all too long, just look at the pictures like I do, and you get to know it just as well. And remember, too, if you want a movie instead, my dad can make you one with his eight millymeter. Our whole family watches them at night when we get bored. Dad takes the movies, and I take the Brownie pictures, so you won't see me in any of them, 'cuz I'm behind 'em snapping away. But even if you don't see me, remember, this story really is mostly about me.

Now, our old house has really creaky steps and a dirt basement that's kind of smelly and where little mushrooms grow. I'm glad there's a little light bulb down there. And down there's a big coal furnace with big, red-hot cinders in it. Dad puts 'em under the car tires in the snow to get the car out of the barn. So you have to have a coal furnace to make those, or Dad can't drive to be a teacher any more. You see how everything works? That furnace is huge, but there is no heat upstairs in our bedrooms. And remember, Mom says that keeps the germs away, and we never get colds. She keeps us healthy!

At night you can hear birds and mice running around in the creepy old attic. It's always dark up there, and there's just a little hole in the ceiling that you have to put a ladder up to get there. Just step on the old boards, so you don't fall right into your bedroom. It's dark up there, but one time I found some old bird bones on a board with a tiny beak and no eyes. Boy! What a creepy place! Girls can't go up. You've got to be brave like me! And everyone says that's where all the ghosts and goblins live. There's more up there than in the cemetery.

Our new house doesn't have any fireplaces like Cathy's, but it's got the only big, iron dinner bell around 'cept for Pearl, the little old lady up the road. We can ring ours at the same time to let her know we're home, and then she knows right where we live. Our bell always rings at six o'clock for supper, so you can run home as fast as you can, or you just get bread and water!

Mom always says, "No dawdling!" I was born a dawdler! Mom even says it took me forty-eight hours to come out. I'm not sure where she thinks I came from, but I made it out! Mom said, "It was hard labor." That means hard work! I know just what that means, 'cuz now I'm a really hard-working country boy. I'll tell you about all the hard work they made me do later, but now I'm just having fun thinking about our new house. Sometimes you just have to have a little fun!

But anyhow, about this fireplace thing. I think it's funny 'cuz the McGeough's old house down by the mill has seven fireplaces. One in every room! So I know why our house is so cold. And Cathy's mom and dad don't look so healthy like my mom and dad do. They have white hair, but they are so nice.

Dad has a big chest and lots of muscles. Dad says our fireplaces got all plastered up behind the wall during Indian times so you could hide, and they couldn't see you. Dad knows lots of history! So all we have is that big, old coal furnace down on that basement dirt floor with lots of fire sparks and real red clinkers you can see through the little glass door. When the hopper backs up, Mom yells "Tommy" or sometimes "James Thomas" real loud, and the house gets all full of smoke. You know you'd better get down to that coal bin fast and shovel that coal into the hod and throw it into the hopper as fast as you can to cover up that smoke, even if you can't see anything with all that smoke! And that is just one of my jobs! I sure learned a lot about coal smoke, hoppers, and clinkers fast. I learn how to smell for smoke and how to cough it up out of your lungs. If your eyes sting, you know it's time to fill 'er up again!

Our house has low ceilings with lots of little sticky-out points of dirty white, stucco plaster like it's wanting to stick and itch you all over. I never saw anything but flat plaster before, but out here in the country, you see everything. This plaster lets the rain fall right on you, 'cuz lots of it has fallen down. Rain drips right on your head. It's a big job to help Mom put pots and pans all over to catch the drips, but I'm Mom's big helper. Drops get so big that you can see holes in the ceiling with this funny, steel honeycomb stuff behind it. That helps a little bit. But lots of little pieces of plaster fall down on the floor and table. But you know I like surprises! It's really exciting to see whose plate those little pieces fall down on. Sometimes it's a big chunk.

At supper we sure laugh and giggle like kids. When Mom sets that food out, we all sing, "For health and strength and daily food, we praise thy name, oh Lord!" as fast as we can. Sometimes we sing it two or three times, and in rounds, too, if we aren't too hungry. That's the fastest blessing they make! But it's a really good one, specially if your mom really cooks good. If you sing it really fast, you get to start eating faster. It's a lot better than "Little Tommy Tucker, Sing for your supper." That's my name again, but I like us all singing. Now I've been giggling a little bit, telling you about our blessing, and I know that's not right when you talk about the Lord, but Dad giggles the loudest.

And now Dad's being in our family, I'm learning to be a better tricker from him. But Dad's the better or best one. I get those words mixed up. Dad always gets the red *uranium* plate, 'cuz he's the dad, and he says that's what atom bombs are made of. So when I set the table (and that there's really not a big farming job), I always try to put Dad's red uranium plate right under where the plaster falls down. Our table's round, so we can put the plates anywhere we want. Now don't tell him, but I also always give him the fork with the bent up and crooked *tine*. That's one of the first farm words I learned from *pitchforks*. They have tines like sharp fingers. Later on when you jump off in a hayloft, make sure there aren't any pitchforks down in the hay! Or you can just make hay forts instead. They don't hurt you but aren't as much fun if you really like jumping.

Anyhow! My family has the best eating forks. They have a lady on the handle with no clothes on, called Miss Liberty. You can look at her round chest bumps. Sometimes I can't take my eyes off her, but that makes me eat a lot slower just like Dad, and he is the slowest eater of all. I think he's peeking at that fork handle all the time. Every year I get older, I look at that fork handle lots more and more. I sure love it, though, when Dad finds that bent fork on his plate every time and says, "How did I ever get this fork again?" Boy! I'm a good tricker. I may be a better or best one, too. And my poor dad laughs and says he was always cursed, whatever that means. Nothing good ever happens to him, but he never gets mad. Not even when a big chunk of plaster falls right on his plate. He looks really scared, but then he winks at us and says he got a second helping! He laughs until his sides hurt. We all laugh! No wonder he's such a good teacher and tells so many stories. All the kids like him so much!

**Wow! Look at those bumps! You can see why
us boys, Dad and me, eat so slow.**

He taught me how to climb up on a chair and pull a little piece of plaster just a little bit out. That way at supper just Dad and I know what plate it's going to fall down on. That's a trick just Dad and I know! Now let me tell ya! Dad doesn't teach just telling stories sitting around in a little children's circle looking up dresses. He teaches big kids. Mom says, "Dad is the best pretender," and now I'm starting to pretend a lot more like him, too. Other dads don't pretend much. They're just always serious, and their cheeks look like they're hanging down and falling off. Now I pretend lots of things to talk about, and I try not to smile. And that's not easy to do! Try it sometime! Sometimes I even pretend to not tell the Truth. Nobody else can do that!

Dad can really tell funny jokes. I'll tell you one of them to tell you what I mean. Like the joke I told you about when he drives. He says, "Be really quiet because the corn has ears." Gosh! He's funny! Mom says, "That's corny!" Well, of course, Mom! That's why it's about corn, yaa! Sometimes Dad pats Mom on the bottom when she says that, and then she gets the joke, too, 'cuz she'll smile and giggle and gets all red and looks right into his eyes when he pats her like that. Just a little pat. Not a spanking! I'm the only one who ever gets one of those. Dad is just a better or best joker than Mom, but Mom can really giggle good. And Dad just keeps patting her and telling those jokes over and over and over until Mom says, "Stop it, Rex!" Mom just can't giggle anymore!

Now here's one more. I get to laughin' lots, and it's hard to stop. Now, Dad was in China after the war driving China men in his boat all around out west up to the front to fight some other guy in China, so they could have a war, too. So he knows all about dentists in China, 'cuz he didn't drink much milk in the navy and got bad teeth. We kids drank it all up, and the cows weren't giving us much then. There weren't as many farmer men to milk them, too. They were off in the war. And his teeth fell out.

So when we ask him, "What time is it?" he says, "Just like the China dentist says, 'Tooth hurtee.'" Get it? It means your teeth. And Mom would say, "Oh Rex! That's an old one!" But they aren't that old. I have one that wiggles sometimes. I don't think Dad needs to drink milk anymore. He's got these new teeth he calls choppers. He can take 'em out and click 'em real good! Yep! He sure is funny. And he sure loves to go places. When we boys are in the boys' room and ready to go out, he says, "Shake the dew off your lily, and let's go!" Don't know what he's talking about, but it sure makes me laugh.

You know something! I never call my dad "Daddy" like lots of kids do, 'cuz Dad has a big chest and strong arms from being in the navy. He is just different! Even his name is different. I never heard anyone else called Rex Waldo. Have you? Mom says Grandma named him after some old man that writes books in Boston. When I was first born, Dad says he helped Mom make me a baby when he was away in the navy or at some school teaching. Like I said, I think I came half out of my mom's tummy and half out of my dad's. And two halfs of me make a my whole self. So that's me! Other moms mostly make all the babies all by themselves. You can't fool me about this stork bird carrying babies around in a basket. That's dumb! I know all about where babies come from! Mom says I'm the spitting image of Dad. My dad can do everything! He knows the very first name of every chipmunk and squirrel on our farm. And like I told you, I'm a lot more than just half of him. That's the Truth!

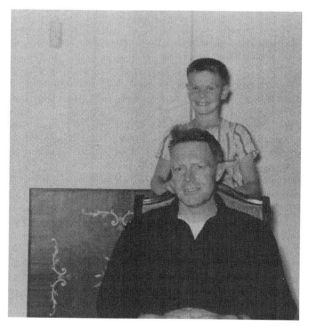

You can tell Dad and I are just the same. Dad gets to sit down 'cuz he's older.

Dad sure can explain you things in a fun way. One time one of our big, woolly sheep got stuck in the stream, and he said, "Sheep make great sponges. They can dry up the whole pond!" Another time Dad was taking red-hot clinkers out of the furnace, and it exploded. He came up to the kitchen, and his face and hands were all burned, so Mom drove him to the doctor fast. When he came home, he said, "Because I had red hair, that's the only way I can get a tan!" And you know what? He kept these little pieces of falling-off skin in his desk drawer for a long time, telling me, "That's part of myself I'm keeping for later." He sure could explain things, but I'm not sure if it's always like it's sposed to. Dad! You silly old goat!

Anyhow, 'cuz we are kids and have more years to live and won't die or get sick, Sue and I sleep upstairs with no heat. Sometimes the windows have so much ice, you have to scratch a hole to see outside. It gets so cold, I wet my bed and feel all warm for a little bit. It feels real comfy til you wake up, like a warm river. That's terrible! I'm just not a baby anymore! I sure hope the other kids don't find out! You know how they like to blabber it around.

In the morning the floor's so frozen, you run downstairs to the bathroom to brush your teeth as fast as you can. Then jump right into the kitchen where the oven's on, and it's toasty warm. In our brand-new house, we have to keep the toilet seat down, 'cuz we have two girls in our family, and they can fall right down the toilet. We don't want to hurt anybody! Specially the girls, 'cuz Dad and I are tougher! Girls can get lost that way. But if they do, what a scream! Now me, I'm growed up tall and can stand up tall and tinkle now sometimes on my tiptoes. Don't even splash now. We only got one toilet, so some times Dad and I cross swords with our tinkle like soldiers and pee red if we eat beets. We have big wood stairs and railings right in the middle of the house, too. I learned how to climb over the railing, taking a shortcut to get upstairs faster. I love shortcuts! That's the only way to get anywhere! I'm always in a hurry!

Now, the fastest time I ever made it over those railings was when my dad chased me. I had just done the worst thing in my life. I'll tell you, but please don't tell anybody else! Sue yelled, "Tommy's swearing! He called me a 'son of a bitch!'" Well! Pinky Freeman says that every time he burns his finger on a red-hot horseshoe. Boy! Dad ran after me, and I climbed over that railing the fastest I ever could. Real fast I said, "Son of a fox, son of a squirrel, son of a cow, son of a gun, son of a skunk." So what's the difference? And I was telling the Truth, so Dad let me go that time. I always tell the Truth! Swear on a Bible, but Sue won't let me even swear any more. She's mean that way. I can't even cuss like all the big men do down at the mill. How am I ever going to grow up?

But Dad never spanked me my whole life. I think he spanked everyone too much in the war when he was fighting everybody over there and got tired of it. Mom did a few times, though. One time she made me go out into the woods to find a switch. I found a little dead one that was falling apart, so she made me get a better one. She always gets a tear in her eye, and it gets all red, and she looks so sad, but I never cry, even though I get three swats. They aren't hard ones, but I feel bad when Mom's upset with me.

Dad really likes me a lot. Yep! We are a lot alike, but he's a little bigger, and my face isn't scratchy like his. I sneaked his razor one time, but I didn't see any hairs. They're hard to find! Anyhow, my dad lives with us now when he's not driving the Green Hornet or being a teacher. I think he's going to stay with us forever. But I need to tell you about all the other grown-ups in Fowlers Mills, so you'll know them when you see 'em!

Now I found this secret hiding place in the hayloft on top of the box stalls. Nobody knows you up here. Boy! I'm thinkin' our new farmhouse sure looks old and rickety. Plaster's falling down, tar paper on the roof's going to blow off, and porch windows are broken. Hope our new house doesn't fall down. But boy! We sure have lots of fun in there.

Dad sure says funny things, and we all laugh when plaster falls down on him. I'm going to be like Dad, too. I think it's OK if he breaks Mom's rules sometimes, if we don't get hurt and have fun. Mom's happy about it, too, but we sure know Mom's rules to make us behave. Dad knows them, too, but it's OK. Sure looks crummy, but I sure love our new house. I thought we were just going to be cold and sleep in it and not have any fun, but we sure are. I didn't know that before we moved in. This old barn looks crummy, and hay smells, too, but if we get any animals, they'll love it. They'll have their very own rooms.

CHAPTER 4

THE GROWN-UPS

Let me tell you about the grown-ups. They don't do much around here. They just sit and talk and eat most of the time. We kids do most of the work! They just live here, 'cuz us kids are so busy all the time. Now, here the people and houses aren't all lined up on sidewalks. There aren't any sidewalks! And all these people have real names, so you really know for sure who they are. Not like Mr. Steffy or Mr. Smith down the street who you only know just by their names. But Fowlers Mills people have real names that let you know what they look like. They have names like Pinky, Pearl, Dart, Mr. and Mrs. Partpart, Saloma, Lil, Merle, Shorty, Red, Hinie, Toots, Grandpa Reynolds, and Grampa Kobleha. Names like that! Now, Pinky could have been called Mr. Blacksmith, but he just looks like Pinky. I already told you about Mr. Partpart with two last names both the same. Why not just call them two parts. I mean, these parts both live in the same house across the road from the cemetery, so they can keep an eye on it if their sheep die. You learn a lot about dying on a farm. Animals do it all the time!

The Partparts are older than our family, and they have eight sheep and a nanny goat that Tippy and I love to chase all over the pasture. Sheep are so smart they just put their noses in another sheep's tail and just keep running around going nowhere. When we get tired, we stop and drink right out of the little pasture stream that goes right under the road to make our stream and pond. The sheep have to drink, too, or they fall over when Tippy really chases them hard. Boy! Tippy can run and bark better than anybody! She is the best, and she never falls over chasing sheep even when she bites their toenails.

Way up behind Partpart's house are caves and lemon squeezes to climb all around. You really have to dig your fingers into the rock to not fall off. Right across the road, there's an old house that used to be a one-room school before they built our two-room one. Like I told you, the Eboshes live there with all their pigs. All sorts of them! Fat and small and squealing all the time. When they get loose, it's so much fun to catch the little ones. Wow! When you fall them on the ground, you just do your better or best to hang on. Sometimes Big Louie grabs them by their *snouts* to make 'em squeal louder. Now, that's another farm word I'm learning. I know there are lots, but I hope you can keep up. Anyhow! Big Louie never wears a shirt, so the pigs don't see him coming, but he sure can call those pigs, "Suuuieeeeee, pig, pig, pig!" so loud you can hear it all over the hillside up into the woods. He slops 'em up with lots of slop in the trough to eat and get them fat and big enough to go live other places. But most of 'em just want to run and hide from Big Louie.

Now, behind our new house is an old interurban railroad. We call it the right-of-way, and what's horrible is my cutest little sister Kathy tells my mom to take our new baby Mary Beth and throw her over the bank to stop her from crying. You shouldn't do that! That's after Kathy was borned and another cutest little sister Mary Beth got born. I'll tell you later about them being born, 'cuz that was a really close race, and I want it to be a surprise to you. We play with Kathy all the time. I put her on my back and ride her like a horse all over our farm, and she never falls off, 'cuz she can pull your hair really hard. She just loves lots of exciting things. I found her a little field mouse one day, and she carried it around in her little hands all day long until it just didn't move any more at all. Boy! She's fun and loves animals, too.

But anyhow, this old right-of-way has old wood railroad ties and old iron spikes. I love to walk on these ties without missing even one to see if I can find any of these old spikes to bring home. I have a snapshot of some I'll show you. I love this old right-of-way 'cept when the little Louie Ebosh boy got lost on it, and all the people had to come out and look up and down the whole right-of-way til night. We all thought wolves had eaten him, but there he was, sitting all alone on a railroad tie, just looking at the stars. I wanted to be the first to find him, so I could be the winner, but he just was there like finding himself. Everyone was so happy, and all the men had these big glassfuls of brown stuff with bubbles to drink, and they were the happiest of all! This may be a grown-up game like Find Little Louie or something. Anyhow, little Louie didn't even get a spankin' that night. He was just too tired for it and just fell asleep. But all those men sure got happiest all night.

Now, next to this right-of-way, Grampa and Gramma Kobleha live in a little brown house. Gramma never moves one bit and always sits really quiet in her same old kitchen chair and looks out the window with a babushka on her head all the time. Her grandson Bobby says she had a long car ride from Bohemia a long time ago and never talked after that. I think she's lonely. Grampa Kobleha has a big, old-fashioned green car in the driveway that never moves. He always washes it a lot, and it really looks more like an automobile than just a car. He doesn't wash himself. He always wears a dirty, old hat and gets real mad when Tippy runs in front of the mill and barks. Tippy doesn't like him. He yells "bulash" or something like that. That's one of the only words I can't spell yet. And when he yells, he throws a stone or a grain brush right at Tippy to make her jump. But old Tippy is too fast for him! He's kind of scary with a big hairy mustache, but he used to be the mill owner, and I think it was sad for him to have to give it to Bobby's mom, Lil. She is the best at baking fancy cookies and cakes, which Bobby and I like to eat a lot, they're so good.

Grampa Kobleha is always in the mill and chases us off the feed bags, yelling that same bulash word again. I don't know if his mother ever taught him any other words or how to smile. I don't think so. I think he misses Bohemia and might not like Fowlers Mills like I do yet. It takes a little while to get to know country life.

But he keeps the key to the mill pond dam locked behind our house, 'cuz he is the only people who can walk behind his house to turn that iron wheel hard to not let all that water run out so fast. Then the water goes down the millrace right to the mill and down the shoot and over the waterwheel to really make it go around. Funny! Just closing up a little dam does all that! Boy! What a racket! It only takes a few minutes, but when he does that, the whole mill shakes. All three floors! Big belts go running all up and down through all the floors, and it makes so much noise, and flour is flying all around. Makes your hair white. Maybe that's what happened to Cathy's mom and dad living too close to the mill. Boy! You sure don't get excited like that in the city! All you do there is play in the yard, skip rope, play hopscotch, walk past a house, say hi to somebody you don't even know, go to school, stay on the sidewalk again, and go shopping. Wheww! Boring!

Then down the dirt road, over a small iron bridge over the little Chagrin River where the catfish sit on the bottom doing nothing in the sun all day, real close to the mill is that other Tommy's house. Another year it was Beverly and Harry's house when their mom and dad moved in, so their dad could be the miller. If you aren't careful, you can fall off their side porch right into the millrace. Nobody else in Fowlers Mills ever moves from their house 'cept that one. Everyone else just stays in their own house 'cuz it's theirs.

Fowlers Mills Road down to the mill.

Before the next miller, Tommy's dad was the miller. He was in charge and kept busy all the time, moving boards in the millrace all around like I already told you. That would let the water go in all different directions. He'd also sweep the feed off the floor a lot with a big broom to keep it shiny. He was always so busy. Then at night he'd walk across the road to sleep in his house. They only had two bedrooms in their house that was almost right over the millrace. Don't roll out of bed there! Just joking. Nobody ever did. You know what? If I can't be the best farmer, maybe I could have his job when I grow up and be a miller.

Right in front of the mill, there's a little grass circle with a big stone hitching post. The only horse I ever saw tied up there belonged to our Amish neighbors, the Millers. Their big racehorse gets spooked lots and shakes all over. We'd tickle her with a long piece of grass, but better watch out for her hooves. Get you right in the beanie! Right around that mill is where all us kids play every night til it gets dark. Every summer I get a lot bigger and jumpier, and I get so I can run and jump right up to the top of that hitching post with no hands. If you wait til all the kids are all looking, they can all see you real good. But you gotta wait for just the right time. Don't want to miss the top, and don't try it if you don't want a split lip. It's not for babies! I have lots of stitches to show you, but I didn't get more than seven at one time. Most on my elbows and hands, but I got five on my knees, too.

Now, on the other side of the mill, Carol lives with her little brother Bobby and her dad Hinie. That's another Bobby. I told you about Hinie before, 'cuz he really acts like a little boy. That's why I put him in the kids' part. But he really is a dad. Most dads are grown-ups. Like I told you, Hinie works really hard in Cleveland, and when he comes home dirty, all he does is just sit in that big, dirty chair in his dirty underwear and drink beer, 'cuz he worked so hard. I snuck some one time, and it tastes funny, but it makes you work hard and gives you lots of energy.

Carol has a mother, too, but like I said, she's real quiet, and her lips don't open, only to eat and yell at Hinie. And I don't even know her name. She smiles and just wears an apron all day and cooks dinner. That's what all the mothers in Fowlers Mills do all day long. They just cook dinner all the time.

You may already know, but they got the very first television with a big bubble in front of a 7-inch screen to make the picture really big. Hinie loves lots of cowboy shows of Hoot Gibson and Johnny Mack Brown, which I really love, too. But before Hinie comes home to sit in that chair, us kids all watch *Uncle Jake's House*, *Howdy Doody*, and *Gabby Hayes*. Boy! Gabby can really blow a lot of that Puffed Rice and Wheat out of that cannon all over the inside of that television. I love that and love it when he says, "Altoona, Pennsylvania," 'cuz he doesn't have any teeth. He is so serious, and I like him a lot better than that goofy man Uncle Miltie.

Now, Howdy Doody is the kind of boy who moves around on strings and has lots of his own friends like Flub-a-Dub, Flibberty Jib, and Clarabell who is a trickster but doesn't talk and just blows his horn. My favorite one of all is Princess Summerfall Winterspring. Funny how you make best friends with a silly puppet on a string. I really like Howdy, and I like that Pinnochio guy we saw in the outdoor picture-show movie, too. That's the place they put a movie up outside the car, and you sit inside the car and wipe the fog off the windows, so you can see it and try not to bump the things on the windows that talk to you, and people run up and down the cars getting food to eat. We saw *Bambi* there, too. Sometimes if you walk around, you can see a big boy and girl in a car lying down in the back seat. They're all alone with no mom or dad there to make them even look at the movie. We have to tell 'em how it goes.

Now, the princess is so pretty! I think she likes me a lot, but she also likes Buffalo Bob a lot, too. He combs his hair better than me, too. He puts some of that Vitalis on it. I wish she wasn't make-believe and could live right here, 'cuz I think about her all the time when I go to sleep at night. She's beautiful! But I really need to tell you all about the real, alive Fowlers Mills people.

Like I told you, Sue's friend Cathy lives right next to the mill, and her mom and dad both have white hair and are almost one hundred years old. But they are so nice, like more grandmas and grandpas. They always take care of me if I need them to. But their house is older than they are, and it was built by the other Fowler brother and has a fireplace in each room.

So one brother, Hiram, liked to keep really warm with lots of fire-places, and the other brother, Milo, wanted to keep his house really cold, so he didn't build fireplaces in our house. And he was more scaredy and wanted to hide from Indians all the time behind the walls. I don't think Milo ever got a cold germ. I think two brothers in the same famly would build the same house, but they didn't. I don't know their mom and dad, but I know Milo wanted to be a farmer like me and get away from that mill. And he didn't like to chop wood all day to make fires. There's more stuff than that to do around here. He didn't want to chuck wood like a woodchuck chucks. I don't know why I said that, but I thought it was funny! But you know what's funny? My sister Sue and I are just alike. We do everything the same. We like to run, play jacks, and walk on stilts, and we were born together before the war. So we're just alike 'cept she'll be a mom before me, 'cuz she's older. Can you believe it? So I don't know why those Fowler brothers weren't just the same, too. They had the same mom and dad.

Now, across the mill, Bobby's mom and dad live in a big white house. That's where Bobby and his little brother Georgie live, too. Bobby taught me everything about the mill, like how to climb on feedbags and not put too many holes in 'em and how to go barefoot. His feet have really tough, fat skin on the bottoms, and he doesn't hurt one bit to walk right over sharp stones. But boy, mine do! That's why I love to jump on these really soft and squooshy, colored flour bags. And I'm more of a jumper. Bobby took me all over the mill and down inside the big waterwheel when the water wasn't pushing it around. He can go anywhere in the mill, 'cuz his mom and dad own it, and his grandpa is Grampa Kobleha. You remember it's Bobby's mom Lil who makes the best and biggest cookies that Bobby eats and gives us one sometimes. And 'cuz they own the mill, Bobby and Georgie get the most presents from Santa Claus. Santa can find their house on Christmas Eve, 'cuz he sees that big hitch-ing post. Our hitching post is just a little, tiny white one, and we don't even have a fireplace chimney. But we can't help it!

Now, in a little old house up the hill is where Pearl lives, and there are big blue spruce pine trees all around that make Christmas trees. She is the only other people with a big iron dinner bell like ours, but she only rings hers on New Year's Eve. So ours is best! Pearl wears pretty dresses she sews out of chicken feed bags with flowers all over them she gets from the mill. She has a husband Pinky who has really old, wrinkled skin and no hair on his head. Just big curly ones in his nose!

Pinky spends the whole day helping in Farmer Carroll's barn or in his blacksmith shop. You remember him? I never saw him put a shoe on a horse foot, but he would hammer a lot of red-hot horseshoes, and one time he burned his fingers and started talking just like a real preacher, yelling, "Holy Christ," "Jesus Jenny," and "God dammit," and all that stuff. He was yelling out all of 'em. He didn't forget anybody in the whole church. Boy! You could hear him all over Fowlers Mills. And he doesn't even go to the church. I don't think he needs to, 'cuz he does all his preacher things right there in his blacksmith shop.

Now, he can't run or climb too fast, but he taught me how to hold all these cows' tails, so they don't hit Farmer Carroll in the face when he's milking. Pinkie says sometimes you gotta hold 'em real high to keep 'em from kickin'. He went away somewhere later, just somewhere else, and I sure miss him, 'cuz he was the best teacher about cows. Dad said they keep the town hall flag at half-mast for him, so he knows where to go. Old Pinky just knew what cows liked to have their tails held up higher or down lower and just how to talk to them. Say just the right things, so you don't make them feel bad. Get them to moo not so loud. He always says, "They're happier than a pack of possums." Sure makes them feel good! I don't think possums are as big like cows. He doesn't talk a lot, but he sure shows you lots of things. Like Mom says, "Actions speak louder than words!"

Now, Pearl also has a good friend Dart, who has a real old Model A car, and while Pinkie is holding cows' tails still just right and helping Farmer Carroll after dark, Dart's so nice, he drives Pearl up to the cemetery by our house and stops the car. They just stay inside the car and don't do anything at all. We tried to peek in the car one time, but you couldn't see their faces, 'cuz they were all squoonched down and not sitting straight up in their seats like you're sposed to. Pearl always has a big smile on her face when she sees Dart. Boy! He must be pretty special and precious, like Grandma says. He has a real red face, a big bushy beard he can pick food out of, real bushy red hair, eyebrows that aren't combed, and little grandma glasses on his nose.

Everybody always smiles funny when they talk about Dart, and all he ever says is, "Hi ya, fella" and "Yep." Like Mom says, "He's more action than words." I guess that's like Pinky. That's why they probably both like to see Pearl a lot! Now, when they never get out of that car all alone up in that creepy cemetery, I'm always thinking if they're OK. But Mom says, "That's not necessary! They don't need any help!" Sue says, "They're spooning and pitchin' woo!" or having some picnic or whatever those kinds of games are. Pinky's good at pitchin' horseshoes he made. But Mom said Dart is an old skinflint and at least should take Pearl to the outdoor picture show up by route 44 to see *Bambi* or something! Everybody loves *Bambi*! Maybe Dart and Pearl will take me, too.

Next to Pearl and Pinky, Merle and Grandpa Reynolds have a big house and the Reynolds General Store. Merle has a mustache and can butcher a whole half a cow behind the meat counter. Back there are some big fat cats sitting around and a big, wood butcher block with lots of pieces of meat all over it. One cat always sits on a big roll of baloney, eating and licking up little scraps of it just to keep that baloney roll clean. Everybody has their job in the country. Even cats! Ours is a barn cat, and its job is to catch mice. Don't really even have to feed it. There are also some chickens back at the meat counter with no feathers on them. They have beaks and bald heads and sometimes hang by their feet. Their eyes are all white, so they can't see too good. And lots of fly paper is hanging all around back there, so that's where I practice my counting all the stuck, dead flies on it. They "Stick to it" like Dad tells me to! There I go, saying dumb things again! It's just like Dad and me, I guess. We think up dumb things just for fun!

In Reynolds Store, there are also lots of cans of food and boxes of cereal way up to the ceiling, and if you can't get one with your hands, Merle takes a long stick with a hook and some tweezers on the end and pulls one down. Plop! He catches really good and taught me how to use it to catch all kinds of cans and boxes in one hand. I think that really taught me first how to catch a baseball so well. If you want a can of hash, there it is! Oops! If five of 'em fall down, you gotta run!

Now, this is the good part! One glass case in the store has little pieces of candy. Two for a penny and five cents for candy bars, and

Merle can make you a milkshake from a pint of ice cream and a quart of milk and Hershey's Syrup he gets right off the shelf. He doesn't even have to look at a book to make milkshakes. Grandpa Reynolds is so nice to me, 'cuz when it gets to be Thanksgiving, he gives me a whole quart of Halloween ice cream with a jack-o'-lantern in the middle of it, and at Easter he gives me the Christmas ice cream with a green Christmas tree in the middle. For that, all I have to do is help him chip out the old freezer ice. When you're an ice-cream lover like me and Dad, it doesn't matter what holiday it is. I never got any of that Memorial Day ice cream, though! I was hoping for it, but not sure anybody makes that one. You're really not sposed to have ice cream on Memorial Day. It's one of those sad holidays when you shouldn't be having too much fun but sposed to be in the cemetery all day. I was sposed to take it all home and share it with my family. But 'cuz I have some sweet teeth, I mostly hid in the right-of-way and ate the whole quart just myself. Grandpa Reynolds spends most of the day, when he's not giving back money for empty pop bottles, just sitting around in an old gray sweater with holes in the elbows, with the cats around the stove, just picking his fingers and jiggling the skin hanging down from his neck.

Now, on top of Reynolds Store is the Grange Hall. They march around and do stuff up there like square dance and cake walks. But the best part is the musical chairs game! Boy! There's more shoving and pushing little kids off chairs when the music stops. That's the most fun! Push one of those folding chairs over and boy! That makes a noise! We boys like pushing kids down, even if the music's still going! That's more fun than winning the prize!

Across the dirt road from Reynolds Store, Farmer Carroll lives with his mother in a big white house and in his barn with all the cows, Bossy, Whitey, Grandma, Little Jersey, and all the other ones, and Tom and Jerry, his big draft horses from Belgium. And that's more far away than even Cleveland. He likes big horses better than tractors 'cept when someone does spring plowing.

His mom mostly lives in the house, and Farmer Carroll mostly lives in the barn with his eleven cows. Biggest herd around! He milks before the sun comes up when the cows are still sleeping. Now, he's not a kid, of course, but you wouldn't tell it, 'cuz he's so short and skinny and doesn't dress up much. They say he's about fifty years old but looks more like one of Santa's elves. He wears the same overalls every day and only takes one bath a week like me. His breath smells like old fish and tobacco spit all chewed up. Never goes anywhere 'cept to cross over to Reynolds Store to get more ginger ale and tobacco. He calls it bacca.He only drives horses and doesn't got a car!

His nose has a lot of little holes in it, not just the the two big ones everyone has. And he always keeps his eyes all squinshed up, and his eyebrows and nose have more hair than his head. Farmer Carroll doesn't talk too much—mostly twinkles his eyes, smiles a lot, chews tobacco good, listens, and talks to his cows a lot. He likes his mom and cows more than anythin'!

He sure can spit this gooey, smelly, brown stuff in a line way out of his mouth. Makes like a bird noise doing it, too. I learned to spit, too, but not as good as him. I'll have to learn real good how to chew this tobacco just right. He keeps it in a little bag to give to Tom and Jerry. And I have to grow a big cheek like him, too, when I get older and lose some more teeth like him, so I can get that spit out there faster. We can talk more about that stuff later, 'cuz you can't learn all about this barn stuff all at one time. There's just too much! And you really shouldn't talk about spittin' stuff around lunch time, 'cuz I ate half a bag one time and forgot to spit it out. Boy! Was I ever sick to my tummy!

Now, way behind the barn in this big field is a big pasture of alfalfa and wheat and a sugar bush for sweet maple syrup way up on the hill with all the maple trees. There's also the biggest manure pile of all. We can talk a lot more about manure later, 'cuz it's the best, and that's how you really learn a lot about farming. There's a whole lot to learn about manure. Makes you grow up fast. And you already know maple syrup and manure really don't go together anyhow.

And of course across that big highway called Mayfield Road was our school, my church, town hall, and the community house. If they didn't make me go to all those places first, I'd probably already be a farmer by now. First they make you go to school, and baddest of all, in Sunday school they make you learn all those verses. I just can't tell you all about that now! But sometimes you just have to do what your mom and dad and those grown-ups say!

You see everything's busy here, don't you? You can't learn everything about Fowlers Mills in one day, but I wanted to make it like a picture for you of everything I can. And I know you liked the way I got out of that city and am free now to do anything I want, 'cuz now the war's gone, and Dad's home in our family, and everybody can do anything they want to. That's what Dad was in the war for! Dad got us freedom! Try to do good, but of course if it's freedom, you can do anything you want. Bad things, too! You get to pick one! So be careful like I am!

And I had to be in that Cleveland city so many years, I was getting really tired of it. You can tell it was wearing me out! Now we can finally have real margarine and everything and all the animals and candy we want. Not just one dumb dog or cat like those kids in the city! Just like that kindergarden song "America the Beautiful" says it when you sing "Hammer Ways of Grain" and "Spice and Skies" and all that stuff. Yep! Out here you can do whatever you want! Boy! It feels so good! That's what I really wanted you to know. And anyhow, Mom knows that, too, and she never tells a lie. Lies can be more fun and let you keep secrets, but if Mom catches you, like I told you, you have to go to the woods and find a switch. And it better not be an eenie-teenie one! It's got to be a real, live, strong one. Nothing wrong with that! And I'm getting a lot stronger, too, now, living in the country. Just look at me and all my muscles!

I'm climbing that ladder up to that secret hayloft again. I didn't know about all these new people in Fowlers Mills. Everyone's not all the same here. Each people is his own self. They all look different and do different things. You learn that when you see them. In the city they just walk on the sidewalk and then go back home. Sometimes they say hi to you. Sometimes they don't say anything. Out here, there are only sixty-four people, but they're all more busy all day long. I didn't know there were going to be so many people in one place. It's more fun 'cuz you can go anywhere you want to and talk to them. Nobody tells you where you have to go. You sure find lots of new stuff when you move, if it's in the country! I'm not sure, but I think they might make you go to school out here, too. And now I'm getting to learn how to talk to animals, too. Like Tippy! Tippy and I are a lot like each other, too. I guess you just learn all this country stuff.

Our family sticks together on the farm.

**See how we take care of the little children. Isn't
that a great mouse I found Kathy?**

Kathy was lots of fun and a real job, too.

That's my West Virginia Grandma and Grandpa and us kids.

Little Kathy. See what I mean about Kathy being gabby.

We really had a big job with two little sisters. See what a tiny hitching post we had. And that barn had lots of secrets.

CHAPTER 5

FIRST DAY AND
FIRST GRADE

The first night we go to sleep in Fowlers Mills, it is so cold and blowy out. It's so cold that all the little birds and mice run all over the attic and up and down the walls, so they keep their feet warm all night long. It's so creepy that Sue and I have to sleep on the same mattress with four or five blankets on top of us. I'm going to help Dad set up all the beds before New Year's comes. Sue's scared, but I'm not til I see this big bat fly out a small hole in the attic. Sue tells me that's where they put people before they put them in the cemetery next to us. Maybe some people are up there now. Why do we have to live next to the cemetery? You can go play hide-go-seek somewhere else. Sue sure learned a lot about Fowlers Mills and our new farmhouse, but she's older than me.

What a surprise in the morning when Mom shows me a letter that sweet old limpy Mrs. Ramsdel sent from my old school, telling me how much she misses me, but she says I will really like my new school. I don't know how she knows, 'cuz I am not sure I will. But I sure miss her, 'cuz I'm getting nervous about seeing all these new kids. I don't know if they're going to like me, and here I'm really trying to be good. But maybe they'll really like some of the things I can do already. Things like standing on my head and making duck noises. Even though my tummy's all turning around, I help Dad put up all the beds. My job is doing bed slats. That's what I'm best at!

Sue's new friend Cathy, the girl I was talking about who lives down by the mill in the other brother Fowler's old house, came up and took us down to meet all the new kids in those four millhouses down there. That's where I first met Bobby whose dad owned the mill and his little brother Georgie. They both have new snowsuits.

I had grown a lot from being at home from the hospital, 'cuz I ate lots of Post Toasties and Wheaties, and Mom made me eat a fried egg every week. Now my pant legs don't even go all the way down to my boots, and all that snow gets cold down into my shoes and socks. My snowsuit is so tight, I can't bend over to buckle up my galoshes. I can't even move my arms. Those galoshes get your finger pinched, too. Kids need help bucklin' up sometimes! It takes me so long, and Sue keeps saying, "Hurry up 'cuz I'm in charge of you!"

Boy! She can be so mean to me sometimes! But she really knows how to take care of me, and Mom says that's Sue's job. I hope I get that job pretty soon! I want to take care of my own self, but Sue says I'm just a little shaver. I could poke her eyes out, but I won't today. To make us grow up big, Mom makes us eat this big spoon of castor oil every week. And Mom's rule is "Don't spit it out!" Tastes like fish juice, but they put something orange in it so we don't gag. Some people really do want to help the little children, and it does make you grow!

Bobby's rich 'cuz his dad owns the mill, and like I told you, they got a lot more Santa toy presents than we did. He showed us every one of 'em. I wished he'd stop it, or I'll break 'em all up. And I met a pretty girl Carol, who's in second grade, and her little brother Bobby. So one Bobby was too big, and the other one was too little, and that's how you tell them apart. Partparts! Just joking you! We have a big Bobby and a little Bobby. That's too doggone many Bobbies in one place. They should have picked other names. Of course Carol's dad Heine with his big hinie was sitting in his big easy chair again, keeping warm in his undershirt and shorts all the time. Taking it easy again. And there's another Tommy, who his mom and dad didn't name him right, 'cuz of me. I already have that name. He doesn't say much, but he's just there, too. He has an old snowsuit, too, 'cuz his dad's only the miller, but he has a hat with earmuffs already on it, and he's only five. So that's the new kids!

I'm not sure I'm going to like these kids. We play this stupid Fox and Geese game up by the mill and throw some snowballs, but the snow is so deep, it's up to your bottom, so nobody can run very fast, 'specially Bobby. It's pretty boring. I can really run fast, 'cuz I get all Mom's castor oil, so I just hope I can show my whole new school just how fast I can run. I hope I'm the fastest, but there are lots of other kids coming by bus from everywhere there is in Munson Township. And Dad says Munson is five miles square, and that's huge! Bigger than most countries. Boy! I hope they're not very fast! Maybe they'll all be nothing but girls. I'm getting worried, 'cuz my snowsuit is too small. It's so tight, and snow gets my feet and toes all wet and squooshy. That can really slow you down a lot when you run.

Anyhow, this deep snow is melting, and the millrace is getting really high and moving really fast, too. They say the millrace is running! I don't know where to and don't get it, but that's what they're all saying. I still don't know much about this millpond, millrace, water shoot, and waterwheel. All this mill stuff that Big Bobby already knows, 'cuz we just moved in. I can't believe that a boy not as old as me knows all that stuff I don't know. It just isn't fair! That didn't make me feel very good. But anyhow, I can run faster than him and really jump high, too. I have been jumping all my life, so I need to show all those kids how high I can jump from one big stone on one side of the millrace to that other little stone on the other side. Hey! Watch me really jump far!

<hr />

Well! This is just the baddest thing of all my life, and it's all their fault, too! They made me do it! My snowsuit was too tight, and nobody even helped me put my sneakers on, too. Well! Those are the things that made me miss that other stone, and I fell right in the millrace, and my little, too-tight snowsuit and those big old galoshes and buckles dragged me under the water for an hour, and then my head finally came up again. And wouldn't you know it, right there in front of me, bobbing around, was a wood pole and my big sister Sue up on the bank, pulling and yelling at me.

This is not the time to be yelling at anybody. It isn't my fault, you know! I'm not a scardey cat! I wasn't scared or anything. I don't remember everything about that like I always do. I know I've said some bad things about my sister, but she is so strong and a tomboy, too. (That's funny. They named that after me, too. They name everything for me! Tom turkey! And someone told me tomfoolery, whatever that is.) But Sue pulled me right up the bank by the top of my snowsuit. And Dad was so funny again that night. He said if I had been wearing a barrel like the little old lady going over Niagara Falls, I wouldn't get wet! His jokes always make me feel better. And you know what? If Cathy hadn't been cheering, yelling, and jumping around so hard, Sue wouldn't have been so strong to pull me out. I think Cathy really likes me a lot. And Bobby was scared and screaming so loud, he ran away to tell his mom, so he wouldn't get his snowsuit wet, but he didn't run very fast. And all his mother did all day was just bake cookies anyway. And he never came back to help save me, 'cuz he was eating cookies again.

Darn! I really wanted to be the best new kid here. I should have gone sledding all my life and never done anything else. But if you're fatter than me, your sled goes faster. It's not fair! And don't you know it? Now my sister Sue is the biggest hero in Fowlers Mills. Everybody knows Sue and Harry Truman now. That's all they talk about! Every one of those sixty-four people is talking about it all day long up at Reynolds Store. Merle wasn't even cutting meat anymore. Just picks little food pieces out of his mustache and talks all the time about Sue saving that new boy. That's me! They should lock that store up tight and not let anybody in.

And for days at church, all the people in Munson and Preacher Kheenel praise the Lord for Sue saving my life, and he knows what he's talking about, 'cuz he's a farmer, too. He should have just only praised Sue instead of the Lord, 'cuz Sue really was the only one who really saved me. The Lord was just standing there looking down from on high, like preacher says. Not doing anything. Just up in the sky! Sue could have left me right in that terrible millrace just bobbing up and down, and I could have shot myself right over the falls. But then Mom would really be mad at her! But Sue never gets spanked anyway. I mean, who does everyone think is going to farm our new farm now? I feel like the dumbest person in the world and the biggest baby, and here my sister Sue is the biggest hero in the world now. More than even General Ike in the war. The whole world is going to talk about her forever. It is getting so bad, I have dreams about going over the mill falls that make me wet my bed. Now all the kids will really laugh at me in first grade, so I'm not going there at all. They can't make me! I'll run away. You'll see!

Well! That's all the people in Fowlers Mills thought about and talked about all day long for a long time. All sixty-four of 'em! That's all you may be talking about, too. There are sixty-four people now, 'cuz we moved in four more in my family. This is the horriblest way to start my brand-new life, and we only moved in two days ago.

Now, this is really getting bad! Right away I want to go right home to my mom so bad, 'cuz she makes everything all right. But 'cuz I'm all wet and cold and shivery so much, they take me right straight over to Cathy's mom 'cuz they live right next to the mill, and they have a huge fireplace in every room, and the biggest, hottest one of all is in the kitchen, and you remember I told you about that Hiram brother always building fireplaces, don't you? You can tell I'm getting really nervous, 'cuz I can't stop telling you that long bunch of words. Gotta get my breath! Anyhow, they try to call Mom, but these old ladies won't get off the party line, so right then and there, Mrs. McGeough takes all my clothes right off me. And there I am as naked as a jaybird! Not even my boots on, and she wraps me all up in a big blanket. They say they can't see me, but I'm there! And Betsy, our mixed-up dog Tippy's mom, and Cathy and Sue keep walking in and out, so they can peek at me. I don't mind a dog seeing me, but having Cathy see me is horrible. I know she likes me a lot, and she is so pretty with red hair and freckles. Boy! She smiles at me a lot. I don't know if I can ever look at her again.

And Heine, next door, never got his hinie out of his easy chair to come over and help. Some of that stuff he drinks would taste so good right now, 'cuz I am so thirsty. Our cat ran away once, but I didn't know much about dying. But I wish I could have, right there with no clothes on. Don't even care if I die with my boots off either. Nothing on! Maybe Sue should have just let me go over the falls, and I'd go away for a long time. But she loves me so much, even if she is a little snarky at times, and I'd sure miss her. I love her so much, 'cuz later on she taught me how to pitch like Bob Feller. Boy! What a dumb way to start! I know the kids won't like me now, but at least Mom and Dad and Sue and Tippy do!

So New Year's comes, and the wind blows part of our roof off, and we ring the big dinner bell to make the New Year come in. Pearl rings hers, too, down in the valley, so that makes the New Year start down there, too. And Mom and Dad get a little silly drinking some of that smelly orange juice, and Dad pats my mom's bottom again a few times. She just giggles and gets red and looks at Dad kind of funny and says, "Oh Rex!" That Dad is so funny! He just knows how to make Mom laugh.

When my little sister Kathleen got born almost exactly nine months later in October, all they did is laugh all the time and say, "Boy! That sure was a whopper of a storm last New Year's Eve!"

"Yah! It sure was a good one! Whoopee!"

Now I just don't get it! They got to calling my new baby sister Kathleen the New Year's baby even though my newest little baby sister Mary Beth was really the baby born on New Year's Eve four years later! Kind of mixed-up! But there sure was a lot of wind and shaking going on upstairs that night. And that's right where Mom and Dad's bedroom was. Boy! They were noisy! They could have falled through the floor. Anyhow, that's what New Year's Eves are good for! Making lots of noise! Don't they know you're supposed to be quiet after you put the children to bed? If I was Mom, and Dad spanked me on the bottom, I'd be mad, too, 'cuz you're not supposed to spank a girl like that. Just bad boys like me! They shouldn't have drunk all that funny orange juice, either. It's not good for you! Sue and I just drink Vernor's Ginger Ale. So it gets to be 1948 just after we ring our bell. Thank God we got the New Year in, even if nobody else did!

◆

But all I can think about now all day is going off up the hill to that new schoolhouse. Boy! Am I getting to be a nervous Nellie again! This school thing worries me a lot more than some old roof blowing off!

So this is like it is! Our new school has three grades in one room and only two rooms in the whole schoolhouse. I'm in the first grade, and Sue is in the fourth in the big room next door. The rooms have these funny old desks with funny designs on the side that say Sears and Roebuck. You can see through them, so you can't hide anything in there. And they have inkwell holes, like old-fashioned things or something. I have my new Christmas wood pencil box with two number 2 pencils inside. Better than anybody else's! Don't want to take my pencils and eraser in a crummy oatmeal box with that Quaker man's face on it. The kids laugh at you. They think you're having breakfast. That's dumb!

Mom told Sue she better take my hand across that big Mayfield Road to the other side, so I won't get hit by a car. That's the lookin'-both-ways road, but I just want to shut my eyes and not go at all. Now, if you remember, Sue already saved my life one time, so I have to do it. And would you believe, Cathy takes my other hand, which I kind of like. But this is embarrassing, stuck between two girls, but they cross me over to the other side, past the church, town hall, and up the steps into our new school. And then Sue and Cathy let go my hands and go off with the big kids to the other room and Mrs. Zepp over there and leave me all alone by myself.

**That's our new school and coatroom windows with
two rooms and three grades on each side.**

I feel sick all over, and here I am in the coatroom all alone. I know sometimes I talk too much, but I really am shy, and now I'm really getting nervous. My brand-new pencil case is full of sweat, and it falls all over the floor. I can hear all of the kids inside, talking about all their new presents from Santa. They're so noisy and excited about Santa. Boy, I'm not! That doggone Santa should have just stayed at home just like I should have! But that bossy Mrs. Claus made him go! I just want to hide inside my snowsuit. Darn thing is too small. I take the longest time to take it off, pulling and tugging all over really slowly, even though I really don't have to. And I can hear Mrs. Van Orsdale (later we call her Mrs. Horsetail, 'cuz she was more like that) telling the kids where to sit and to shut up and keep their mouths quiet. Boy! She could yell! Boy! I miss my mom, and I want to be so brave here, but I'm sure not doing very good.

And Ruth Ann, a first grader I never met before, keeps saying, "Come on, Tommy! Don't be afraid!" Mrs. Van Orsdale asks me to come inside, but I just sit there in that coatroom bench all day long. I want to hide behind the coats, so nobody can find me.

So she went back in to teach all three grades in one room, but Ruth Ann stays right beside me the whole day. She has a beautiful smile and pretty, dark-black hair. Really pretty! She is so nice to me, and I think I might be falling in love, but later on all the boys say you can get cooties if you sit next to her, and I sure don't want those germs. You remember, I was already in the hospital and almost died two times. I sure hope that thing they call the cootie catcher works. Make 'em out of construction paper.

There are only five boys in my grade: Bruce, Jackie, me, David, and Dickie. Sue's room has only four other kids in the whole sixth grade: Tommy, Don, Joyce, and Hilda. That lucky Tommy went right into the United States Army after the sixth grade, 'cuz he is so smart and grown-up and knows a lot about girls. Boy! We're so proud of him! He's so grown-up, he can blow beeps out of his armpits. He even has a fuzzy little mustache, and I think Mrs. Zepp likes him 'specially so much. That's why he stayed back so many years in her same room. She didn't want to let him go!

Ooh! I'm so glad when the bell rings, and I can go home and worry all by myself again and go to the bathroom some more and more. I must have wee-weeed in my snowsuit. That's kind of a baby word. I've got to think of another one, but I can't spell it yet. I asked Mom if I can go back to my old school in Cleveland Heights, but she said it's just a little too far to walk and that Mrs. Ramsdel already said good-bye to me.

Now the next day, things get better, and I'm really trying harder. My teacher says her church is having a fish fry in Claridon. I have no idea what a fish fry is or where's Claridon, but I tell Mrs. Van Orsdale that my whole family can go, and she lets me take four tickets home. We all go, and I take Mom and Dad right up to Mrs. Van Orsdale. I know now she will think I'm the best new student ever. But two weeks later, report cards came out, and mine said all Bs, even in deportment. I don't believe I didn't get any As, so I went right up and asked her. She told me I had only been there two weeks, and she didn't know me well enough yet. Well, that made me mad! Your teacher's supposed to know who you are right away. I mean, who else did she think I am? Winkin', Blinkin', and Nod! I sure don't look like those other dumb kids. That's making me really feel bad. I know I have to show her, so in a week or so she starts telling us about the valentine box. Well, I yell right out, "I'll do it," 'cuz I'm really trying hard. Then I got Mom and Dad and Sue to help me. I have never seen so much of that red-and-white crap paper you can twist and stretch all around and glue all over. So I know now she'll think I'm the best student ever!

I begin to like Mrs. Van Orsdale. She's kind of grumpy sometimes, but she starts to smile at me a lot. After lunch she reads story time to us while we sit in a circle down on the floor, and she sits way up high in her chair. I can't help it, but I try to sit where I can see up her dress. What's up there? Her legs are kind of wrinkled where her garters are, but I never even told my best new friend Bruce, 'cuz I don't know if Bruce will see it like me or not, and I don't think you're supposed to do this. I peeked in Mom's drawer one time, so I know what garters look like. I just hope nobody sees me do it. I also found some caramel candies in Mom's drawer that make you lose weight, and I ate the whole box, but nobody knows that, either. They were so good. If I eat the whole box, I wouldn't be any pounds at all. But don't drink that Milk of Magnesia stuff that's in the bathroom. I mean, it tastes really good like peppermint, but it says M O M, and I'm getting to know those letters mean just for Mom. That stuff gives you the runs, too. Makes you run really fast. I'm going to give her some caramels back, though, when I get some. If anybody sees me peeking up at story time, I'll turn really red.

I know I don't remember any of those reading stories, 'cuz I spent more time looking way up there and not listening, but I never told anybody until now. I'm a boy who likes secrets. Some kids even make noises out of their bottoms, sitting around at story time, like beeping or something. Well! They hold their noses and giggle but not me. I sit there really quiet. I like secrets! But you and I are getting to know all the new kids, so you know who it is anyhow. A burp kind of sounds the same, but it's out the other end.

I'm really beginning to like this new school. It's lots of fun! I get a desk right behind Peggy. Mom says she and her brother George had left the Amish, and I thought that's strange, 'cuz the Millers and Bylers are still Amish, and they didn't leave. And where are you supposed to leave them? Peggy has big pigtails and eyes and two big, beautiful front tooths. She always has a big smile on her face to show them. Her long pigtails are yellow and come right down to the front of my desk. I know you're not supposed to, but I start to play with her pigtails, and she turns around and smiles right at me. Just like Mom smiles at Dad sometimes, like when they drank that orange stuff on New Year's. And I can't stop smiling back til I tie one of her pigtails into my inkwell. I couldn't untie it, so Peggy and I decide to cut her braid in half with her scissors. She looks so pretty now with one long braid and one short one. I kept her hair in my desk, 'cuz I thought about her a lot even when I was supposed to pay attention. And we smile for each other a lot more. I think I'm just having more troubles! Mom and Dad probably should have made me talk with a grown-up, but I don't think they have any around here.

After Valentine's Day it gets warmer outside, and Farmer Carroll starts his *maple sugaring, tapping trees,* and *boiling sap*—all these syrup words. It's the spring thaw! You know spring is coming 'cuz I start to sneeze. Mrs. Van Orsdale says that's the time teachers need more time to put more stuff on the chalkboard, so we get more recess. That's the time I can't wait for! We go outside in the schoolyard, and everybody jumps around and runs and gets muddy. And then we all get in twos and threes and start wrestling and try to pin somebody. I never wrestled before. Not in the city, and this is really fun. You just do it all at once and don't have to take up all that time choosing up sides and like playing that stupid Red Rover, Red Rover, Won't Rosie Come Over? And not like chasing some stupid ball around. Wrestling, you can really beat somebody up. 'Cuz I like Bruce and said hi to him, we started wrestling together.

I have to tell you this. Bruce has been a farmer a lot longer than I have, and he is really strong. He can lift a whole pail of water all by his self. And he's got these yellow curls that stick out right on top of his head. Looks like he combs them. He buttons all his buttons, and his shirttails never come out like mine do. There's a kid in every room up in his big white house up on the hill. Has seven sisters and one big brother Bud who has his own Brown Swiss cow. They're all in charge of the little kids there, 'cuz all they got is their mom who always has a baby and stays out back. Bruce believes what you say and never complains. He sits still at his desk all day if he wants to and goes right to work and can think about one thing at a time. I bounce around more. He's a real doer and not a daydreamer or sneaky like me. He likes to make things. When he's got something in his head, though, you can't talk him out of it. You'll get to know him a lot better, 'cuz he always says what's on his mind, and he and I work together a lot!

Well! He got my shoulders pinned right on the ground. He said he learned that from his sisters, but I thought I could flip him over. And if it wasn't for this stupid old snowsuit pinching my arms, I probably could have. But he is strong! Sometimes you think you know everything, but you don't til you find out. And you learn that! His muscles are all inside, too, and you can't see 'em. And here I thought I was stronger than anybody, but dadgumit, that surprised me! Anyhow, I couldn't budge Bruce off at all. I was getting embarrassed, 'cuz all the other kids in school made a big circle around us and started yelling and cheering and jumping up and down. I couldn't give up! They would think I wasn't very strong or a chicken. I was supposed to say uncle or aunt or some kind of cousin to stop it, but you don't just give up. I had to show them something, 'cuz they were all shouting really loud.

Finally the school bell rang, and I sure hope nobody saw the tears come out of me. I'm really too big to cry, but I couldn't help it! I wasn't doing good, and you know what? Bruce became the best friend I ever had! He even gives me my very own purple rosary when I sleep over with him on Friday nights at his house. But I lied again here, and I'm not supposed to! You'll see what I'm talking about not doing so good!

Now we kids all sit together inside around our desks, and I tell everybody right there that Bruce pulled my jacket right over my eyes on purpose, so I couldn't see and had tried to choke me with his scarf and stab my eyes out with his fingers, and that's why I couldn't flip him over. But Bruce's pretty sister Rosie, with long brown hair and in the third grade, touched me and says, "Bruce really didn't do that and really didn't want to hurt you." Well! Rosie is so nice and pretty, and all of a sudden I almost kissed her, but I remember the last time I kissed a girl in that horrible city school, and we got the biggest talk about bad germs. I sure don't want that to happen again. But now I know in this new country air they don't have germs. Only in the city! So I believe Rosie 'cuz I also know the Truth.

That's when Bruce and I become the best friends forever! Can you believe it? Bruce and I fighting like a bunch of roosters, and now we're best friends! Later, we even have our new babies together! We borned them at the same time! Every day we'd ask, "Did your baby come yet?" I don't how he did it, but his baby came out three days before mine. Boy! Bruce and his family knew how to make lots of babies, 'cuz so far they have seven kids, and all we have is three. I know that Bruce boy is faster than he looks. But my baby sister Kathleen is so cute with big eyes and lips and fluffy hair, and she loves to pull Tippy's tail. Most babies I know just dribble out their mouths, but not Kathy. She doesn't breathe when she eats. We called her Kathy for short, and she's not too tall, either. She's so much fun! I'll tell you a lot more about her later.

Dad told me about Bonnie Prince Charlie, and I told Bruce that. He just never figgered out how you can name a baby boy Bonnie, so I guess that's why they called their new baby girl Bonnie. Then another Prince Charlie was born in England a couple weeks later, so Bruce changed her name to Bassie cuz we liked fishing so much. That's history like Dad teaches kids.

But I do remember better when I was all grown-up in the fourth grade. That's when I really got to kiss Rosie. You can remember things better when you're out of first and second grade and can see back on 'em. The three of us were walking up the Mayfield Road hill to Bruce's house. We were single file with Rosie in the middle, 'cuz the road was a busy one, and sister Rosie is a girl. And 'cuz Rosie's a girl, she said, "Let's pass on a kiss!" That's better than just going ahead and fast kissing. So I kissed Rosie, and then she kissed Bruce, 'cuz he's a boy, too. Wow! That was something I'll never forget! Her brother Bruce didn't seem too excited, though! I don't know what's the matter with him!

Mom says Bruce being my best friend is the best thing that ever happened to me. And Bruce and I talk about lots of serious things. We talk about things like: "What's hell like?" "Do your brain and heart grow as big as your stomach and legs?" About this "going to heaven thing:" "Why do you have to wait so long to get there?" "Why can't we have it now?" and stuff like that.

Bruce says, "You go to hell if you don't say the rosary," and I'd say, "What if I don't have a rosary, or just say 'rosary.'"

Then he says, "We'll make one," and I'd say, "What if we don't have any beads?" or "Maybe I can sneak some from your mom." He makes more things than me. But we did lots of religious talk like that! Bruce says his rosary is really a lucky charm. I sure need that! I could use two of 'em! I'd talk like a Methodist, and he'd talk like a Catholic, so he has lots more things to say than me. I only have a couple of things to say about that.

Boy! When he talks about that purgatory thing, that gets scary. Don't know what it means, but it sure doesn't sound fun! Bruce and I got to figger all this stuff out! Maybe you have to get more purple beads or make a bigger rosary for that to stay out of there. I'm going to have to learn a lot more Methodist things to say. Hard to find 'em, but I guess they're there somewhere. Why didn't I know that everyone in Fowlers Mills doesn't go to the Fowlers Mills Community Church? I thought you had to go there if you live here.

I talk to him again about having to wait for this heaven thing, and he tells me all the things you have to do first to get there. I'm not sure I'm going there anyhow! Sometimes I just can't wait long enough for anything. And you have to be the first one to die to find out, and I'm not ready for that thing. I don't want to be the first to find out. Sometimes it's better to be the last kid in line. This ain't no lunch line we're in here! We spent more time talking about that kind of stuff than we did our school workbooks. And sometimes it was just country stuff like, "Can a fish swim backward?" And stuff like that. I don't know if we ever got any good answers. Mom probably knows all this stuff anyhow. We shoulda talked to her about it, but this is more kid kind of stuff. I sure didn't find it out in Sunday school!

And you know what? Bruce really believes me about things I say even if I don't know what I'm saying. He's good that way. Yep! He's a good believer! I'm a better daydreamer than a believer. That's why I let him wear my cousin David's new hand-me-down black-and-white-checked, furry jacket. I told Bruce it was from a real buffalo my grandfather had shot in Virginia. My grandpa was a good shooter. He was the second-best shot in Virginia. I don't know why I lied a little here, 'cuz that grandpa really lives in Huntington, West Virginia, and not Virginia. I just made that up! But 'cuz he is my new best friend and believes me, I let him wear it for two whole weeks. I can see how proud he is, and then he lets me wear his. He even wears it in the lunch line. He never takes it off. It makes him so handsome. Bruce puts the coat collars down flat, but I wear the collar up high, 'cuz my ears point up like a fairy. I think all the kids want to wear my jacket, but I only let Bruce wear it, and I'm sure glad to do it. Everybody sees we're best friends now!

One time we were reading out loud, and I started to talk like they do in West Virginia with a funny twang. And Bruce said right out loud that I sounded like I was from down South, and I told the whole class right there that I was from Virginia. But you know we really moved in from Cleveland. But Bruce could believe so well. He was the strongest, and I was the second strongest. I couldn't let him down, but I just seem to have more trouble telling the Truth. Telling the Truth just doesn't sound so good to me. It's too boring, and believe me, you never want to get bored!

Bruce and I spend lots of time together playing in barns, shooting Osage oranges in bent-over trees like the Romans did, camping out, and building fires sometimes with flint and steel. But you'll hear a lot more about Bruce and me, 'cuz we are friends forever. We know what we're both thinking. He knows all about me telling you all this stuff even before it's on the story paper.

You know what? We even got a little blood scratched on our wrists and tied them together with a grapevine. That's how we became blood brothers just like Cochise and all the Apaches did in that Western movie. I'll tell you more about that later, 'cuz Bruce and I are best friends for life. Everybody who's a best friend should mix their blood up together. You know, with Bruce's blood in me now, I can wrestle a lot better. Mixing up each other's blood is how you get some better things in you. I'm not sure what Bruce got in my blood, 'cuz he never started to lie much like me.

I love to stay overnight in his big farmhouse up the hill, 'cuz he has six sisters and one big brother, Bud. And we even put on the best make-up plays, and I got to kiss Rosie one more time right on the lips in a play we make up. Don't want everyone to know about it, so I'll tell you more about it later. Then all of us would say the rosary all together around the big bed right on our knees with his mom there. She really smiles about that. Then we put her right to bed in the back of the house with the new baby, and off we go and have more fun. No one ever makes us go to sleep, and we never do. We play all night! That's how you learn every-thing—by trying things out and playing around. Taking a chance. You don't have to do it, but you just want to. Work's different! Gotta do it!

Later on when we got a lot older in the third and fourth grades, Bruce and I would stand all the other boys in baseball. Just the two of us make one team! I'd pitch, and he'd play the outfield. He gets the only one glove we have. The Rawlings! That glove can catch anything, even dirt balls. Always put lots of Neat Foots oil on it, so that glove never drops anything. Bruce and I take turns batting each other in while the other kids just run around chasing their balls. One of our balls doesn't even have a leather cover on it, just a bunch of wound-up rubber bands! Boy! We two are a real team! We just know how to pull together like two draft horses!

Later on in life, we talked and thought a lot and figured out there was just too much swearing going on in our school, and that really went against our religion. You've just got to stop that before it gets out of hand or out of their mouths. Well! We started as soon as we could, washing kids' mouths out with soap. I'll tell you more about that later. Bruce and I saved the little shrimps from the mean bullies, too. We really knew how to beat up all those mean little bullies! Make 'em bleed all over!

Beat 'em up really badly! Break their bones if we have to. Yep! Nobody's going to be beating up those little kids! So we just beat 'em all up really good. Those little bullies better grow up fast! Now we really were going to be the best and nicest boys in that whole school, but you'll see later.

Now I'm not sure I should, but I have to tell you about what happened one time. I'm not so proud about it now. But Mom says you have to listen and keep your ears and eyes open and learn from your elders. That's people older than me. And you know kids that don't listen just grow up to be lumps and take up space. And always tell the Truth! And that rule's not easy to do. That's something you probably learn a lot later in life when you're older, 'cuz you know grown-ups always tell the Truth. They don't even know how to lie. Mom doesn't talk a lot, but she has a rule for everything, like, you think about it, don't whine, don't think you're better than anybody else, help somebody if they're hurting, and tell the Truth, and that's the one I'm trying to work on most right now. That Truth one is the toughest one for me!

One day it was real springy out in the schoolyard, and I know, 'cuz it's sneezing time. I like spring 'cuz Mrs. Van Orsdale likes it and doesn't make you work very hard and gives you more As. Well! I get to watching the fifth- and sixth-graders like Tommy S., you know, those older ones. They're doing something I know takes lots of muscles and really being brave. They are actually holding on to the ankles of the older girls like Carol and Joyce and twirling them around, so their dresses are flying up over their heads. You can actually see their unders if you're that kind of boy and want to look really hard. The girls scream and giggle so loud, and Tommy S. is so strong and brave, and that's why I think he joined the army after the sixth grade. He was the best! He spent about ten years or more in Munson Grade School 'cuz everybody likes him so much. He is almost like everybody's dad. He was like a real man teacher. I feel so proud 'cuz he was Tommy S., and I'm Tommy T. I'm hoping I can be a lot more like him!

And I got to thinking. What a great way to show these lower-grade kids what I can do to get them to like me best, just like Tommy S. Well! I started a "Pull Up the Girls' Dresses" campaign right there, 'cuz I wasn't strong enough yet to twirl them around by the ankles. I can't tell you where I got that "campaign" word, but I think I heard it from when Mr. Truman and Mr. Dewey were shouting on the radio at each other to see who could get the better job, and they kept calling that a campaign. Every grown-up has got to have a job, you know. I already knew in 1947 that my job was to be the best farmer in Fowlers Mills. So Bruce, Jackie, David, and I got busy and started pulling up dresses. Dickie didn't do it though. We sure had a lot of work to do! That job seemed more important than just sitting under the swings to watch the girls who swung so high. Us boys wanted to be the first to swing up over the bars. That's a dare, like climbing the highest tree, jumping on the pond ice to see it break, or jumping way up in Bruce's barn rafters to land on the hay, hoping there's no pitchfork in it. Only boys do the dare things!

Girls just swung high enough to show their unders. This campaign thing was a lot more fun than just showing our things behind the pump house. We did really good at this until we pulled up Nancy's dress. Boy! Was she strong, and she can really hit hard! She couldn't read so good, but she sure knew lots of arithmetic and was in the third grade two years, but she was extra smart. She could add and subtract better than anybody. She didn't do so good in spelling bees, but she sure knew how to stop our campaign. And it really got bad when we pulled up Joanie's dress, 'cuz she was the church choir teacher's daughter, and she told the teacher on all of us right away. That's what church people do. They tell on you! And then, thank goodness, snack time came with juice and graham crackers, 'cuz after all that work we did on our campaign, we were really hungry.

I got to share a desk with a big boy, Billy, a third grader. He's long and quiet like a soldier! He was the only boy in the third grade that played baseball. Rosie smiled at him a lot. He has yellow hair, too, and girls like that the best. I wish mine was yellow and not all bushy brown. Billy follows the rules just right, too. He doesn't touch the girls like we did. Boy! I can't even chew now, 'cuz my jaw hurts bad where Nancy hit it. It's OK to hit a boy, but it's against the rules to hit a girl. Never hit a girl!

And then, right in front of the whole class, Mrs. Van Orsdale said, "I know a nice new boy who did something very bad, and I know he'll never do that bad thing again!"

I hid right under the desk, and Billy poked me and said in a really loud voice like only these third-grade boys have, "That's you, Tommy!" Well! I turn all red and never have been the same again! Can you believe it? Right in front of the whole class! And Billy gets all my gram crackers and orange juice. I just want to vomit! I feel horrible about myself! Now nobody will ever like me or play with me except Mom and Dad, and that looks stupid. Bruce won't want to be my best friend anymore, and I can't come back here to this school again. It's not going to be easy. I'm just going to have to live in the woods!

———◆———

Well! I finally got over it. It wasn't easy! Spring's coming 'cuz I'm sneezing again. The river's flooding all over our road, and there are flowers like wild ginger, bloodroot, trilliums, May apples, and all that weird stuff starting to grow. There's a jack-in-the-pulpit flower, 'cuz you have to have a church one. Can't pick trilliums or jack-in-the-pulpits, or they die. One time I won a Snickers bar for naming the most wildflowers. Candy bars really make me do my best even if naming flowers isn't too exciting. If you don't get candy, I don't try so hard. Buds are coming out, and this means summer is coming, and I can get out of this crummy school and go off to the Geauga County Fair! It's the oldest one in Ohio. I can't wait going off! Yippie!

At fair time I had the biggest chance to do something really big. It was art, 'cuz there is going to be a special school art exhibit at the *fair*. That's another one of those *F* words, like "farms," "fishing," "fairies," and "fun." I like the *A* words, but all I can think of is "art" and "apples." Yep! Lerning all my letters to spell real good now!

You can tell I was good at art and going to the fair.

Well! I knew I could really make the best picture ever in the fair. The teacher must've known I could really draw, 'cuz I got a big piece of oilcloth and a whole box of eight crayons just for myself. Not just two or three but the whole box! So I crayoned two red barns, two horses in the field, two bales of hay, two trees, and two goldfish in one stream. I was drawing everything in twos, and I got so excited, I just couldn't stop.

And now Mrs. Van Osrdale yells, "It's time to put your art supplies away and do your first-grade numbers; second grade, get your readers; and third graders, you work on your workbooks, and when you finish that, help the second graders with their readers." Well! I can't remember if it was exactly morning or afternoon, but don't you know it, all of a sudden I can't see anything. That's what I told the teacher. I went blind just like that, and the teacher was so worried, she let Peggy say all my numbers to me, like two plus two, out loud, so I could add them up in my head, 'cuz I couldn't see anything. I was lerning to spell really well, too, so Peggy would just say the letters, and I'd get the word, too. So then after numbers and spelling, 'cuz I couldn't see words and read, I got extra time to go back to the art table in the corner to work on my fair picture again. This was going to be something really wonderful, and everybody in Geauga County would be there and see it. Boy! Peggy was so nice to me. She said all the numbers I couldn't see out loud for a whole week.

But I began to get nervous. Somebody was going to catch me and not believe me. I really got worried, 'cuz I heard something about Mom going to take me to Dr. Thomas in Cleveland to find out what's wrong with my eyes. I didn't know what was going to happen! I never got to sleep all those nights, thinking about what I was going to say to Dr. Thomas, except it's funny he and me have the same name. Yep! Everybody's getting my name. Like Dad says, "No tomfoolery!" And there's Tommy Hawk, too! And that book Mom reads that says, "Tommy this and Tommy that, and Tommy don't you dare!" I'm not sure he's going to laugh at all that or not. But at least I didn't wet the bed. I don't have to! I'm just scared all the time and wee-wee all day long!

It takes an awfully long time in the car to drive there. I wish Mom would slow down. But when we finally get there, they have me look at all these letters on the wall. Funny looking *E*s backwards and upside down. They need to straighten these letters out, so somebody can read 'em! I fool them, though, 'cuz I can't even read any of them big or small. Never told them, but I really could, 'cuz I know my alphabet really well. Then Dr. Thomas came in and made me look through all these big machines. Boy! Was I really glad to get out of there! I don't know what he did, but anyhow, I came home with Mom with a little piece of paper to get glasses with a plastic frame and a nice little brown case that snaps shut with a little pink cloth inside. I look pretty weird! Like somebody else when I wear them. Mom says I'm nearsighted and have an "a-stick-is-in-em," whatever that is. They told me my eye was bumpy and crooked. So what! I saw a dead pig's eye once, and it didn't look so round. And Dart's eyebrows are so bushy, you can't even see his eyes. And he can't even see his beard to pick food and chewing tobacco out!

Well! It's that time to go off to school again, so I put the glasses case in my pocket and run down to the mill. That's when I take off my glasses and put them inside the case, snap the darn thing shut, and hide it behind a tree. So nobody knows I have these stupid glasses when I get to school. I sure fooled them! You can't really run hard and wrestle with glasses on anyhow. No one fights with glasses. You just don't hit a kid with glasses on!

One time they must have fallen out of my pocket, 'cuz sometimes I just ran too fast down that path up the dirt road to the school. Well! One day Sue found them in the snow and gave them to Mom. Sue did that 'cuz she cared about me so much, and you know Sue was already a hero before me in Fowlers Mills. Boy! Was I ever mad at her for that!

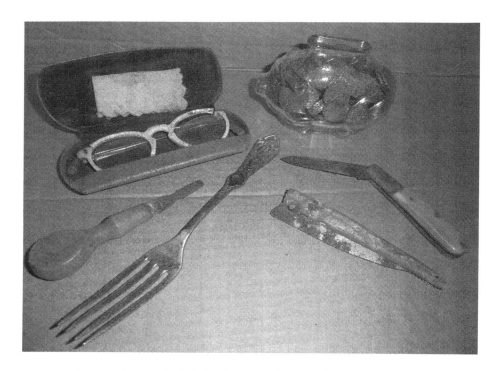

Those glasses didn't look so good new, either! That's my piggy bank for hiding all my money so nobody steals it.

One day Mrs. Van Orsdale asks Mom, "How's Tommy doing with his eyes?" 'cuz I can see all my numbers now.

Then Mom asks her, "How are the new glasses doing?" and the teacher says, "What new glasses? Tommy never wears glasses."

Gosh darn it! Nothing ever works out for me, and I'm trying so hard to be the best boy. Mom even got a penny postcard in the mail reminding her to bring me back for a visit with Dr. Thomas. Well! I sure didn't have any more jokes for him, and I sure wanted to really give him a big reminder right back!

I wanted to say, "I'm tired of visiting you, I'm not comin' back, and that's that!" I think he's catching on to me. Now, this time I can just tell there's going to be lots of trouble.

I should of stayed playing with Jackie and those boys digging big hunks of dirt out under the community house next door to the playground. They love to run all these silly toy trucks and cars around that hole that goes halfway under the floor. Jackie just loves cars, trucks, machines, or anything that moves. Those boys are always making these noises like trucks going "boom chug-chug boom beep-vroom."

Jackie is so smart! He can tell you what kind of car it is just by hearing it drive by with his eyes shut. Like a Hudson from Packard or a Chevy or a Desoto or a Ford. Boy! Jackie can even tell a Model A from a Model T or a V-8 from a Chevy V-6. Heck, I thought a V-8 was a can of tomato juice. And with a Studebaker just setting there, I can't even tell which way it's going 'cuz it's got two fronts on it at both ends. I'm better at telling what people are thinking about. I got him one time, though, when it was a Nash and one time a Willys. We got a Willys after our Gray Goat car died. Boy! I hate dying! Of course Jackie could have been lying, too, and peeking with his eyes only half-shut. I don't know if he's a good fibber like me or not.

But then all these mothers got all worried, 'cuz mothers do that a lot, and they thought the community house was falling down, so they made those digger boys stop digging. But I really think their moms' arms just got too tired washing all those dirty clothes on those washboards and having to hang them all out to dry. That's the only other thing that mothers do all day, besides cooking and worrying. They hang stuff out to dry all day. Just don't ask anyone to come over after school if your mom has her underpants and girdle out on the line to dry. That's really embarrassing, and it's hard to look your friends in the eye. Sometimes you gotta get there first to make sure! That's another good thing about running fast!

Now, I don't know much about cars except our '35 Plymouth, the Green Hornet, and the '37 Dodge we called the Gray Goat, but every time I go over to play at Jackie's house over by Sand Hill, all we do is push these little cars and trucks up and down the same stupid dirt pile and say, "Vroom! Vroom!" all the time. It's kind of boring, huh? I'm just not a car kind of boy. I only like to ride in them, especially if it's ours. I'd rather peek through all his mom's drawers and can't wait to get a glass of orange pop. They have lots of it, and that's Jackie's favorite pop. But me, I'm more a Vernor's Ginger Ale boy. Jackie moves around all the time, all over. He's a squirmy action boy. Jackie's kind of like the other side of Dickie. Dickie's quiet and follows the rules. Put 'em together, and it works out OK!

You never know where Jackie's going to pop up. One time the teacher even tied him in the front-row desk with his own belt to keep him from walking all over the room, but that didn't even stop him. Walking around like that, he doesn't even need any desk. Sometimes that's when you get the most things done. He can have my desk if he wants. I sure don't want it! He's so squirmy and curious about everything. Too curious to pay much attention to rules. I don't think he knew they had any! Sure loves to talk a lot. Jackie's sure a good and smart guy, though, and we sure think he's pretty funny. He's real exciting so you don't get bored so much at school. Full of the dickens! Not quiet like a Jack-in-the- Pulpit boy. His head is really big like the rest of him. Biggest boy in class! That's why the teacher paid lots of attention to him. He sure was a fun boy!

I don't know why they don't make him take some kind of juice or some pill or something to keep him quiet. Kids shouldn't get away with anything! He was a PILL! But the only pills they have are ASS-BURNS. Hey, people! We don't talk like that in Fowlers Mills! That's a joke! And those pills don't slow you down anyhow. A sixth grader told me that first word means your bottom. Doesn't sound like it, though. That's funny! Or they can give Jackie a shot like I got in the hospital. All fifty of 'em, right in the bottom. And maybe that'll quiet him down. Sure didn't quiet me down! Boy, I yelled! But he has a bigger bottom than my little skinny one, so it won't hurt him so much. I mean, look at me! I get that dumb castor oil and iron once a week, but it doesn't slow me down. It just makes you gag and go faster. I don't think something like that's ever going to quiet Jackie down, and he can have all of mine if he wants. Maybe it'll run the runs right out of him! Watch out! Mrs. Warner could sneak it in the soup. She puts everything else in there! Even some of her hairs go in there when they fall out. But Mom says I'm a lot stronger for all that castor oil, and I sure am. Just look at me! It takes a lot of muscles to push a wheelbarrow full of garbage all over the creek bridge and bury it, but that's just another one of those tough jobs that farmers have to do. You know it's not really like work if you pretend it's Captain Hook's treasure box. And boy, I could pretend! Arrghhh!

Boy! School days are almost over now. I can't sit still. I am so excited 'cuz the big Geauga Lake Amusement Park picnic is only one week away. And just to be good so I can go, I'm wearing these stupid glasses just for reading these silly books about Dick and Jane and their stupid dog Spot, and I don't really need my glasses, anyway. I can see more of them than I really want to. This book is really stupid anyway and says the same thing over and over, like you're dumb or something. And it isn't very funny anyhow. It just says stuff like, "Dick jumps, Jane jumps, Dick runs, Jane runs, Spot runs, Joe runs, Bruce runs, and Bob runs." Everybody runs! So what! Gives me the runs. Gives me the jumps, too! Anyhow, I'd rather run all over than read this silly book. Mom's right again! She says, "Actions speak louder than words."

That's what I mean about reading stupid books. I'd rather be doing something special than read about it over and over and over again. And remember, I was blind one time, so I can have trouble reading too many of those dumb words. Don't want to be blind again. You have to be care-ful! And this is why I don't do better in deportment or what Mom calls conduct. I don't even want to work on that thing!

I already cleaned out my desk and brought my special wood pencil box home. Now school's over, and summer's going to be forever! No more shoes and sitting still in desks. The very best thing about schools is getting out of them! And Mrs. Van Orsdale even gave me a big, scratchy hug for a good-bye. I think she forgot to shave, but she sure was getting nicer!

Anyway, the mothers' club gave us twenty little red tickets to ride a whole bunch of rides at Geauga Lake. They made lots of really sweet, red Kool-Aid, too. That red Kool-Aid gives me so much extra energy I can run all day long. Fast, too! At least moms know what's best for you! They always have the right answer. At least, that's what we tell them. One of our biggest jobs is to make moms happy. Of course, there's a whole lot they don't know what we know. It's the honest Truth!

Every ride was one ticket that cost ten cents, except for that fast, clickity, old, wood rollie coaster that cost two tickets. It looked like it's going to fall all apart, and when you got off, you were awfully glad it didn't. There was one guy there in the fifth grade who always had his hair combed to a point in the back with Vitalis or Bear Grease on it and a T-shirt rolled up on his shoulders with cigarettes in it. Not the good kind. Not Lucky Strikes that make fine tobacco like my dad's! Can you believe how angry that boy's mom would be if she knew he didn't smoke the Lucky kind. The other kids thought he was really cool 'cuz he had a girlfriend. I think he's one of those city guys. Someone even saw him smoking cigarettes behind the church, of all places. I don't see him much at recess, 'cuz he's got a girlfriend who he always walks with, his arm around her waist. She's the kind of girl who always falls down and needs lots of help walking and doesn't look too strong and has to lean on him a lot. Those two kids always play their games by themselves behind the church, probably secret games, so you really can't see them much. They might be playing a lot of helping games, 'cuz that boy really likes to take good care of her. I hope she gets to walk better soon.

Well! That boy took ten rides in a row on that rollie coaster, and then would you believe, he vomited all over his girlfriend, himself, the seat, and the whole rollie coaster and even got some on us down below 'cuz we were watching up from the bottom. I thought it was bird stuff dropping on us! And Bruce and I even gave him two of our very own tickets 'cuz he said he didn't have enuff. We're the real givers in our school. We like to help all the kids. And he looked like he really knew what he was doing and was a lot braver than us because he was a fifth grader, and other kids said he was really cool. This whole thing was scary to look at, even for old Bruce and me!

He couldn't stand up, and the girl he took with him couldn't ever stop crying. I cared a lot and thought maybe she could lean on me awhile. I felt sorry for them, so Bruce and I got lots of rags and napkins and helped clean them up. We sat with him until he could stand up and not be woozy. He had one of those crummy tummies. Don't know why, though, but we took turns holding his head up like my mom always does when we get sick. I always call her Mommie when I'm sick, because she gets to us faster that way. Well! His girlfriend went away off somewhere. We couldn't find her anywhere. She probably had to go wee-wee in the bathroom really badly. And old Bruce and I never peek in girls' bathrooms! No, sireee! We're not those kinds of boys. And then she probably couldn't find her way back. I think she must have got lost or something.

Well! Lunchtime came at last, and Bruce and Jackie and I were so hungry after helping so many kids, we ate so many hot dogs and potato chips and lots of that good old potato salad that Mrs. Warner had made the night before. We ate every bit of that potato salad. It was so yummy, we couldn't stop! Boy! Mrs. Warner knew just how to put that big old pot of potato salad right there smack in the hot sun all day with all that yummy mayo just goooing it all up to keep it extra good and really warm and tasty. Looked like it was sweating. Made it taste a lot sharper on your tongue. Wow! It had a good bite in it! Boy! She could really cook well!

And you know Kool-Aid is just the right thing for you! You should drink as much as you ever can. We even had fifths and sixths of it just to get some extra energy. You know, we got so much energy we couldn't even sit still. We were jumping all over the place. Of course me, the highest! We ate plenty to keep us really healthy. We ate as much as we could, because after all that hard schoolwork all year long, we sure deserved it, and we sure wanted to grow up big for the summer, to get those muscles up! But for some reason, and I don't know why, we got the worst tummy aches and puked all over, just like that fifth-grader guy. I'm not sure if the other kids thought we were really cool or not. Boy! I felt hot! Gosh, that picnic was the most fun! That Geauga Lake Park is the most exciting place in the world!

I felt bad for Dickie, because his mother wouldn't let him go. His mother was so nice, but she's from Chekoslovakia, and there are no amusement park rides there. And she sure didn't want him to get all sick with germs and stuff. And the reason Dickie never gets sick is because he eats so many pastries his mom makes all the time. That's what they mostly do in Chekoslovakia. They just eat lots of pastries, and that makes you really healthy all the time.

She must have been pretty smart, because Dickie sure is. Dickie even has a big Adam's apple that bounces up and down when he talks, so you know right there he's really healthy. And you can guess, too, he sure has a pretty skinny neck. He is long and so skinny, his breastbone touches his back. Like a hole there. He could lie down, and you could put a whole glass of milk in that chest hole. Dickie doesn't cut up.

He's like the cowboy sheriff on TV who rides tall in the saddle and is always saying in a really deep voice, "Pardners, let's help those settlers burning up in that log cabin down there." Does the right thing! He doesn't talk much, but he sure knows how to follow the rules! Never gets scolded, and teachers don't have to keep an eye on him. Not one of those tricky troublemakers! Or maybe he is, and we just don't know it! He runs mostly in a straight line and doesn't zigzag around like Jackie and me. I don't think he knows how to lie or pretend stuff. What you see is what you get!

Dickie. See how scrubbed he is. Teeth brushed and hair combed. He was gooder than me.

Wow! Dickie has the cutest little sister Janet with blond hair and beautiful cheeks. I think I can marry her some day, but she's so little and shy. And she never asked me not even one time to marry her. And you know what again? I may be just like Farmer Carroll and never get married at all, anyhow, and just live with Mom. Nope! Dickie never talks a lot, so his Adam's apple wouldn't bounce around too much. He just says, "nope!" and "yep!" He just talks in one-word things. Not a best-spelling-bee boy like me. But he sure knows all the answers for those arithmetic questions the teacher asks. He even came to school one time with this thing he called a slide rule. Looked to me like a fancy ruler, and we pretended pirates and swords with it. Said he got it 'cuz his dad's a carpenter who measures boards. Made my new pencil box look kind of dumb!

But anyhow, summer's finally here, and I won't see Dickie again til next year in second grade. I miss Dickie, but he lives too far to walk to his house, and he never gets into trouble. Going over to his house to play is like going way out of the country. It's all the way to Route 44! That's a busy road and that's why Dickie plays more in his yard and doesn't run all over the fields like I do. And even though I don't like school when summer's over, I always like seeing Dickie again. He just seems to do a lot more things right than I do. He doesn't get scolded and isn't fidgety like me. I have a fidget problem! Jackie's got one, too.

Dickie didn't have to sharpen everybody's pencils over at the big sharpener on the wall like we do. I think I'm the best pencil sharpener in the grade! Dickie just sits really still at his desk, sharpens his pencils right there with his very own little sharpener and doesn't run around like Jackie who can't sit in his seat very long at all. Dickie's yellow hair is always combed. I don't even have a comb. And Dickie never went to school in his pj's, too, like I did one time when Mom's washboard, wringer, and agitator were all broken, and everything else was dirty. I know everybody was laffing at me in my pj tops. It really didn't look like a sweatshirt, after all.

And now my hair sticks up like a big haystack on my head, and one time the teacher was talking about this poor raggedy boy who never had his hair cut, and I know she was talking about me and that big haystack on my head. Bruce said that was me, too. I don't like haircuts. It just hurts too much, especially when Grandpa doesn't sharpen his hair clippers. Don't like those Saturday night baths any better, too. Rub-a-dub-dub, three men in a tub. Hey! Not three! It's only just me in there, and I still don't like it at all.

And that's why I want Amish haircuts with a bowl around my head just the way Johnny, Andy, Eli, and Jonah have. Amish people are always thinking up the best new things ever. They only need half a curtain on their windows. We have to have two. They call us English people and we just do the same old things over and over again. We English people are just like everybody else. Nothing different! I mean, if you can't think of those new kinds of things, you just don't go anywhere, do anything, and just sit around and get bored. But not them! They have the most fun, especially Andy. He even raced a car down the dirt road with his horse and buggy and crashed it over, but he wasn't hurt. Not old Andy! The Amish know how to be safe! And Constable Kieffer helped him get out of that smashed-up buggy. And big sister Saloma babysat us and had four friends there, too. Two boys were Amish, and the other two weren't. They had so much fun jumping over our little hitching post and tickling Saloma and rolling around on the ground with her. Just having so much fun! More than me!

One of the Byler brothers, Alfred, got ringworm one time (although I've never ever seen one of those worms up close), and they cut his hair right down to the skin without a bowl. Then he had to wear a sock cap, so I thought that's pretty smart, too. And Andy has a little sixth finger on his right hand, the one you throw with. So you know he's extra good at throwing baseballs, and everybody Amish just loves baseball. They have all sorts of new and wonderful things. Wish we did! But Mom says, "Be thankful for what you've got," but I never was. This has really been a hard year! Maybe second grade will get better!

Somebody might find my secret hayloft, so I like to go up the hillside next to the cemetery under the apple tree where it's really quiet. I can think real good up here and see our whole farm. Nobody pesters me. First grade is over at last. I guess I made it. You know, it didn't start too good. They thought I was dumb falling in the millrace and Cathy seeing my bottom. And it was me who was that scaredy kid hiding in the coatroom, 'cuz the kids would make fun of me. And then Bruce rasslin' me down and keeping me pinned. I thought if I pulled the girls' dresses up like the big boys, everybody would like me. And then I pretended I was blind, and they made me wear those stupid glasses. I did some bad things and got a D in conduct. But I made the bestest friend forever after he beat me up, and I lied to the whole class about it. And he has a really pretty sister, so maybe first grade really wasn't so bad. I sure needed a best friend. Maybe I tried too hard. Try to do the good things, but it's hard to know what they are. Boy! There are lots more surprises out here in Fowlers Mills than I thought!

You can tell what a job I had with animals.
Glad my sister helped a little.

Kathy grew up loving my goats, too. She really could march on that
dirt road! You can tell I was in charge of her and my goats, too.

CHAPTER 6

FREEDOM AND SUMMERTIME

Well! Old Bruce and I both saw lots of us this summer. Summer's when you do almost everything, and you're doing stuff all over the place. Nobody tells you what to do or when to do it. It just happens whenever! It doesn't matter! Everything just gets all mixed up!

I called Bruce Bruster the Rooster because he walked so tall with his yellow, curly hair sticking right up on top. Not falling down and pecking around like a little chickie hen. I call everybody lots of names. I used to call Bruce Brucie the Goosie, but that was before I knew him too much. I change the names sometimes, because everyone's still all the same anyhow. It doesn't really matter! It's fun to try and change lots of things!

But in summer, first you get Memorial Day, and that's the way summer always starts because you get one more of those really big picnics and lots more Kool-Aid. Sometimes we have orange-and-green Kool-Aid, but I love that really sweet, red-color, cherry Kool-Aid the best, because it makes you run a lot faster. And we have so many hills, pastures, and woods to run around to get anywhere, even if you don't know where you're going. Remember, now! We don't have any sidewalks, so you can go anywhere out here you want to. It really doesn't matter!

But before the picnic, we kids always do something very serious. We go to two different cemeteries. One far from the church and one right next door to our farm. That's rite where I want to be buried, really close to our house, so everyone can find me, and I can see everything that's going on. That's the last rite thing I want to do! And Bruster and I and the other kids carry two heavy pots of red geraniums at the same time and two little American flags on little sticks in our back pockets. And we run off really fast to every single grave there ever was and put a pot rite on top of it.

Old Mr. Chris Bogaski, who looks after the cemetery, drives around in his old Model T all around Munson Township. Boy! Mr. Bogaski talks and talks. He talks so fast, his little white hair that looks Amish wiggles all around, and he has lots of hairs in his nose and ears, too. And that's why he can't hear very well. You have to shout, "I'm here! Over here!" to get another pot, and you just can't keep these graves waiting. He has the reddest nose I've ever seen with little bumps on it, and it has big blue lines all over it, too.

He tells us there are lots of dead people under the ground, and all of them are soldiers. I even thought I saw some little girls' names on some of the stones in the cemetery rite next to our house. Probably little girl soldiers! They knew how to scratch and fite mean back then, too! Some stones had no names at all on 'em, so if you ever need a cemetery stone, there it is for you. Nothing on it, so just carve your name on it like you do your desk. You might get famous, too. Our cemetery has four huge beech trees with smooth gray bark and lots of civil war soldiers and even one soldier in the Revolution War. That there is two more wars! Hope we get some more!

Mr. Bogaski even tells us a story about two Riley brothers who climbed way up to the top of the church steeple and put a American flag rite on top and said, "Don't ever take this down until we get back!" I know Mr. Bogaski would be up there next to 'em, and me, I'd be rite up there behind him.

But then you know what he said? He said, and I can't forget, "They never came back," 'cuz they were shot in the civil war by some cannon balls. That's sad! But boy! This war stuff is exciting, but you've got to be careful, or you won't have a good time in it. Don't be a Riley brother! I have no idea why Mr. Bogaski had tears coming out of his eyes. Big ones, too! I just don't think he was having much fun that day!

But old Bruster and I were so excited, we ran as fast as we could with those geranium pots all over to beat all the other kids. Because we knew when this cemetery thing gets all over, that biggest-ever picnic starts, and summer really begins. And lots more Kool-Aid. It's about time!

Of course in summer, Mom makes you hoe the garden for an hour every day. Mom does lots of things like parching corn, canning tomatoes, and making those sweet watermelon rind pickles and string beans. We always eat the spring peas up in only just two suppers. And it was my job to throw on all that Rotonone white powder all over the eggplant to keep the bugs off. It makes your hair and face and arms all white, but I don't care, because no bugs ever get on me. We weren't supposed to get it in our eyes or mouth, because Farm Bureau says it can poison you and make you dead. But you have to do your farm jobs. You can't be a baby and whine here! And I have lots more jobs on our farm like burying the garbage and of course cleaning the barn and box stalls and getting all our manure out. I'm good doing manure stuff up in Farmer Carroll's barn and ours, too. I do a good job on both our piles. We have a pretty good one. You have to do all your farm jobs first, but then you get to take your shoes off and play as much as you want all day long. That there's freedom! Just like "America the Beautiful" says!

Like I told you, Bobby always had the toughest feet, because he walked on a lot of gravel at the mill. He didn't run around a lot like I did, but he thought a lot. I wish I could walk on gravel, but we just have dirt and grass up on our hill, so the bottoms of my feet always hurt. I just can't toughen up, and I feel like a sissy. So I just wear my same old sneakers til they get pretty smelly, and Mom makes me leave them out on the back porch. They even make Tippy sick!

Anyhow! First I'm a farmer, but I'm also getting pretty good at fishing. Grampa Koblaha is the best and leans over the bridge and catches bullheads and drinks something out of this big bottle all day long. You can see those fish all piled up at his pail, and if we look too close, he says that word "boulash" again really loud. That's his favorite word, but I think he knows some more of 'em. If we're looking into that pail too long, he puts his breath on us, and it smells so bad, you almost fall down. The fish just lie there and don't flap much, but they all get a little jumpy, too. Sometimes he fishes so much he can't even walk straight after that.

He walks home with his fish pail in one hand, some bullheads on a rope, and that empty bottle of something smelly in the other hand, and almost falls right off the road. You can tell he needs a nap fast.

For this fishing thing, all you have to do is find a little hatchet and chop down a little tree. Bruster and I chop down a new sapling every time, because we always lose the old one. Put 'em somewhere and just forget. Dad's hatchet is so dull it takes forever. And for about a dime we can get a bobber for both of us and then four or five little hooks and sinkers. I can't remember exactly if it's four or five hooks, but Bruster and I split a nickel for 'em, and off we go. Those little sinkers are small enuff you can chew 'em up really good, but somebody said you'd better not, because they're made of lead and would make your blood heavy. Make you dead! And then when Mom wasn't looking, we'd sneak into the back door of our house and take a big stick of margarine. Not that old war kind that you had to press so hard to make the butter all yellow but the real stuff! And an old frying pan, one paring knife, and some matches. Of course being all grown-up now, I had learned to use those matches just the right way now and not burn a hole in my jacket like back when I was a little squirt. Boy! We'd cook up all those fishes and if we weren't full, we'd rip corn right off someone's garden and chew it raw right off the cob 'cuz it's so sweet. You gotta have dessert. And coming back from fishin', we hide all these fishin' things in the barn for next time.

We were good at secrets, like on the television show *I've Got a Secret!* and Groucho Marx with this silly duck dropping down on a rope with the secret word. We hid lots of stuff in the barn. We even hid pictures I found in an old *National Geographic* of girls with no clothes on. We hid 'em in a big tin potato-chip can up in the hayloft to look at when we grow up old. Not even my sister or any other girls in Fowlers Mills knew where we hid 'em. We shouldn't have done that, but we did! Sometimes you just have to go ahead, get things done, and do what you think is right. Good thing nobody was good at smelling potato chips. That old can really had that potato-chip smell and grease inside. You can get a good licking for that!

But now back to fishing! I've been thinking too much about potato chips here! Now, one time Bruce and I even tried to use some old tennis rackets we found to bat fish out of the water that were splashing down below the mill dam in the spillway. Nobody played tennis. There wasn't even one tennis place in Munson Township. But that didn't work, and all we got was all wet, splashing each other. I think that's because the strings were all broken, because we sure could bat pretty good, old Bruster and me!

We'd usually start fishing under the bridge down the little hill, and we just made this one promise to us. If we didn't get a bite or even a nibble in a few minutes, the fish were just not biting today, and we moved on really fast to the next fishin' hole. You just have to keep movin' in this fishin' thing, because these fish are really smart. Especially the ones with the big heads. You think they're not looking at you, but they really are. They know exactly who you are and where you're standing! And that's exactly why some moms and dads keep those little gold ones up on a table in a little round glass bowl. That's so they can keep an eye on the children and splash those little squirts if they misbehave. At least, that's maybe! Somebody's got to watch those kids all the time! Fish can see you a mile away, especially when it's sunny. And their lips move a lot, so they talk to each other all the time. No telephones! They just do it through the water. And if you take a hook out of their mouths, they look you right in the eye and really don't like you so much for that!

If it's sunny, you get a lot more bullheads than bluegills, because bullheads stay down at the bottom and are a lot lazier, and their mouths are a whole lot bigger for worms. Sometimes they stay in the same sunny spot all day. But bullheads are a lot of work! You have to take 'em all the way back behind the barn, pound their heads into a board with a nail, and pull off their tough skins. And don't let their little sharp whiskers get you. Sometimes Bruster and I both have to pull real hard together on one pair of pliers. Remember! We're a team! But bullheads are just too much work, and they taste like mud, 'cuz they live in that ooky, bottom muddy stuff. Bluegills are the best eatin'!

Yep! Bruster and I work really good together. We know exactly how each other pulls. I think up a lot of silly things, and Bruster can always find just the right tools and make sure we get things done. Old Bruster and I are really good at starting things. A lot better than finishing 'em. A lot of things we only do half of. But then you have to go on to another thing! At least I do! I'm more of a daydreamer, and Bruster is more of a one-thing doer. We both got our parts, like Partparts! Mom says Bruce and I were just meant for each other! We're kinda like half of each other, too. You know? Maybe we should build a house or log cabin together and always live right there by the rules of the woods. We always know when the phone rings exactly which one of us it is.

Anyhow, back to fishing again. I told you summer gets all mixed up! Different things all the time. Anyhow, you never eat sunfish. We always scaled bluegills and ate those and chubs with no scales on them. Chubs are easy because they're just little nibblers, and we just fry 'em up whole with their heads on. Sunfish are real pretty, but some big guy told us you always throw 'em back 'cuz they're sour. They have to eat, too, so they bite your hook. So I don't even know what a sunfish really tastes like, but they sure are pretty and yellow and shine up in the sun real good. They can move their lips up and down really good and flap 'em a lot. Sometimes getting that hook out of those sunfish, you had to slap 'em around really hard, but that really hurts 'em a lot. When you throw 'em back, they don't look so good, trying to swim, flopping around on their sides and hurtin'. And if you squeeze 'em too hard, they'll spit on you. Or something comes out of their tails. Don't blame 'em! It's just best not to mess around with sunfish. Just let 'em be! Fishin's kind of like makin' friends. You let some go and just keep the good ones.

Anyhow! We have lots of different, special fishin' spots only Bruster and I know about. After fishin' the iron bridge over that little Chagrin River, we go behind the mill under the waterwheel where the water roars and splashes so hard falling down from the millrace. Now we go to all these fishin' holes in just one day, so you gotta keep up! And you probably can't forget how horrible that was so long ago when I fell in that millrace in that too-small snowsuit. Everyone's still talking about it! I can forget most everything all the time, but I just can't forget that even if I try. Behind the mill we really can't hear us talk at all. It's so loud, and the water makes the fish so dizzy. They can't even get their breath, and that makes fishin' there not as good as the next spot we call Kingfish.

Fishin' hole behind the mill.

Now that Kingfish spot is really good, and we stay at Kingfish a real long time. More than three or four minutes at least! It's like a bend in the river out in Farmer Carroll's cow pasture and makes a really deep pool where you can swim, too. It's really deep, and the river moves really slow here, and there are lots of cattails around.

One time Bruster and I were going fishing there, and we saw this big boy, Johnny, who goes to Chardon High School, swimming in there with some girl who didn't even have a bathing suit on. Now we boys know that's something you shouldn't do, because that's the way snakes and turtles get to bite you. We kept really quiet and hid behind the cattails, but old Bruster tripped and made a splash down, and boy, they went home really fast! It's like, where did they go? Bruster needs to learn how to be a little more careful on that. I'll try to teach him to be more patient.

Well, they left so fast, do you know, that girl left her T-shirt behind. We thought we'd take it home and give it to Mom because we stole her margarine, and this would be something nice for her. Yep! Old Bruster and I really know how to share nice things. But at least that girl with no shirt didn't get no turtle bites, and we can do something more important here than what those big kids were doing. Just splashin' around and rasslin'! Why don't they grow up! We're keeping this best secret fishin' spot just for us! Our next stop for fishin' is way past the Kingfish 'cuz they aren't bitin' here today. You see the way I'm talking a lotta fishin' talk now?

Don't spread it around, but we go way back to the mill pond behind our house to just above the dam spillway where lots of fish may want to swim through it. That's the best place in the whole world. It's so deep because the dam wheel is locked, and only Grampa Koblaha has a key to that padlock, 'cuz you see, he was the mill owner before Bobby's mom and dad owned it.

I almost forgot this part, but I can tell you it now. First you have to dig for worms. Big, juicy night crawlers who love living in our ma-nure pile by the barn. That where they're really happy! We dig and grab worms and manure, all with just our very own bare hands. Better than a shovel 'cuz you can feel 'em good, too. They'd wiggle a lot, so you gotta be fast to get a real handful, because you didn't want to squoosh 'em. Nope! Our fish like 'em fat and juicy! They're not like us. They're picky eaters, those little fisheroonies!

Sometimes we try to catch minnows in our stream under our wood plank bridge, but they're hard to find 'cuz they hide in the shade, and grabbing into that manure pile with our hands and swooshing worms all around is a lot easier. And that's a fish's favorite food. Also, if our big, fat, black pet snake Stanley has gotten back from the winter after being away and is sunning on the plank bridge, he gets in the way, and that makes it a lot harder to get those little, itty-bitty minnows. Sometimes you have to step on old Stanley's tail and throw him off. But that's the kind of thing that slows you down. Then you have to pull back a plank to drop a bucket down to scoop out the minnows. It's just too hard, and we really don't have a lot of time anymore. We just have too many things we have to get done. Our days are just too busy! We aren't just sitting around taking time off like old Stanley! And you know what? These poor little minnows are like babies and so cute. Just like tiny little fish that smile all the time.

This was a dumb thing to do, but Bruster and I saw a dumb movie once where a bunch of cuckoo people were dancing funny and having a party, and one man they called a flapper swallowed a goldfish. Right there in front of us in that movie. So I got to thinking to put one in my mouth and let it wiggle around a little before I spit it out. Now, you can't treat live things like that! I mean, what kind of people go around putting raw fish in their mouths not even cooked? And we aren't ever going to be any dumb movie stars, anyway. We're real live peeple, just like those *Life Magazine* pictures show you.

One time this man with a fancy fishing rod and long rubber boots up to his chin drove all the way out from Cleveland and told me I'd get fifty cents for fifty minnows. Wow! A penny a minnow! Lots better than that professor guy from Cleveland giving us a penny for every spring peeper we could catch, so he could run a test on 'em. You'd creep up on 'em back on the millpond bank peeping away, and then they'd shut up and be as quiet as church mice. Never got a one!

Well now, I ran as fast as I could straight back to our little stream, which goes under the dirt road, and finally caught fifty minnows in a pail and ran straight back to find that man. I couldn't find him anywhere, and that really made me mad! I couldn't believe he said he'd give me fifty cents and then just drove away and didn't even say good-bye. That's what they do in Cleveland! So I'm glad I'm not there anymore, and I worked so darn hard to catch every one of 'em. Next time I'll make him get his own bait. That guy is a cheater, making us kids work so hard for nothin'! He can take his big fancy car and go back to Cleveland and stay there! Those cute little minnows must have been really happy, though. All fifty of 'em were still smiling up, so everything works out! Made me feel good!

When we got older, Bruster and I did lots more things with our fishing. We had to pay a lot more, but we made big money now. We could still buy two, three-sided hooks for a nickel apiece and catch some frogs back on the millpond and cut their legs off and cook 'em. They called it gigging frogs, but nobody liked us to talk about that too much, and I didn't blame them. It was a horrible thing to see and do! Those frogs looked so sad with no legs on and not smiling any more. You shouldn't hurt animals. I almost gave up fishing after that, watching those poor frogs croak. And worse than that, I was sneaking too many things from Mom's kitchen, like salt and flour and more sticks of margarine for all our cooking. Kids should eat at home more and not go eating out so much! And you really don't have to steal food! Hope you're thinking like me.

Well! We did get some pretty good cooking fires going, and once we almost burned down this old barn, but Bruce threw his coat over the fire before it got away. Bruster and I just thought we shouldn't be eating our lunch out that day because it was raining, so we ate inside. And you should be careful, anyhow, 'cuz hay makes good tinder. One time these little jerks, Georgie and Beverly's little brother Harry, were playing in a barn and burned the whole darn barn down. Somebody had even butchered a deer in that barn and hung it up by a rope on the rafter. Boy! That poor old deer meat really got cooked extra well done! That was one of Grandpa's how-do-you-like-your-steak-cooked words.

Wow, though! Was that ever exciting! We all got to watch from the school coatroom all the black smoke blowing up and going right up to the sky. We should put those little jerks in a circle and take turns spanking 'em! Sue calls me a jerk sometimes. Not sure, but I don't think it's a nice word. It's really dumb if you're little, though. You should never play with matches, and that's something your mom or dad should always tell you! That's the rule, and you'd better listen and obey them or else!

Now! This is one thing, and please, please don't tell anybody. Don't forget your good words like please if you ever want to get something! But I have to tell you this! One time old Bruster and I untied Klatkas' rowboat on the other side of the millpond in their pasture across the big road from Bruce's house. We didn't steal it, 'cuz we don't do that stuff anymore. It says not to in the Bible. That's one of those commandments. Funny, 'cuz in church we sing, "Steal away to Jesus! Steal away home!" Now, it may have been OK for Jesus to steal away home but not us. I mean, you only say that stuff when you play baseball. I don't think Jesus ever played baseball much.

Now, we'll just borrow it for a little, 'cuz we really need a boat badly right now and will put it right back again. When you need something bad, you have to do it right away! Old Bruster rides in the back 'cuz he's stronger, and I get up front where I can see and stand straight up like George Washington crossing the Delaware, just like you see in our school's picture on the wall. Of course, I'll probably be the famous one someday like George. Old George and me! We don't carry any stars and stripes over our shoulder like George did. Not putting any of those little, teenie cemetery flags in our back pockets, either! That really looks stupid! And we need all our hands for rowing hard and standing up looking out where we're going. Bruce couldn't see in back and wanted me to sit down, but I had to see where we were going. We just got right to work! We weren't showing off here! It was exciting, though, with Bruce rowing as hard as he could to get us right out to the deepest water. We wanted to get right next to that dam spillway where I know the big fish are, but nobody ever told us that dam was opened up with the whole mill pond rushing right through it. You gotta let people know that! They can die that way! It's not funny!

That's George's picture in our schoolroom.
Don't know why it wasn't in his.

That's just like Bruster, rowing hard in the back, and me in front, knowing where we were going. Right to the dam to fish. It was just Bruster and me and not all those other guys. No flag for us, 'cuz we were too busy. I don't know if George stole that boat, but he did two things at one time. He chopped down the cherry tree and crossed the Delaware River. He was something that way!

That's the dam! That's me with the big fish. Watch out, little fishies. Thank goodness Bruster and I didn't go through it.

The spring floods made a lot of water go higher and higher, and the water started turning all around, and so did our boat. It got to spinning. We were a little scared. At least Bruster was. I wasn't really, of course! But we worked well together, and sometimes the only way you get famous and get your name in the history books is if something really horrible happens to you. And Bruster and I weren't chickens. At least, I wasn't! Who's scared of being dead anyhow? I mean, we had our cemetery right next door where we could keep an eye on it. Boy! We paddled so hard and started screaming so hard, too. Boy! We were really sweating, and we finally made it out of there. At least, we thought so.

We got free, but really it was like this. Grampa Koblaha heard us yelling and screaming and came running really hard to close up that dam with that dam key and yelled "boulish" all the way at us again. Now, I'm really sure that word's not a good one! At least he didn't have that smelly bottle with him this time, and he wasn't running crooked. I guess they didn't trust old Bruster and me anymore, 'cuz the next time we tried borrowing that boat, it had a padlock on it. Somebody really mean must have ratted on us! We should have sunk that dam boat! We heard somebody talking about a death spiral once, and I think that's what old Bruster and me were in. That's when the rowboat gets sucked into the water, and you go through the open dam and don't come out the other side. That always turns out bad, unless you can really swim hard upstream or grab a pole. Boy! I had never been so scared in my life, and I will never do that again! I didn't wet my pants or bed, I just couldn't sleep all night!

Anyhow! The Bible says, "Thou shalt not steal," but I'm not thinking that means everybody. Not like old Bruster and me, too. We weren't stealing, just borrowing, and that's the difference right there! It seems we just don't read that Bible enough or not well enough, 'cuz we just did that against the rule. And that's that!

Now, I could go on and on like parents do, but that's enough fish stories here! And 'cuz my real job in life is really to be the very best farmer that ever lived. I mean, that's the only reason we all moved out to Fowlers Mills anyhow! Farming is going to be my whole life. You've got to become something when you're a grown-up, and the time is going by way too fast. And you can probably tell already I'm not doing so well. That's a bad rhyme! But not doing so good at all!

First, I need to become Farmer Carroll's best barn helper with the cows. He needs lots of help. After having such a horrible first grade, I did make it to the second grade and needed to make something really big out of my life. I also need to get busy collecting some of my old baby and children things and start keeping them in a special place in the barn, like old toys and stuff to put in a muzim for when I become really famous as a farmer. Then everybody in the world will know all about me. And the teacher will ask the children, "Who was the best farmer?" But don't you dare put those toys and stuff next to the potato chip can, 'cuz those dirty pictures wouldn't look good at all in Tommy T.'s Famous Farmer Museum!

And for sure, the next time we need a boat in a hurry, we'll buy one straight out of the Sears and Roebuck catalog for twenty-nine bucks with all that big money we're getting paid now. When it comes to that millpond, we're staying on top of it next time!

Work's done now, and up on our hillside, I can see the whole world. Summers are so much fun, and you can do lots of things if you get your gardening done and be home for supper when the dinner bell rings. You forget what time it is, but you're free to try anything you want. Some things might be bad, but you don't know til you try. So you've got to think more and pick good things. I mean, summer's lots of fun with nobody making you sit still, but you can get in big trouble, too!

CHAPTER 7

FARMER CARROLL AND
FARMING

Now that I'm older and past the first grade, it's good to tell you more about farming out here. I started to act more like a farmer should. Weekends came, and all the people from the city took these long Sunday drives, 'cuz they had nothing else to do. Well, I got this big pitchfork and hay rake but not a scythe, because I wasn't big enough yet. An older boy I knew tried to sharpen a scythe and got eight stitches in his hand by using the whetstone the wrong way. Coulda been me. Anyhow! I wear this dirty old straw hat and extra-dirty dungarees and stand out in the field, right close to the road by our house, so when these city people drive by, they can see me working like a real farmer.

The father always slows the car right down, and the mother tells those kids in the back seat all about these farmers, and she says, "See how hard they work in the hot sun all day!" They just aren't playing all those silly hopscotch games all day like you do!

That's a girls' game anyhow. Gotta have sidewalks! The poor kids are probably awfly bored. They're saying, "Let's get outta here!" If moms and dads would just have more kids and listen to them better, they would learn a lot more! But they just keep on driving and talking too much. But if you're a kid, you really should behave better in the car and quit picking at each other. You should think more about making your mom and dad move out to the country and becoming farmers, too. It's the way to be! Let 'em be a little free!

Yep! Farming's going to be my whole life! I even began to think up new ideas like pulling a scoop along with a rope to pick up all those little manure piles behind the cows' bottoms in their stanchions in Farmer Carroll's barn. That would make this all this manure shuvlin' go a lot quicker. Better on your nose, too! Kind of a shortcut. That's what I like! Like running through the pasture for supper or up and down the stair railing, of course! Like one of them Slinkies!

Stanchions was one of the first new farm words I ever learned from Farmer Carroll, and he's a man who don't say a whole lot. He only talks a few words. He just works all the time and still spits this gooey, brown stuff out of the side of his mouth and milks cows all the time. He is an action-speaks-louder-than-words man like Mom likes. Boy! He can really teach you! Heck! I wasn't talking as much either anymore. Just working too hard, I guess. Around cows you can be as quiet as you want, 'cuz they think their own thoughts and don't care. They're not yapping away on the telephone all the time like some old ladies I know. They're just thinking about their own happy days and what each other's doing today. Happy like a pack of possums! You see, you can really learn a lot here! Cows make all those hamburgers, too! But not ours! Did you know that? Now I just hold the cow's tails while he milks, and they moo. Pinky had taught me well. He told me not to hold the tails too high 'cuz those cows can shoot out gas balls. Sometimes you can't tell if it's Farmer Carroll or the cows. Either way, it smells bad. Pewwww! Boy! Think about those Saturday night baths. Mom should be scrub-a-dub-dubbing Farmer Carroll down! He might have drowned, too, like me when he was little and be scared, too.

I have to tell you, Farmer Carroll has a big bump on his nose and a lot of curly hairs inside it, so he can't smell so good. He's got more hairs out his nose and fallin' out his ears than the four of 'em on top of his head. On his arms those hairs and big blue veins poke way out, especially when he squeezes those teats. I think that makes him really really happy, 'cuz he always has the biggest smile on his face when he milks. He loves it so much, he can milk all day if we don't have to stop every now and then for ginger ale. And those big, rubber farm boots never get taken off. He has 'em on all the time! So stiff you can't pull 'em off! I never got to see his feet, and I don't think he had any shoes to wear anyhow. Farmers always just wear boots. His socks had to be smellier than mine. They can stand straight up!

I must have really showed him a lot, 'cuz he told both my mom and dad in Reynolds Store, "Tommy's quite a worker! Yep!"

I don't mind him bragging about me, 'cuz he is the best farmer in the whole wide world. If he doesn't have me, he's got to get somebody else, or he can't get all those *teats* pulled. It was just too much! Teat-pulling is a tough job. "Teats" is just another farm word. Mom calls them "bosoms." We got to calling them "bazooms" for short. I might have told you that already. If you get tired of all this, just go to the end to see what happens. Can you imagine cows with bosoms? Yipes!

Farmer Carroll is different. He always keeps this tobacco in his left cheek, even though he grabs things with his right hand like me. He can spit farther that way, 'cuz he can hit a barn cat a mile away. He could spit right into a cat's ear. They put their ears up when they're taking a break and catching mice. But those sneaky, old, slow-walking barn cats don't dare do that around Farmer Carroll. Noo, sireee! And barn cats don't get their own names. Just "damn cats" is enough for them, and that name changes all the time, too. I mean, look at me and all the names I had for Bruster. Like I said, first Brucie the Goosie, and now Bruster the Rooster.

At first I thought something was wrong with Farmer Carroll's cheeks, but when he spit far, thank goodness, that cheek got lots smaller. His left cheek is the biggest and the best one he's got. Even though I'm right-handed, I hope I can get a really strong left cheek like him. And you know what, he never eats. Just like my West Virginia grandma! Never eats a thing! Farmers just don't have time for that! He just grabs a bag of that tobacco and gives some to Tom and Jerry and eats the rest all himself. He only drinks ginger ale. That's all! If he ate more, he'd grow bigger. He's got big hands for milkin' though. He says manure makes everything grow big and he touches lots of it. But you've got to be a little guy like him to sit underneath those cows' bosoms and pull hard. He let me *strip* a teat to practice sometimes. Just showing me how! Letting me get the feel of it! He sure could pull those teats fast on that little stool down below. If he had gotten any bigger, he'd have to get his very own house and not live with his mother all the time. But she really takes good care of him.

And Farmer Carroll doesn't spend too much money, either. Nope! One time I helped Mom in the March of Dimes, and he gave one dime for himself and one dime for his mother. Just like it says in that march! He sure knew how to save his money. He didn't need any old dime saver for that. He just kept it all his own self. Well! They got their giving pins for that, but Mom thought it was kind of stingy. But that's why they call it the March of Dimes, not pennies! Most people give at least a quarter, but he's got lots of cows' mouths to feed, and all the other people only got to feed a few hungry kids. Of course, he doesn't need a wife to cook for him, 'cuz he already has his mother. I probably won't need a wife, either, 'cuz I got my mom, and my mom's got me!

'Cuz I'm the hardest worker, he pays me the best of all. He pays me in real Vernors Ginger Ale—half a bottle for him and the other half for me. When those watermelons riped up, he split one of those beauties clean open, again half for each of us farmers, right down the middle. And we'd spit the seeds away out there like chewin' tobacco. He taught me how! I was really getting a stronger cheek, too. Yep! He was a good teacher! We were just like workers together, everything half-and-half like it should be. Yep! Me and Farmer Carroll! That makes me just want to work harder. Let me tell you something! He paid me plenty! Where else can you get that much ginger ale and watermelon? Had a strawberry patch, too! But when he said he put the best, fresh manure on his strawberries, that didn't taste too good to me. I just put sugar and milk on mine!

Lots of times I jumped out of bed in the morning and ran all the way up the hill way before breakfast and ran right into that barn to hold all these tails again while he sat there and milked. I got to know whose tail I was holding with my eyes shut. Now that's something even Jackie telling exactly what car it is can't do, I bet! Sometimes he hit me in the eye with a squirt of that warm, sticky milk, just to make sure I was wide awake. OK, you can't sleep on the job! Yep! Just like Farmer Carroll, I'm getting to be a lot better worker and not talking much, too.

One thing I'm really good at is riding that manure trolley all the way out the barn and pulling on that rope at just the right time to pile all that good, fresh manure right into his big pile and not to get a whole lot on myself. Now, that's the one thing I do a little better than Farmer Carroll. His manure pile is a lot bigger than our little family one in our home and smells a whole lot sweeter, too. Now, you really have to pull that rope just right, or you can get thrown in there, too. That's why I always wear my baseball cap. Just to keep my hair clean! And remember, I don't like baths too much. You can get your hair wet that way and soap in your eyes with those bath things. You know? I'm using that "manure" word a whole lot more now, too. I'm becoming so smart in this farm stuff. It takes an awful lot of practice!

You know what's amazing, though? You can tell every time when those cows are eating sweet alfalfa or just regular hay, like Timothy. You do it just by smelling that good old manure up really close. This is the kind of stuff you learn by being right there in the middle of 'em. And horses' stuff smells a lot more horsey than cows. You don't have to go to school to learn all this. And this is exactly all the important stuff all farmers need to know! Yep! You don't need to read books about it; you've just got to get right into it! Great Grandpa T hauled a lot of manure every day so that thing runs in our family, too. He wrote it down a long time ago in this little book so he wouldn't forget what he was doing all day.

**Great Grandpa T's diary. We both know a lot about
hauling manure and that's one thing why we got the same
name. Jim whoever has gotta know that stuff, too.**

And that's why we know it so good. We farmers learn that really
good manure also has lots of different flavors, shapes, and smells. Kind
of like ice-cream cones do!

I don't know how important this is, but we really didn't get enuff of that ice cream, except like I told you when Grandpa and Merle Reynolds cleaned their freezer out at Christmas and gave me the Halloween ice cream with a pumpkin in the center. They chose me because I helped chip out the old ice. Yep! I was a really good ice chipper, too. That ice cream's never exactly on the right holiday, but it sure tastes good. I ate a whole quart myself once down in the right-of-way, but I may have told you already. Merle gave me a Klondike once and told me to take it right home, but I stopped and played by the mill, and it melted all over my unders and dungarees. Forgetting too many things! Just too much happening again right now! Getting mixed up again. And we're not talking about food any more here, either! That's enough!

I'm also really, really good at bringing the cows home from the pasture for their inside dinners and milking time. They are so smart! Probably the smartest animals in the world, 'cuz they all line up right behind Bossy and go single file straight to their very own stanchions to be milked all over again. They like being milked as much as Farmer Carroll likes milking 'em. They're really smart, 'cuz they can do two things at one time. They can give milk and eat at the same time! Not many of us can do that! I'm starting to think a whole lot more like cows do. They love being milked except when they kick the bucket over to let you know that's enuff.

My dad says, "Don't kick the bucket until you're old enough!" He's so smart, I don't even know what he's talking about.

You know? It makes you feel really good giving those weenie, little kids lots of milk to drink and those cows getting their teats pulled, too. All at the same time! Two things happening at once again. They all have four *teats* 'cept for Whitey, and he has an extra little, bitty one that makes him five, but it never got milked at all. That poor little teat got left out like a runt in a puppy litter. I think it's good to talk about these farm words, 'cuz some of you may have never seen these things before, and you may be stuck back in the city. But you've got to drink your milk, too! You don't want to be a runt!

Working with cows is not easy! Once I saw a cow plugged up and having a real bad time. He was dribbling out of his mouth and screaming a lot, and finally the vet came. The first thing that vet did was get all dressed up, looking just right for his job, and put on these long rub-ber gloves. Took him a long time! Then the vet, without even telling the cow, pushed his hand into that poor cow's bottom right up to his elbows and mustash and pulled and pulled. Farmer Carroll even pulled the vet by his overalls 'cuz he's so strong. And would you believe it? Out came this baby calf that was four times longer than any calf I ever saw, and he didn't move at all, either. They said he was *stillborn*. He wasn't just stillborn. He was stretched! Boy! He sure was still, though. Didn't move a bit! I think he was what they call still dead. I know he wasn't still alive. Too bad, 'cuz we could have gotten so much milk from that calf when he grew up, 'cuz he was so long. Maybe the vet stretched him too much. I don't know. You've got to be careful there! That's the thing I'm trying to teach Bruce. How to be more careful! That's just not the way you get new babies to come out. Everybody knows that! Just think if they stretched my prettiest little sister Kathy out of my mom's bottom like that. She'd be too tall and too skinny. You've got to put a little weight on those heifers!

Farmer Carroll's cows are like best friends. Everyone is different. Their cow fur is all different colors. Grandma is a black-and-white Holstein. She's been around awhile, a lot longer than me—sixty years or so—and she is so patient. She's in the first stanchion 'cuz she expects to get milked first, too. Heck! My grandma has that grandma cow's same name and wants that, too. And Grandma let Farmer Carroll know that! That makes a lot of sense, 'cuz she's a girl kind of cow, and Mom says, "Girls always go first!"

And then there's Whitey—all white with lots of muscles and really big and strong. He stomps a lot and doesn't listen to you so good and stops and eats lots of tree leaves on the way back to the barn. I really have to keep a close eye on that guy. I think he thought he was better than me. Whitey's the best giver of milk though—a whole pail. But he needs to listen to Mom's rules more: "Don't think you're better than anybody else. Don't forget it. And don't dawdle." I have trouble with that last one.

And then next in the line is a Brown Swiss we call Brownie. He can be mean and pushy, shoving everyone else out of the way all the time. If you aren't careful, he tries to reach his head over to eat someone else's hay. That's just piggy like a real porker! Everyone should just eat their own food, don't you think?

And then there's little Jersey. She's so gentle and has big, beautiful brown eyes that look at you so sweetly, you just want to go hug her up and kiss her. She doesn't give lots of milk. Not even a third of a pail, but it's so creamy tasting. More like a milkshake and not like water. You just dip your finger in the pail and pull some out. That's the best way to try some.

Of course, if people don't want milk warm and sticky, we carry it down to the milk house to cool it down. Then we pour it in big milk cans to carry down to the side of the road. You might be tired of hearing about cows, but there are about five other big Holsteins that don't do much, and you get a little bored, 'cuz they finally get milked last. They just follow Grandma along. Then there are a couple of yearlings, calves, and a heifer in some box stall over there whose names I never learned anyhow. They were over there somewhere, like in somebody else's family.

That's enuff about cow milking and working with manure and barn stuff, but I'm also good at haying. When it comes time to make hay, Farmer Carroll hands me over the reins to drive Tom and Jerry and the hay wagon smack out of that big barn door. When I do that, I feel like I'm the king of all Fowlers Mills, and I yell, "Gid up, haw, gee, whoe" and all those big words only big Belgian draft horses know. It's some kind of their own Belgium talk. Farmer Carroll told me these big horses came right from Belgium or some place over there. That's a long way away, so I don't know who drove them to Fowlers Mills. Horses are a lot better than tractors. Don't need tires and no breakdowns! Don't need to fill 'em up with gas, either! They just give their own horse gas back to you the old-fashioned way! That's the way you get work done around here!

They're both brown and reddish, but Jerry is bigger and pulls harder on the right, and lazy Tom doesn't do much at all on the left. That's why the wagon goes all crooked to the left sometimes. Whoa there, Tom! Even if he's lazy, someone has my name again. I'm still good at gettin' my name all over. Everybody has it! I told you I'm really good at driving horses, and I have to, 'cuz I drive 'em down bumpy and dusty old Fowlers Mills dirt road, past the mill, and turn left, past the little iron bridge and right-of-way, or old interurban railroad, if you want to call it that. It's the same thing. Same things can have lots of different names, you know, but there're all just the same anyway. Then I drive them horses right across from our house, right on up to the hayfield. They know and go exactly where they want to, but I'm still in charge of 'em. It's a long way, and it takes a long time to tell you that, so you might want to look at my map to find out where you are and how you get there. I know that I'm right up here, but it's easy to get lost in Fowlers Mills. I mean, there are sixty-four different kinds of people here, too, and that's a lot!

I can see Klatkas' silos way off in their pasture, a big one for silage and a little one for corn. Not even beside each other. I don't know why they just don't just mix it all up and have just one silo. Thinking about too many silos gets everybody all mixed up. Hard to know which one to go into, and you can fall in if you go too high, too. That's why when they try to feed their own cows, they get all "cornfused" like Dad says. Farmer Carroll knows farms so much, he doesn't need any silos. He just knows what to do and only needs that manure trolly.

Now, haying is pretty tricky! First, Farmer Carroll pitches that sweet-smelling, new-mown hay way up high to the wagon, and I drive up just a little bit at a time. That hay gets so high, I can hardly see Farmer Carroll, but he keeps on pitchforking. I've never seen anybody pitchfork like him. He pitches it up so high, and you can't see him down there, but he always yells up, "How high can you jump, Tommy?" He's so nice and cares an awful lot about me. He knows I'm a good jumper and can jump way over that pitchfork, 'cuz it's sharp. Remember how I practiced a lot, putting finger marks on our living-room ceiling.

Good thing I'm way up over their big bottoms when I drive those Belgians. You know, everything from Belgium is really big. I can see better way up high here, but watch out when they lift up their tails and plop. Goes all over the wagon wheels, but you drive right over it. You really have to steer here, or you slide! It's worse, though, when it's just gas! With a flashlight you can see inside their stomachs from the rear. Sounds like a train whistle! Boy! It makes your eyes sting, and what a smell! Peweee! Those're big gas balls! They make you want to jump off that wagon, but farmers don't just give up and quit! Just hold your nose and reins tight, and ride 'er out!

Hey! When you're through haying, those horses are really ready to run back to the barn. Watch out. Farmer Carroll yells "Hold 'em back, boy! Keep 'er tight." Heck! I'm not holding nothing back! I'm kind of like that Ben Hur guy in the movies. Run 'em fast! I mean, this job isn't for kids, let me tell ya! Better and faster than tractors! Don't need tires and rearview mirrors! No breakdowns! No filling 'em up with gas, either! They already got a lot of it inside and just give it back to you the old-fashioned way like I told you!

The sun out here is so blasted hot, and I sweat like a pig. Then that moldy hay smell gets in my nose. One time I just saw all dark in my eyes out here. It looked like night all over and little twinkling stars. This ain't no "Twinkle, Twinkle, Little Star" song thing here, either. I was seeing real stars! But my head hurt counting 'em so much, I just fell right to sleep. Well! Farmer Carroll tells me he pulled me down and filled me up and splashed me all over with cold creek water right out of the pasture and saved my life right there! That's exactly how you save an overheated hog when they get heatstroke. You learn that in 4-H! He made me suck lots of sweet clover to make me feel better. He knows I like that sweet stuff, and I sucked 'er dry! Sure did!

Got right back up there! Could see the sun again and kept on driving those horses! And Farmer Carroll kept on shouting up, "Give 'em rein, boy! Giddyup." What the heck was he shouting about? What rain? My head was funny but I had no idea. Yep!

We talk a lot about all kinds of things like, "You there, boy?"

"Yah, I'm here."

"Giddyup, boy."

"Yep."

"Whoe!"

Yep! We talked and talked all the time about lots of really important things! Yep! I tried to show Farmer Carroll a lot. He was the best teacher about farms! He sure cared a lot about our cows and Tom and Jerry. He taught me how to work hard, and you know what? His mom never made him change his clothes or take a Saturday night bath like my mom. He wore the same old shirt and overalls with suspenders every day. They got pretty smelly sometimes, but with that bump on his nose, he couldn't smell too good anyhow. He'd fall over if he could.

I don't care if I'm pretty smelly, too. My toes and not my nose are smelling more now, and I'm spelling more now because (not 'cuz) I'm getting older. See how those words rhyme! This really gets tricky!

Of course, here's something you don't ever want to do. Never jump right on to a hard, old cow pie when you don't know what's underneath it. Might be soft! Not hard and dry yet. Now, that can make your socks pretty smelly! I mean, that's a real surprise! I like surprises, but take your time in knowing this stuff like I'm trying to teach Bruster!

Here's something pretty amazing! Both moms have only one son, just one, living with them—Me and Farmer Carroll. And that's why we're so good! Moms really take special care of their only boys. I want you to remember all this when you think a lot about Me and Farmer Carroll together!

I can almost see Farmer Carroll's barn from way up here. When Bobby meted me to him when he was sitting on his little stool under an udder milking those cows, I didn't know we'd get to be such good friends. He looked funny and so happy and only talked to cows back then, saying "Git up, Bossy!" He was their best friend, but now he's mine, too. He loves milking his cows. Doesn't have to count every cow and jabber away about it. He just does his job! He taught me all about cows and every barn job there is. Shows me how and lets me try stuff my own self. That's how you get smart about farm stuff. You don't learn it in school. Yep! Just showing you, taking a chance and doing it is the best way. He knows exactly what I'm thinking just being around with him. That's how best friends are!

CHAPTER 8

BASEBALL

Well! It's no secret. I love farming, but now I am going up in the grades, and everybody in Fowlers Mills and Cleveland, too, knows that the Cleveland Indians won the world series in 1948. Who wouldn't know that? Anybody who goes to Reynolds Store knows that, and that's all they talk about up there anymore. Everyone's talking about baseball. It's all I'm beginning to think about. It's like I'm on the radio program "Charming Children" or "Mrs. Francis" when the lady says, "Today, children! Let's talk about baseball!" That's all!

This next summer, Farmer Carroll and I work really hard on our big farm together, but working there I'm thinking in my head all the time about Larry Doby, Lou Boudreau, Mickey Vernon, Jim Hegan, and all those baseball guys, but most of all, about Bob Feller! He's only about ten years older than me, but they call him Rapid Robert. Like me, he grew up on a farm and threw real hard against the barn door. He could put holes in it out there in Iowa. I'm throwing balls everywhere now. When I see a stone, I throw it. So I know I can be both the greatest farmer and baseball pitcher at the very same time. Two things at once again! I can't stop dreaming about baseball even in my sleep.

The cows began to know that, too, because I was getting things all mixed up now. I got all their cow tails mixed up sometimes. Well! That hurt their feelings, you know. Cows have a lot of feelings, but my mind was on baseball. I kept thinking Farmer Carroll was going to make a good catcher, because he squatted down like catcher Jim Hegan when he milked. His barn boots even started to look like shin pads. Even old cow pies started looking like baseballs, and I wadded 'em up and threw 'em around. Now, I have to tell you. That's just not keeping your mind on your work. Where's my life going here?

Everybody knows you only throw cow pies flat, like plates, unless they're soft and fresh. You can spin 'em, too, if they're hard and dry. That was a new game we made up where you twirled the really flat, dry, round cow pies all around and caught 'em on the fly. If they were just fresh and sitting there, they would splash all over you if you jumped on 'em. That was why in baseball, if you got 'em really hard, you could use 'em for home plate. Just don't get a fresh one! Dry 'em out a little. Be really careful! Learn it like Bruster! This may be all you really need to know right now about cow pies. Remember, I'm always right here to help you learn as much as you can. And listen up, people! Now we have two things to talk about—baseball and farming!

This summer, the first thing I did in the morning, before breakfast even, was run straight out to our rural free delivery mailbox. I'd pull out the Cleveland *Plain Dealer* and rip that thing right open like a Christmas present and go straight to the sports page to see if the Indians won and if Larry Doby hit a home run. That's the only reason Dad got that paper home delivered. Sometimes I already knew it all, because I listened to Jimmy Dudley on the radio. But that's more something you do if you're an old man or working on a car or sitting on the porch, swinging and drinking ice tea. I almost became Larry Doby.

That's mailbox RFD #2 for all the newspaper baseball news.

Jimmy talks a lot about that famous beer, Erin Brew. Sometimes just hearing it makes me thirsty. Jimmy says, "It just cools your mouth and tastes so good! Have an Erin Brew!" But Mom won't let us do what Jimmy says, because she thinks we're not old enough. You have to be in the upper grades before you can drink that stuff. But what she did buy me couldn't have made me prouder! It was one of those shiny, blue-and-red jackets with a big, smiling Indian face right on the front, right over my heart. That's when I first knew I was going to be just like Bob Feller. I believed him to be me wearing that jacket.

Sue's favorite Indian is Jim Hegan, because she says he's good-looking, and she's eleven. When girls get to that age, like Sue and Cathy, they giggle all the time and start whispering about boys. Sue liking baseball is a strange thing, because only boys play baseball. But us boys don't hopscotch or jump rope. If it's a picnic, then the rule is girls can play softball but can't throw hard. Hard to figure out! But anyhow, I'll have to tell you, Sue can squat down in the dirt and catch just like Jim Hegan. Cathy doesn't squat so good like Sue and doesn't like baseball much, either. She likes to cheer and jump around. All we have is a wrinkly, old, round orange catcher's mitt that doesn't even have a pocket in the middle of it. Dad found it in his school. Sue pounds her fist and shouts funny things like, "Pop it in here. Show me what you got," and "Chuck it to me, baby." A bunch of silly things like that. I'm already in the second grade, so I know that's dumb. I don't know where she ever learned to talk like that.

We played catch in this little flat grass by the tire swing, and she'd call balls and strikes. She was good, and I got faster and started throwing the balls right through that tire swing to get a better aim. But then I had to run around and pick 'em all up every single time. And I had three different balls. When you get tired of running around for your balls, you have to sit down and rest, like between *innings*. Keep an eye out for all these baseball words. Most of my balls had the *horsehide* coming off— *bad stitching*. There, I'm using these baseball words again now.

You see something here? I can talk both baseball and farm animal words at the same time now. I'm throwing balls everywhere now. Even threw one through the porch window one time. That's when my dad taught me all about glass panes, glazer points, and putty, and how to fix it. He even taught me about using my head more. But picking up all those balls you throw can get pretty boring, but somebody has to do it if you're going to be like Bob Feller. Then I begin to throw against the barn door, so I don't have to run as far. But that's kind of lonely, because nobody can watch me except my goats, and they don't even pay attention. They're still just kids! Get the joke? They just chew grass or maybe the horsehide off my ball. They'll eat anything, those little goaties!

Now I'm getting so good at pitching that my sweet old West Virginia grandma with the cute little rabbitlike nibbler nose and a baseball, I mean a ball, of hair squooshed on top of her head, and my grandpa of course, too, sent me a brand-new Rawlings pitcher's glove. That's 'cuz everybody in West Virginia knows how fast I pitch, and I haven't even pitched to a real batter yet. Boy! The first one I pitch to is really going to be surprised to see me out there with a brand-new Rawlings glove. He'll be looking so hard at that glove and won't even see me throw nothin'. And now since I got the only glove in Fowlers Mills, the very first one, my dad gives me the best idea. He says, "You have to break it in!" That's more baseball talk. You have to keep the leather nice and soft with lots of Neats Foot Oil on it, so it won't get old and crack. That's another thing he learned in the navy in the war. By cracky!

He must have learned an awful lot there—things like folding his socks up in a little ball, how to smoke cigarettes right to the last part, say things like "dadgumit," and everything. You've really got to be so smart in the navy to learn all about these best things that make you really healthy. He learned about everything when I was just a baby. I didn't have to help him at all back then. He just learned it all by himself. He smoked Lucky Strikes 'cuz they make fine tobacco! But when all his teeth fell out because he didn't get enuff milk in the navy 'cuz us kids drank it all up, Dad stopped smoking. Just like that! Now, that's a Lucky Strike, if you know what I mean! Sometimes Dad puts his choppers in his right hand and makes 'em click, and Mom puts a rose in her teeth like a dance. Boy! We sure got a laugh out of that! Lots better than that dumb "Sentimental Journey" dance stuff they did!

Dad says I have to sleep with my new glove under my pillow to make it flat, and that makes the leather softer, too. Dadgumit! That first morning, I sure had a lot of oil dripped all over my hair and sheets, but it sure worked good. That glove was so soft, and it kept my hair from getting bushy all day. Some kids even thought I got a new comb at home. I smelled like car oil all day. At recess next year, I let everybody take a turn with my new glove and that little old orange catcher's mitt, too. That lumpy catcher's mitt with no pocket don't catch so good, but works for just sitting down on it like a pillow if you get real tired.

The boys really like me a lot for my gloves. Life's getting a lot better! I had the only glove until Eddie Spagetti, I called him, moved into our school in the third grade. At least he didn't have that bad name like a Peter to tease him with. He's left-handed and has a huge trapper's mitt or first-base glove that's so big you can wear on both hands if you want to. Or you can put it on your head like a hat if the sun's too hot out there. Lefties are like that! They eat funny, write upside down, and do everything different. Eddie tried really hard to be a country boy, but he just had too much city in him. He was a good sport, though, and jumped in and took part in anything. He had a big, wide smile and black hair with the best crew cut. And doggone it if he didn't go right to work trying to be number one with Roberta! His house was right over the pasture from ours, and his and Jackie's dad drove all the way to work to Cleveland every day. I could run from his house over the pasture down the right-of-way to my house in ten minutes. Just before the dinner bell rang in time for supper. Never missed!

I made up new names for everybody: Bruce the Goose, Eddie Spagetti, Jackie Quackie, and Dickie the Quickie. Later on I changed Bruce's name to Bruster the Rooster, because like I said, he walked straight up, and his hair was curly on top. He didn't have a comb, either. Get that one? It's about roosters' combs. It's getting a little tricky here. Of course I called myself Tommy Salami, because that's what my old neighbor in Cleveland, Mr. Shulman, liked the best. Mrs. Shulman gave me the biggest, fattest, best sandwich of it ever one time, with mustard on rye. I can still taste that salami today! I'd love to burp it up again and smell it again if I could! I will always love and never forget those city folks for that.

Now I'm going to tell you about the biggest excitement that summer! Somebody in Dad's school knew every Indian that ever was and gave my dad free tickets to see my very first Indians baseball game right down in Municipal Stadium in Cleveland. My hands got all sweaty I was so excited. Even though Mom said it was really hot and sunny outside, I still wore my Indians jacket and baseball cap just like Bob Feller wears. We walked right through the ticket-taker man and through all these dark tunnels, right up to our seats that folded down, and there I saw the most pretty grass and some man named Emil Bossard and lots of other guys pulling rakes and rolling things all over the grass. One man was even painting white lines on the dirt. That's to show you where to go. There were lots of other people there. Not just Dad and me. Lots of other men were sitting in seats and wearing white shirts and ties I didn't know you had to wear; some were smoking cigars that stunk and drinking out of these brown bottles full of Jimmy Dudley's Erin Brew Beer. Just like on the radio! Boy! This was exciting.

I looked but couldn't find Jimmy Dudley. My dad said he was telling everything play-by-play up there somewhere. I know Jimmy is a good friend of mine and really likes me, because he says so on the radio. He talks to me and says, "It's sure good to be with you again! Let's all us fans sit back now and all have a big cold glass of Erin Brew!" And of course I was the best fan, and I was thirsty already! Boy! Jimmy is such a nice guy! I couldn't hear him talk so well now. It was just too darn noisy!

The two men cheering and having lots of fun in front of Dad and me were brown, and I told Dad so. I never saw brown people before except Mr. Dillard at Grandpa's college in Berea. Dad says, "Everybody's a different color if you look really close." Well! I didn't have to look really close, because he's right. Dad's redder than me. His hair was red, too, when he was little. That's the very first time I've ever seen people colored different from me because you know I'm not very colored yet. I wonder how you get more colored. You can when you get a little older. Grandma's got big brown spots on her hands, and Dad's getting some, too. I'm only eight, but I'm getting a little reddish-brown and trying to get more brown freckles, too. I'm just colored a little different now.

Those men made friends with me and turned around, smiling at me a lot. That's what baseball is supposed to be like! I smiled back, even though I'm a little shy. Baseball makes you not get so shy! They got me to cheer a lot louder, so every time they cheered, Dad and I did, too. Boy, that was fun! We just all cheered together at the same time! My dad and our new friends even got one of those Erin Brews from that man yelling, "Cold beer here!" I think Jimmy had him bring some over to Dad and our new friends. I think that's the very first time Dad ever had one of those. All I got was this teeny-weeny Coca-Cola bottle. Three gulps and you're out!

Never figured out why you get two cents for turning in that tiny little bottle. You get more for the bottle than what's inside costs. I thought Jimmy Dudley might come over to sit with us, because he's such a good friend. He can have one of these beers with us, too, but he was up there being the radio talker and couldn't come over to our seats that day. But we were having so much more fun with those new friends, anyway! And Dad was really funny after Jimmy gave us those beers. Dad giggled a lot but didn't tell his corn joke. Our new friends and my dad really loved those beers, though. And that "ice-cold beer here" man kept coming back to say, "Hi, there! Another?" lots of times. He must have been one of Jimmy's best friends, too. I guess my dad was old enough for Erin Brew. I wasn't yet. But I will be in a couple of years, probably when I get to be a third grader.

Most of the time, we just sat there and watched the players take turns running around the field and throwing the ball around. I got kind of bored 'cuz Bob Feller wasn't pitching, but then, all of a sudden, our new friends in front of us started jumping up and screaming, "Here he comes!" I had no idea who was coming, but I jumped up and yelled really loudly, too. That way I got to see better, too. And then this little, tiny, red car someone called an Austin-Healey drove all the way across the grass and over second base, and out the door came this long, skinny man they called Satchel Paige. Our new friends said he was about fifty-four years old and had been sitting out in a rocking chair in the *bullpen* a long time. Not a cow pen like I work in! And I know the difference there!

These new friends know everything about baseball! I'm just hoping they'll be with us the next game. These guys can really teach you a lot if you listen, and they know I'm just learning baseball. I asked them if they would come to my school and be our teachers awhile about stuff like *spitballs*, *wind-ups*, *knuckle balls*, *stretches*, *lead-offs*, *pitchers' mounds*, and things like that. We gotta learn so much! The kids should put away all their workbooks and readers for that. I know our teacher's going to be glad, 'cuz she loves baseball. And I know Eddie Spagetti really needs this, 'cuz he's a lefty and needs to learn to become a southpaw if he's ever going to be any good. All this stuff is really important, but I'll see these men at the next game anyhow.

Well! Mr. Pitcher Paige got up on this little dirt hill and bent over to tie his sneakers really tight, just like Mom tells me to do when she says, "Don't forget to tie your shoes!" I don't know if his Mom told him to or not, but all of a sudden my dad yells out, "Here's his shoestring pitch!" Now I couldn't see it, but they said he threw the ball right out of his shoe really fast, so the batter never even saw it, either. No one saw it or hit it! They probably could tell what it was by the big pop in the catcher's glove. Kind of like Jackie's eyes closed and knowing every car going by. The catcher almost fell down. The batters probably should keep their eyes open all the way on that pitch. Boy! I never heard so much yelling! A lot louder than any noise in Fowlers Mills, except when that mill waterwheel was turning all around real noisy.

And I got to know every Indian there ever was. My favorites were Larry Doby, Mickey Vernon, and Dale Mitchell, who batted left-handed, so he was really closer to first base by a whole step so he could get there faster. Doesn't seem fair, but it's not fair I'm only eight years old, too. They should have made me older by now, so I'd know everything. I was learning a lot and can catch pop flies good like Larry Doby now, and that right there is a lot more important than anything you learn at school. Larry and I both ran and jumped a lot alike. We're not the same color, but boy, can we both catch and run fast! I really have to study all this baseball stuff if I'm going to pitch for the Indians. I learned I could be the bat boy, but I live too far away in the country and just can't be to all the games on time. I guess Mom and Dad don't know what an important job that is! The Indians just won't be able to play the games without me there, and then they can't win the world series again. That's just not fair for me to do that to that whole Indians team! You don't make trouble for the Indians like that! That's just not right! That's one of Mom's rules again!

But I know every single one of those Indians know who I am, because on the radio Jimmy Dudley and I always cheer the loudest, especially with my brand-new Indians jacket and ball cap on. And you already know I have the only Rawlings glove in Fowlers Mills. I'm still really serious about working with Farmer Carroll, but even when I ride that hay wagon or manure spreader up there all around, all I can think about now is baseball!

And to show you how much I was thinking baseball, when I got my dad's old Kodak box camera that really takes pictures, I even took a picture of my new baby sister Mary Beth sitting on the couch with my baseball hat and glove on.

See how excited babies get about baseball! Mary Beth has my ball cap and glove on if you can see that far. Had to stand way back 'cuz you can hurt a little baby's eyes bad with a popping flashbulb. I was blind once and it's no fun!

That just shows you how much baseball means to me, like it's supposed to! You have to teach a new baby that kind of stuff when they're really little. Babies don't think a lot, but sometimes that's all they have on their minds—baseball!

Anyway, all of us kids went barefoot all summer even though the bottom of my feet never got tough or dirty yellow like Bobby's down by the mill with all his gravel walking. But I didn't complain, because after we did all our chores like hoeing in the garden and stuff, we climbed all over the caves and lemon squeezes back of Partparts and chased sheep in the field with Tippy until one fell over and didn't move anymore. It was really still!

We threw lots of stones to get a stronger baseball arm. We all hid behind the cemetery stones at night for hide-go-seek games and caught fireflies or lightning bugs in Mason jars to make lanterns. That way they all light up and you can get lots of looks at things all the time like a flashlight. Not just one little look here and there. We also climbed all over those flower-colored feed bags all piled up in the feed-bag room in the mill, sometimes putting holes in 'em until Grampa Koblaha threw brushes at us and yelled, "boulish," and we got out of there fast; or fishin' every fishin' hole in Fowlers Mills. We just did so many things, I can't fit it all into one sentence. We were busier than all get out! You have to work hard to make your summer really special, because it's too short. It doesn't really matter. Learned lots of stuff you never learn in school. We just had to plan it all out and get it all done, because when the dusty milkweed pods would bust and these little silk threads with seeds on the end start flying around, you just know summer's going bye-bye. And before you know it, that doggone Labor Day picnic's here again. Uugghh!

I usually love hot dogs with lots of sweet pickle relish and Kool-Aid, but at this picnic I always felt a little sick to my stomach. I didn't throw up because I wasn't that kind of boy, and boys don't throw up anyhow unless something makes them do it. But my stomach always started aching, and I just didn't feel good 'cuz school was going to start all over again. I knew Mom would have me get out my sneakers and new school clothes with longer dungarees, 'cuz last year's bottoms are almost up to my knees. Get new white T-shirts 'cuz, they make us dress all up really nice again for school! They make us all line up like a bunch of dodos behind our new desks with those holes on the sides and an inkwell on top. And then you look really close to figure out whose old initials got carved into them last year. I sure hope I didn't get some dopey guy's desk. I didn't carve real deep, but I wonder what dumb shrimp got the desk with *TT* on it.

I never found my special little wooden pencil box again. Probably some jerk stole it, but it doesn't matter, 'cuz now I carry my Rawlings glove under my arm with me all the time instead. And Mom gave me two number 2 pencils again. I think I know just how all this old school thing goes by now. Thanks a lot, Mom! I don't really need any erasers 'cuz I'm not makin' any mistakes. This school seems like jail and makes you want to sneak out, go to the boy's room, and never come back! I'm tall enough now I can stand on my tiptoes to hit the urinal on the wall, but I still splash on the floor a lot. Nobody knows, and who really cares anyhow. Let the other little stupid guys step in it. I've been through this school thing before. I can step around anything! It's horrible!

Here's my lower-grades picture! See how the Amish boys get to sit in the front row, and they're not supposed to smile. My hair got more like theirs. I had a bad day and had to stand next to Mrs. Van Orsdale and Jackie in the third row, 'cuz I did that kindergarten thing again and tripped another girl. Didn't want to, and if you look real close, you can tell I'm not happy. And that Bruce next to Jackie in the third row is showing all his teeth and smiling with all that curly hair combed up on top. His sisters must have done that. Like I told you, Jackie had a big head. And that's Nancy behind me who hit us when we pulled up her dress.

Here's my lower-grades picture. See how long and pretty Peggy's braids are. She's next to Ruth Ann in the second row five kids over from the right.

I can't imagine who ever thought this school thing up, but it must have been someone not so smart, to make us kids sit down at a desk all day long. And up on this stupid chalkboard, all cleaned up now, was "Welcome Back, Boys and Girls!" Well, you're not welcome, thank you! It's not great to see you! Let's you just welcome the girls back! How about that?

That blackboard's a lot more fun when you get two erasers in both hands and make all that chalk dust fly all over and watch all the kids coff. And chalk up all those cursive letters they got pasted on top. Now, that's fun! I love to erase all the stuff off blackboards. If you're fast at it, the kids watch you better. But if you do it too fast, you had to write on the blackboard twenty times, "I will use chalk erasers the right way!" Boy! Summer was like only two days long, and I have to be still with a dumb book in front of me all day long. Just doesn't make any sense at all!

I'm the kind of boy who learns all my numbers by counting flies stuck to flypaper hanging down. I got up to twenty-six flies once. That's a lot! Take two away and you get twenty-four. Now, that's where you learn! And worst of all, Mom hates to see me go back to school and leave her all alone at home with nothing to do. Why doesn't anybody care about the moms at times like this? Moms get lonely, too, because when Dad and I are off working all day, the only folks they get there is the Fuller Brush man and Pete, the milkman. This school thing just isn't the way to become a famous farmer or baseball pitcher. And I'm still going to be both! Merle said they even have baseball farm teams somewhere where I guess you can play baseball and farm at the same time. Wow! Got both of 'em. That's like a double play!

———◆———

Well! I'm back up under my tree in my thinking place. Boy! Those 1948 Indians world series champs get me so excited. Just thinking about baseball makes me forget about those horrible troubles I had and school, too. Hope I get to see those new friends at the baseball game again next year. That's what daydreaming about exciting things does. You forget about everything else and want to cheer until you start thinking about that darn old Labor Day picnic and school starting again. That picnic's supposed to be fun! But you can't daydream and have fun all the time. There's work to do. It's hard, but sometimes you just have to do things you don't like!

CHAPTER 9

THIRD GRADE—FALLING
IN LOVE

S econd grade was just as boring as the first except for baseball and recess and having three grades in the same room with Mrs. Van Orsdale. Now Bruce and I are in the middle grade in the middle seats. We can poke fun at these little, scared shrimps now, unless they really need our help. The girls swing higher on the swings now, so we can see their underpants better, and the cows get inside the school yard, jumping over the fence a lot more. We have to run out of school lickety-split to chase them all back again. Bruster and I are still doing that secret of pushing the barbwire fence down to help the poor little cows out, so you get more recess to chase 'em back in. I can never get too much recess! You know something, cows jump funny because their backs are all stiff. They just spend too much time eating grass and don't run around enough, especially if their udders get too big.

Now, of course, they gave us a new reading book, but it's still that same old Dick, Jane, and Spot. We don't want to know anymore about those guys anyhow. I don't care if I ever see them again. They just do the same old boring stuff all the time and don't even look any older. And can you believe this? They make us all buy these stupid plastic Tonette things for twenty-five cents and try to make us be a music band. Boy! That stupid scratchy sound makes your ears pop! Dumbest thing I ever saw! Cows sound better mooing up front or blowing out gas balls out both ends!

But moving up to third grade is a big thing! Now Bruce and I are a real team together, and all the kids know that! And all the kids coming up from the city see that, too. Because more kids keep coming out to our school now, we have three rooms with only two grades in each room and a brand-new teacher. And we have real writing books now with lines to do cursive writing and not make dumb block letters like the little shrimps. That cursive writing takes lots of brains, because you have to stay in the lines and write in big circles. Well, my circles were pretty big, but I didn't do so well, because I got out of the lines a lot. Girls do it better. I won't tell you my grade for my cursive writing book. It isn't any good getting Ds and getting that "Do it again!" thing. And we got those exciting spelling bees going. Boy! You can tell I know how to spell. And school lunches this year cost way more! They're up to fifteen cents. But every time a car hits a deer in Munson Township, we get free venison for lunch a whole week. Last day of that deer, you only get spagetti and a couple of meatballs which some kids can't find any of. You really have to be on the ball to keep up with all this new stuff. It gets confusing. You even forget which one of these rooms you're supposed to be going into.

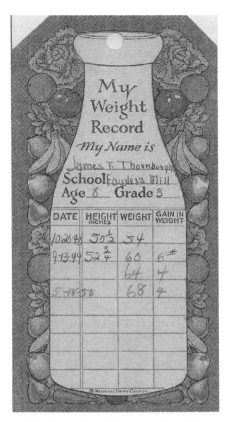

My
Weight
Record

My Name is
James T. Thornburgh
School Fowlers Mill
Age 8 Grade 3

DATE	HEIGHT INCHES	WEIGHT	GAIN IN WEIGHT
10-20-48	50½	54	
9-13-49	52¾	60	6#
		64	4
5-18-50		68	4

© NATIONAL DAIRY COUNCIL

**Hey, look how big I am in third grade. All that milk gives
you muscles. And James is really me, Tommy.**

Then the fifth and sixth grades have to move over to the town hall
next to the church. It's an old, white, wood building with a big stove in
the middle and has only one big room in it. That's all! Boy! This has got
to be confusing for you. I'm sorry, but that's just the way this happens!
Bruce and I didn't plan it that way. You just never know anymore! You
just can't tell what's happening, so be ready for surprises!

That's the town hall where they moved all the fifth and sixth graders and left all the little shrimps behind in the red brick building. And that's Sue showing her tummy.

And we get the new teacher, Mrs. Poutasse. That's not a bad word either. She's the best! She can hit the ball left-handed way up over the trees and out of the schoolyard. She's somethin' else! She's a real southpaw! And she came from Concord, Massachusetts, where most everyone's a lefty. And I went there one time on vacation where we minutemen fought the Redcoats, so we have lots to talk about. I pretended I was one of those minutemen and beat up all the Redcoats. That helped me be a better fighter. We were pretty much the same, except she's taller than me, although my legs grew over my sock tops over the summer. And we both just love baseball! For her, working at teaching and playing is like the same thing!

And she lets me do anything I want to in school. She lets me read books under my desk while she's putting all these numbers on the chalkboard. She isn't bossy, except one time when she was putting all these numbers on the chalkboard and doing something she calls long division. Well! She called on me, and I looked up and said, "What?" And that's the smartest answer when you don't know something. I looked surprised, but she said really quietly, "Tommy! Why don't you put your

Mad Anthony Wayne away, because you'll need this later on." She talked so nicely. Boy! Is she smart! She knows everything. I think she likes me because I can talk about Concord and play baseball a lot more now. We talk a lot of baseball, too. She gave me a kiss on the cheek once, and I really love her for that.

When it really gets hot in the room, she takes us all outside with our readers under the maple tree out back, not in some stupid little circle on the floor like Mrs. Van Horsetail and those dumb little kids did. And Mrs. Poutasse is so nice, I didn't look under her dress, either. I already know that garter stuff anyhow. She doesn't shout or get really excited or anything like that. To show you what I mean, one time she was playing kickball with both our grades outside, and her underpants fell right down to her ankles when she kicked the ball so hard. Well! She just picked them right up and went right behind a big bush and came right back to keep on playing again like nothing happened. And she smiled and winked at Bruce and me, 'cuz we were the only ones who saw it. She really didn't need to wink at us, 'cuz Bruster and I know all about that stuff more than the other kids. Well! I really think I'm falling in love with Mrs. Poutasse and the way she winks at me.

But I'm really thinking mostly about baseball. Bruce didn't have a glove, but just the two of us started standing all the other boys in our room in baseball. Of course there were only two older boys in the older fourth grade, Richard and Roger, and they liked more to shoot holes in things with BB guns than baseball.

But it's only me and Bruster on one team. I pitch, of course. It's underhand for the other kids, and I let Bruster play the outfield. Most of the hits are little grounders and only come to me, and I can run fast and tag them out at first base. Sometimes the grass is so high, because Mr. Warner can't get out of his chair in the boiler room to mow it. If it's high enough, they can't run so fast, and it's easy to tag 'em out, 'cuz they can't find that bag in the grass. It was kind of like Mr. Warner was on our team that way helping us out.

When we bat, I go first and get on first or second base, and then Bruster, who has kind of a wild swing at times, smashes him and me home with a long smash. He misses some, but he sure has a big swing. We don't have anybody like Sue to call balls and strikes. Sometimes

Bruster even hits it into the pasture, so we have to run really fast to get the ball before the cows eat it. They'll eat anything, just like goats! We shouldn't have done it. And I think that was Bruce's idea again. But when we chase that ball into the cow pasture, we always pull some of that barbwire fence down again coming back. Then later the cows can get out and back into our school yard again, just like before.

Of course, the cows make more cow pies that way. The hard, dry ones make the best home plates. But make sure they're hard and dry enough and not all mushy underneath. And I guess you know why! Don't you? Of course then we all have to get out of the schoolhouse again really fast to chase them all back again. Yippie! More fun than recess! I don't think Mrs. Poutasse minds. She's a good egg! I don't think that farmer's too happy with us, though. He's a rotten egg! Just like the kind you find behind the couch smelling bad two months after Easter or even like a dead mouse.

One time, and I don't think I'm ever going to get over it, I squatted down to grab a grounder, and the worst thing happened. The whole back of my pants ripped open and split right down the middle. It was horrible! I was so embarrassed, because a really pretty new girl, Roberta, had moved into Munson school, and she was cheering so loudly for Bruce and me in baseball like all the girls do all the time now. They love to cheer for us, or they can go on the swings, too, if they want to, because now they're really swinging high. Whoopee! Glad I don't need my glasses anymore. You can see their unders from here. Don't need those glasses for reading, either.

Anyhow! Back to the ball field with my behind showing, my heart starts to go really fast, my hands get sweaty, and my face must be beet red. I wasn't sure what to do! But I just pretended I had a bad stomachache and walked backward all the way up the hill, so no one could see my underpants. I went past the Town Hall and Reynolds Store and ran all the way home. That's like a real big home run! Boy! What if Roberta saw my bottom? I never could go to that Munson School again! I'd run away. I hid in our barn all day long with my goats and my stomachache. Bruce must have told the teacher, because no one ever came and found me.

So you know I was in love with baseball, and at my school desk, I was thinking all the time about pitching for the Indians and everybody cheering for me and Bob Feller and Larry Doby, Dale Mitchell, Luke Easter, Lou Boodrow, Kenny Keltner, and all those other players. But now I think

I am also in love with Roberta, and being the best baseball player is a great way to show her. You run and kick 'er up really high there for a little extra attention. That's the only way you get these pretty girls to look at you a lot.

Well! Bruce and now Eddie (the one with the first-base trapper's glove) who had just moved in from the city are all in love with her, too. She's so pretty! She has such a beautiful smile, lots of beautiful freckles, and the biggest, beautiful teeth. She has long, curly, yellow hair that almost looks like strings of popcorn. She smiles all the time. That's why we boys like her so much. She winks at us a lot. That makes her dimples bigger. That's all I see, but that's enough for me. I tried to help her all the time with her arithmetic even when she was all done, 'cuz then I could lean over her workbook with my pencil and touch her long curly hair. My hair still looked like a haystack, and my teeth were kind of crooked like Ollie on the *Kukla, Fran, and Ollie Show* I saw when we got our first Philco TV. That's why I can't whistle too well.

Roberta had the cutest talking lisp, which makes me feel like jelly. And I know Roberta was smiling at me most of the time now. You have to be sure about those things! Just looking at someone doesn't tell you what's on their mind unless it's Mom and her mom looks. So I just had to ask her out loud a lot, "Who do you like the most? Me or Bruce or Eddie?" I wasn't ever sure what she told the other boys, but I had to work real hard to be number one. When it comes to girls, you just can't let down any when you're in love. You've got to keep working at it all the time! And that is not just playing around!

The bigger grades were really getting good for me now. A whole lot better! I always ask my sister Sue to ask Roberta to come over to our house to play with her so Sue can roll us around together in a big, old oat barrel in the barn. This is a lot more fun than playing Fox and Geese, I'll tell you! Sometimes we even kiss in the barrel, and our teeth clink. You can break 'em that way and hit your noses, too. It's dark in there. I hoped our teeth wouldn't get stuck together, and they wouldn't be able to pull us apart. We didn't show our things or anything bad like Bruce and I did in the first grade behind the pump house, because I'm really in love now, and I like her smile and lisping the best of all. She winks more now, too. And I'm beginning to think about the big family and all the children we're going to have. She'll make the best farmer's wife. Much better than that stupid "Farmer in the Dell" one! Oh man! That song makes you want to puke!

> The farmer takes a wife
> The farmer takes a wife
> Heigh-ho, the derry-o
> The farmer takes a wife

I really am lucky I have such a great big sister Sue, even though she can really be snarky at times, especially once a month. And she always makes a little red check of it on the kitchen calendar, so she knows. Mom says every month that happens to girls, and you just have to be nice to them. It seems like every month she gets kind of mean and pokes and yells at me a lot, but she really looks after me the best! She makes sure nothing ever happens to me!

She and her friend Cathy were put in charge of lining us up for Mrs. Keifer's children's choir every Sunday morning at the Fowlers Mills Community Church. And Sue's a saver and liked to save money from her babysitting jobs, and my mom and dad even borrowed from her for stamps and stuff. They didn't steal it! They always paid her back! That's what we always do in our family, pay every penny or last dime back!

Now, 'cuz Sue likes to save money, you know, I got this idea to pay Sue a dime every Sunday out of our family's March of Dimes card or Sunday school money (just one dime at a time, so nobody knows), so she'll let me sit next to Roberta in choir. I can't tell you now, but when I'm not so shy, I'll tell you a lot more about all those dimes and nickels later.

But holy goodness (that's a church word), did Roberta and I ever make good singing together! I thought how wonderful it would be singing together to our little children when we get two of them. I don't think I ever learned the words to any choir hymns. I was all jelly inside just looking at Roberta out of the corner of my eye. Every Sunday all the congregation, Fern and Bob Woolcott, Paul and Gladys Varney, and Maude Beech, and all the really good church goers would sit right up in front there in their same pew seats just smiling and staring at us all the time, because Roberta and I were in the front row, too. They just loved the way the two of us sang together. That's the whole reason they came to church! I think they wish they could be in the children's choir again. That's probably where they fell in love like Roberta and me and decided to marry each other, too.

Now, this is something I have to tell you because it's the real Truth, and you always tell the Truth—Mom's rule! I began to think I might not be too smart after all or maybe lazy, because the only song words I knew were rounds of "Row, row, row your boat gently down the stream," which, if you remember, is not at all how old Bruster and I did rowboats on the mill pond! Maybe I just wasn't paying attention. There was also some song like "Let the Ivy Deck those Garden Walls," or something like that.

I'm not sure why, but there's one song I remember well. It's this one.

> Glory, glory Hallelujah,
> Teacher hit me with a ruler,
> I hit her on the beanie,
> With a squashed tangereenie,
> And her teeth went marching on!

That was my favorite school song, probably because it was both religious and American, too! And I'd never sing that to Mrs. Poutasse! Maybe some of the others but not her! No, sireee! Don't make fun of her name, either! But I'm getting pretty nervous now because I can't even get "The Star-Spangled Banner" words right, and for heaven's sakes, that's our United States country song. I can sure spell, but I can't do song words. And you know how it's going to be when I am a great Indians pitcher. Before every single baseball game, I'll have to stand right out there on the field and try to sing that song in front of all those people. I mean, you can't hide out in the dugout, the coatroom or anywhere! I just don't remember songs! I can't remember Bible verses, either.

But now I mumble through The Pledge of Allegiance every morning in school and always stand straight and put my hand right over my heart. I learned it's higher than my belly button now. I don't know if you're allowed to, but I just began to make up any words I could, and it's all different every single time. Nobody but me ever knows that. Thank God! Sometimes when you don't know something, you just gotta make it up. That's better than nothing at all. It doesn't really matter! Try it!

One time we had this music teacher with a little round face, no hair, and tiny glasses come around every week, and he wanted us to put on this Steven Foster play. Best thing about that man was something he thumped, called a tuning fork, which was supposed to tell you how to sing higher. But our voices were squeaking now, so that fork didn't do us a thing! We boys just sang like we always do, not so good!

Well! We boys had to pick a Steven Foster. And about that time, I had to go to the bathroom and pee. This isn't fair, but they took a vote and voted me in before I got back. Those dirty dogs! I need to learn to hold it. Tie it in a knot or something! Never take a pee when there's a vote going on! You have to be right there! Well! I still couldn't learn song words here, so I pretended I needed Bruce to be my brother, so somebody would know the words. I don't even know if Steven has a brother. We just called him Frank Foster. Well! When we started singing "My Old Kentucky Home" up on the church stage, Bruce and I just looked at each other. I thought he knew the words! Thanks! You bugger!

Sure was a short and funny mixed-up song we must have made up! I think there were two different songs. Nobody clapped too much. They were all too busy looking at each other and giggling out there in the church pews. They weren't even paying attention! They should have known old Stevie was a serious guy! But pretty Ruth Ann was Mrs. Foster, and she could really carry a tune, the music teacher said. That fork must have helped her. So we got to sing "Beautiful Dreamer" together and smile at each other again. She just looked me right in the eyes and I wasn't even afraid about cooties any more. That's where I learned to blush. Ruth Ann knew all the words, and I just moved my mouth, and it was like I was loving her again, but I sure didn't tell anything to Roberta about that. No, sireee! That play really wasn't so good! Wasn't wonderful like in the second grade when I was the court jester and had my best only part ever: "Here comes the queen!" Boy! That was a dandy! Everyone smiled at me. Everybody in Munson Township remembers that loudest, best part even today!

Anyhow! The big chance to show Roberta how much I loved her came on Valentine's Day. And we were smiling back at each other a lot more now. That's when you really let somebody special know how you feel. That's why all they talk about is hearts and cut 'em out all day.

Cut, cut, cut! Those hearts look like that red thing you got pumping in the middle of your body. It's just a lot of hard work, but when they're all cut out, it just seems special. You just get kind of mushy inside! And I'm not dumb, because you know that right in school there are lots of sweet candy hearts to eat all day long. You try to pick out the special heart with those special words you really want on those cute little sugar hearts, something that tells how you really feel inside. One you can't tell anybody else. Keep it secret! And if you don't like what it says, just eat it up, and try another one! You always need a little extra sugar anyway in times like this! Anyhow! No more making those dumb valentine boxes with construction and crap paper. All I was just thinking about anymore was Roberta!

Well! I picked out a special valentine for Bruce, too, because I liked him a lot, too. But it was something different with Roberta. Bruce was more like a brother, because we did everything together now, and I sleep over at his house a lot, and his brothers and sisters were like mine, too. At Bruce's house they even gave me my very own purple-and-pink rosary, my own lucky charm. Once when he came to my house to sleep over, we were running around with rosaries around our necks and got them caught in the door and beads went rolling all over. Dad wasn't too happy about that, and it took a long time to pick them all up, and you've got to get them back on the string just the right way.

Dad said, "That's not doing right, and you'd better slow down!" Well! If you're in a hurry, you can put all those different beads on in any way you want to. It really doesn't matter! It's just the prayers get all mixed up, but that's OK for Bruce and me.

Anyhow, for Valentine's Day I bought this special, most beautiful card for Roberta, not just one of those little, teenie, crummy ones cut out of a big piece of paper like you give anybody. Those can't even stand up by themselves. This best one is all folded up and says beautiful things inside. I'll get really red if I say them out loud to you.

And I put a chocolate-covered marshmallow heart I store-bought for a nickel inside. That's the thing that really lets her know just how much I loved her. I won't have to smile at her so hard anymore. Funny! You do that smiling thing a whole lot more when you're nervous. I was really thinking a lot more about us having little babies. We'll have one boy with short, curly brown hair and one girl with long, yellow hair. And my dog Tippy and her collie Lassie will play together in the family and be making babies, too. And we'll all play together in the field all the time like a big, happy family. And that's all what you have to do!

This was the only time Bruce really surprised me and made me a little mad. Bruster! You bad boy, you! I'd chicken-pluck that Rooster's curly yellow hair out! I don't know where he got all that money and that idea, but I just have to know what he's giving Roberta, because his card is extra fat and clinked a little, too. A really big one! Do you know what old Bruster did? And this just might make you a little mad, too, because you know Bruster pretty well by now. He had hidden two quarters, not even just one, but two, into his card for Roberta, and that's a lot of money! What a sneak! You know that's not right!

Even my mom would say, "That's not the right thing to do! Don't think you're better than anybody else!" I know I'm still number one with Roberta, but Bruce and Eddie might be catching up fast.

This is going too far! He sure surprised me. Well! I'll get him back. I really had to think fast, and my head hurt so much, because that dumb valentine box was going past every desk row so fast now, and the cards were getting all stuffed in, left and right. I didn't know if I had time, but I whispered to Bruce just in time, "That's not good! It's like buying somebody. If you want to be number one, just ask her! Don't go stuffing in quarters behind my back!" You don't go buying people. I knew a lot about that civil war stuff, because my dad was a history teacher. The hair stood up on my neck.

Just ask Roberta! She always says yes. She never says no. She's just that kind of girl! And she wouldn't hurt a flea; maybe she will marry me. Get it? I'm so much in love now, I'm getting to say everything more in poems. But it's hard to get the rime righter, because I'm not a Limelighter. Get it? Rimes and limes! My sister Sue had a Limelighter's 78 song album she played all the time. Listen to it now: "Whistling Gypsy," and I hope the next ones aren't bad words, but they were "Lass From the Low Country" and "Joy Across the Land." Wow! But I'm getting in a dither here and getting all tangled up in this poemy stuff and a little confused. I'm not sure what I'm saying!

Maybe I should just say this whole thing in a poem. Forget this farmer and baseball stuff and just be a poet and sit around and make lots of money.

That's what this love stuff does to you. It makes you all twitter-pated like Thumper in the *Bambi* picture show. I wonder who ever thought this love stuff up, or does it maybe just happen to you? Anyhow, I don't think I'm old enough to marry yet. Most of the married people I know of are a little older than me. Heck! Old Farmer Carroll's not married yet, and look at all the fun he's having!

Anyhow, back to money and candy bars, which make a lot more sense to talk about! With all Bruster's money, we can both buy lots of five-cent candy bars now, five of them with just one of those quarters. But two quarters. Wow! Lots of candy bars like Snickers, Baby Ruths, Hershey bars, and Butterfingers, but none of those Mounds or Heath bars, which are my favorite, even though they're awfully tiny. They cost ten cents, and that's just like robbing us kids. Kids just don't make that much money. They just work for ginger ale, remember?

I told Bruce, because there wasn't much time left, that I'd let him wear that new hand-me-down, genuine, black-and-white, check coat made from real buffalo fur for the whole rest of the winter. Maybe all the way to Easter! What a relief that is, because even the Bruster can't say no to that one! And I don't even know much yet about all those other games like Spin the Bottle or Post Office like the bigger kids play. Nobody asked me to play those yet, and I don't even know if they're fun. But boy, am I feeling better about Roberta! Whew! Close one! And I think this whole thing is making me start to get the runs, and I'm a long way from home. Wow! That's those long home runs again! Might never make it! It's all coming faster, but I'm not!

That was one of the toughest days of my life. I don't know anybody who's ever, ever been through anything like that before! But I really like seeing old Bruster in my winter buffalo coat, and he's so proud of it. He told everybody about that genuine buffalo hide with pride. Bruce was picking up a few new big words, too. And now he starts looking more handsome than I do in it, and Roberta starts smiling at him a lot more. She's kind of shy like me, and her face gets red, but she winks at Bruce more now. I got to wear his old coat, but I'm not worrying, because when school's over every day, I got my own buffalo one right back. I mean, you've got to trust somebody! If you can't trust the old Bruster, who can you trust?

And I'm not sure of old Bruster after all. I'm beginning to hate class picture day! It's not fair! Another bad day in third grade. I pushed a boy this time, so the teacher put me right in the front row between Rosemary and Ruth Ann with the long, black hair. Teacher said "Keep your hands to yourself." I was just trying to help. I thought everybody forgot I was blind one time, but there I am with my horrible glasses and smelly sneakers on right in the front row! Kiss my feet and fall over! I'm the only one not smiling and not folding my hands. No, sireee! Those girls were pretty cute, but remember you can get cooties that way even if you make yourself a special paper cootie catcher. I think I already had them by then.

That man that made that name cooties up must have known what he was talking about. Must have been a doctor! Remember, it's the only germ you can get in the country. That lucky Johnnie got out of this picture 'cuz he's Amish! And Roberta got to stand right behind me, so they wouldn't even let me see her. She's right next to Dickie with the nice combed hair and Jackie full of the dickens. And that doggone Bruster is next to Jackie, all smiling with his buttons up just right. Boy, I was mad that day!

**Third and Fourth Grade Class 1949. See how I'm not folding
my hands right. That's why I got in trouble. Those glasses
are sposed to make you look smart, but I don't think so!**

And I'll tell you something else. I never wanted to marry both those girls even though they're so cute. I'm never getting married, anyhow, and I'm always going to live with my mom just like Farmer Carroll!

And Bruster, you old bugger! On picture day in fourth grade, I tripped a kid and had to stand by the teacher again. I said, "Wanna take a trip?" and that kid did. Well, this was really a bad day! Hate these picture days! I'll bust that camera! I stood next to the teacher again for bad deportment. I tried to smile a little, too, but you wouldn't, either, if you had to stand by the teacher again. You can tell I wasn't happy, and what an awful day it was, because I cut out some of the kid's faces with Mom's nail clippers. Only five, though, and not everybody, though I could've. And you can see I'm wearing that same old striped T-shirt again because it's all I got. And my hair's looking more like Johnnie's bowl cut everyday. And there's Roberta again in the third row, smiling away, so everyone can see her and that beautiful hair. She's got all the boys around her except me. The only good thing about fourth grade is that *Singing Wheels* reader where the old fashioned Hastings boy is taking trips everywhere all day. That's all I want to do, too!

And doggone it! There's that bugger Bruster right on top of Roberta with a big fat smile on his face. Now look at it really hard. Darn! He even snuck a tie on. And all his buttons were buttoned and his hair combed up, standing right behind Roberta looking right down at her. What a show-off! They both had big smiles on their faces. He got to be number one that day! I sure wasn't! And up there on his left in the top row was our favorite Congo-Alaska game player, Beverly. I'll tell you about the Congo-Alaska game a bit later. And he even got his little sister Carlene to hold his very own dog right up there in the front row! That's not Tippy. She's better lookin'! Tippy doesn't like to have her picture taken and stayed home from school that day. Probably a tummy ache. You can see the Byler twins aren't being Amish any more, but they still wear suspenders and got shorter haircuts. And that's the new boy Eddie right up in the back with the big smiling teeth and grin. I'd trade places. That wasn't a happy day for me. Who in heaven's name cut some faces out of that picture? Guess it was me. Yep! Sure did! Cut some of those kids right out of there! Made me feel better!

**Third and Fourth Grade 1950. Johnnie gets to sit front row
again between two pretty girls because he's Amish. Now I'll
never know what those kids with no faces look like.**

Well, and I don't know how I'm saying this, because I don't want to
get too motional, but one day we got the most terrible news there ever was!
Roberta is moving back to Wooster, so her father could help take care of
some stupid cows and some eggerculture center there. And she's even taking her little brother David, so now we don't even have nobody to play right
field anymore. I can't believe it! When choosing up sides with the bat, I
always choose David to be on my team, so he can get his sister to like me
the best. And then he was just picking flowers out there and not chasing his
balls getting hit to him. And now, I can't even count on him. What a friend!
David must have even told his dad to move away really quick and not even
tell us, because you know David didn't like baseball the same as we did. He
can't even get his fat fingers around the bat. Boy! This is really bad!

Well! They moved out right after Christmas, and I was so blue.
Never saw Roberta again, and nobody was in right field anymore! Had
nobody to choose last anymore! Nothing ever got me excited anymore.

Mom said I just moped around like a sad sack, and two of Mom's rules were: "Don't be a sourpuss. Don't feel sorry for yourself!" Well! I was sorry! Whoa, there! Be careful!

I never felt so bad in my life! I couldn't wait until sixth grade, so I could get away from here and join the army like Tommy S. Maybe I could go with him, and we would both get way out of here! Or maybe I would become Amish, because they only have to go to grade school. Those lucky guys! I have had enough! Only talking to my goats made me feel any better. They knew how to listen and not talk back. They knew what you were talking about and were the only ones that believed me. They were so smart! Every time I opened the barn door, they beat their little hooves and neighed and really wanted to talk to me. They couldn't wait to see what I had to say. I could think things a lot better in the barn and with my goats. Nobody pestered me like in school. You know, animals talk a lot to each other, too, but they stop and listen to you when you want. Not like old Maude and Fern on that stupid party line.

We talk an awful lot down in my own box stall. Kind of like my bedroom where it's private. But not like Mom saying, "Go to your room and think about it!" where you're all alone. My goats and I really like to think things and talk together. Everybody calls them only Tommy's goats. They lick your face a lot, too. Dad says they need salt, but I think it's because we're best friends. And no having to say, "Please pass the salt!" Just lick your face for it. I hug them a lot, and they just say a little neigh. You know, sometimes the way a goat looks at you tells you a lot more than what they really say. And you don't have to know everything they're thinking. It just doesn't really matter. They just understand! When their ears go back, that's when you know they really want to listen, and you have something important to say. That makes you feel a lot better and makes you a whole lot better boy!

Talking to my goaties helps. They feel sadder for me than anybody else, because they know how to listen and how I feel. But I'm really feeling sad all alone up here on this hill. Roberta's gone, and she took our right fielder away, too. This being in love thing gets you all mixed up. Mom said it was puppy love, but it sure seems more to me than that! I've seen lots of puppies before. Thought this was going to be forever. Loving Roberta is all I thought about! Made me forget all the bad things.

Even school got better. But now! Boy, I'm so blue and lonely. Bruce and I know how we both feel. Can't believe we both tried to beat the other guy to be number one. So what! I guess you don't know how you feel til you get there. Be nice if someone told you that before!

Look close and you can see how I can do two things both at the same time. Take care of my little sister Kathy and read the funnies and all about Korea in the newspaper.

CHAPTER 10

NORTHERN LIGHTS, SINNING, AND PENNY HORSE

My whole life is really going a whole different way now. So many troubles! Kind of like being all lost on some old, windy, back dirt side road or something. After feeding my goats, Nellie and Millie, I sit up on our hillside. It's still way over on the other side of the pond under that apple tree and near the white and red pines. That's just under the cemetery and close to where we plant our corn and potatoes in the summer. That's the place I just think a lot, especially when the sun goes down. I just think better up here. Nobody pestering me! Don't have to go to my room and think anymore. I can just sit up here forever! I wonder about stuff like, what's going to happen to me when I grow up?

Then all of a sudden one night, you just wouldn't believe it! It was still cold and almost March outside. All of a sudden, all these amazing lights with all different colors—blues, greens, oranges, yellows, and reds—started rolling all across the sky off to the right of me, out over the pasture and woods way over the hill. They were going all over the sky up there in one way like a bunch of flags flapping. At first I thought it was an atomic bomb, because I'm learning a lot about Russia and the Iron Curtain. I read in *The Plain Dealer* all about Korea and the thirty-eighth parallel and all that stuff over there somewhere. I almost forgot if that war's still going on. Don't know where the soldiers went. Nobody talks about it much. No pots and pans ever started banging away and nobody's cheering about ice cream yet. I read there were 20 or 20,0000 hurt way over there or something like that, but can't remember how many zeros. Oh well! I gotta read the funnies and *Beetle Bailey* anyhow.

And we sure were getting to know a lot about atom bombs because of those exciting bomb drills when we scooch down under our desks at school. It wasn't just trying to rub up against Roberta or anything like that! And since I'm going to Sunday school now, I know a lot now about heaven and hell. I thought this might be that last day ever and the end of the whole world. Maybe that's God trying to talk to me again; I don't know! You know, I might never see my family again. Boy! They'll sure miss me.

But, you know, I can save lots of people, now that I'm so strong. But the colors keep on going, and it's so beautiful, I just can't take my eyes off them. They just keep moving all over the sky over there. I don't care anymore. I'm not scared either, and I hope they'll never stop. I don't know if this is an atomic bomb or not, but it sure is beautiful. And that's strange, having something so scary look so pretty. But I've got to let Mom know as fast as I can, so we can all hide up in the caves in the woods behind the Partparts' house. And I began to think out loud, "What if I'm not here tomorrow? Who's going to feed my goats? And what about Mom? Who's going to cook dinner? Nobody's going to hear the dinner bell anymore, and Sue—no more pinching me—but she won't leave me, I hope."

So I got up and ran really fast, down past the creek and the barn, and all of a sudden, it's all gone—just that old owl sitting on that locust-tree branch back of the barn next to the pond, just looking and blinking at me. No more lights. Just nothing! All the colors are gone. They stopped all at once. I feel so silly. Like I don't have anything to show anybody anymore.

Well! I keep walking up to the house in the dark and keep looking out over the pasture, but it's all dark. What am I going to show them now? Mom believes me because she always does. Dad isn't home yet, and my sister Sue's really mean, like, "Tommy, you know you shouldn't be telling those big fat fibs!" I feel horrible. Nobody's ever going to believe me again. They'll all think I'm a really dopey kid. All the Fowlers Mills people were probably eating supper inside, so nobody ever saw a thing out there. They're all going to think I'm the biggest liar in the world. Maybe I should just give up and quit. Maybe I should pray harder and not think of candy bars so much and not be so greedy asking for so much stuff in my prayers. No more prayin' stuff like, "Please God, give me a big BB gun!" Nope! I tell Mom about those lights of course. (You have to do that.) I mean, it's best to stay calm! Ask Mom! Rhyming again. But I never told anybody else, because I know they'll make fun of me forever!

But in church, these sermons are awfully boring. I can't sit still, and all I can think about are those darn candy bars. And when they have this Communion thing with these tiny, little, dollhouse glasses of grape juice and little pieces of bread, only moms and dads and old people go up front and eat those. That, doggone it, makes me even more hungry! I thought grown-ups are supposed to share the food with their children. It's not fair! If I'd have gone up to the front, I'd have stuck my whole hand in the bowl and pulled out at least ten pieces of bread. A big, huge handful, before the preacher sees me. And I know that grape juice doesn't taste like blood like Bruce says, because I snuck some once when a bunch of those eenie-weenie, little glasses were sitting all full on a tray down in the church kitchen. Boy! Give me a whole bottle of that stuff! I guess all the old people already had their tummies filled up that Sunday.

You know, I think my dad is having more troubles, too. We both were! It happens to all the boys in our family. One Sunday morning in some awful long, boring sermon, the preacher from the Bible school shouts right out loud, "Brother Rex, will you lead us in a word of prayer?" And you know what? Dad was fast asleep! Not even one word of prayer from him! So, like me, he sure doesn't pay much attention to these boring, old sermons, either. Dad's so smart! I think he learned how to do all that not paying attention from me. And I'm still good at coloring, but I'm not doing that in the songbook any more. And you know, sometimes that old preacher looks asleep, too. His tiny granny glasses hold his bushy eyebrows up. He can't fool us! Sometimes he preaches, "Here comes your maker and holy saver, so get ready to be saved!" Maybe the saver won't save him!

Boy! I'm getting real nervous, because that preacher might call on me sometime, and I'm not too good at prayers, and I'm still kind of shy. I feel really bad for Dad, because everybody turns right or left and around and looks right at us, sitting right there smack in the back pew. And it really smells like pew, too! I'm just rhyming everything now. Can't stop! And poor old Dad was so tired, because all day Saturday, we both had to do most all the church cleaning for a few bucks. Teachers don't make much, you know, and we always need a little extra!

Cleaning church is hard work, and that's what they say is really working for the Lord! And the Lord's somebody who really likes you better if you're doing hard work. I mean, look at all he did in just six days and then told everybody he knows all around to take it easy on Sunday. He's pretty smart that way! He's been up there or all around this place before Dad was even born. But Dad and I don't obey so much, though, because we worked a little extra hard, early on that Sunday morning rest day, too! Way before we even got to read *Little Orphan Annie* and *Dogpatch* in the funnies.

I almost forgot! Back to this working thing again! That church had wasps flying all over, just buzzing around. Well! Dad and I swatted over fifty wasps that Saturday morning. Knocked 'em dead! It was lots of fun to see who could swat the most, and Dad just beat me. He sure can swat fast. He swats with just his wrist, but I swing the swatter with my whole arm like throwing a baseball. I swatted over twenty, I think. It was a good day! We counted every last one and cheered every time we got one squooshed flat. (I don't want to bore you, too, like that preacher does, but later on you'll get to read a poem I wrote when I'm grown-up more into a bigger church and can really rhyme that stuff. That poem right there will really show you how I really felt deep down in my heart about some of these church things I had to work on better.)

Early every Sunday morning, about eight o'clock sharp, Dad and I get up fast and get to the church. Then my big church job is to hang on to that rope hanging down from the big church steeple, pull hard, and then let it pull me up and down off the floor a bunch of times to ring that bell so loud all over the whole valley, so everyone in Fowlers Mills would get up and get to church on time. That's what we call again really working for the Lord! More fun than climbing caves, but that was just one of our jobs! And Dad and I cheer again so loudly every time that rope pulls me off the floor. That's more fun than scrubbing floors for Jesus.

So no wonder poor old Dad was tired out! He was supposed to be sound asleep in that pew. Just snoring away! And Sunday's a rest day anyhow. After all, he wasn't supposed to be on watch like back in the navy. Hey! The war's over! You remember how we started this story here! Maybe I should be on watch for that preacher, though! My job is to help old Dad out, and we both stick together!

One time I got really lucky in this church thing when one of Partparts' sheep, who never had any of her wool ever sheared off, got stuck in our stream on Sunday morning. It took four big men and one of me a long time to pull her out by her wool. She was full of water and so heavy, so that Sunday we all missed church. I think lots of times, "Thank you, God, for saving me from that!" I wish Partparts had lots more sheep like that one. Sheep are so smart; they know what's good for you.

That's when my dad makes that joke again. "She sure makes a good sponge! Amazing we have any pond left!" Boy! He's a good joker and teaches me some jokes, too! He can tell you what he's really thinking about when he gives you a joke and jokes tell you a lot.

But I'll tell you, I'm beginning to worry I'm getting to be one of those sinners that the preacher talks a lot about. I'm not sure how they can tell, but everyone knows. When Gladys, who has the loudest and highest voice in all the church and must be over a hundred years old, sings that solo, "Jesus Calls Me," she's really serious and looks right straight at me. I really never heard him call my name out right to me yet! But she must be pretty upset with me, because her voice gets louder and quackier, and it looks like she's going to fall down flat. Splat! And, oh my heavens, when Gladys sings that solo soprano song, "How Great Thou Art!" she has her eyes straight on me, too. Sure wished she'd sing so low we wouldn't hear it. Get it? Well! This here "thou" boy isn't feeling so "how great" anyhow! Old Gladys must have known I was sinning again! Somebody out there's ratting on me! Or she's doing that Santa Claus trick, knowing if you're good or bad; you know, that kind of sneaky stuff!

But that piano woman Mrs. Rook's not so nice, either, because she makes her husband Jim eat a whole half a big fruit or prune pie every morning. And he's married to her, too. Everyone says it's to keep him going regular! Everybody in church knows all the regular ones, those regular church goers. They all go regular all the time and sit right up front there where they can keep a good eye on everybody. Funny! Mom keeps me regular by getting me up right on time at seven by yelling up-stairs, "Breakfast's ready!" And I'm not talking castor oil here! Nope! Corn flakes and a fried egg once a week.

Nobody in the big people's choir is very nice, either. I just wish we could all go way back to the good old days when Hazel Rook just bangs away on that piano really loud, and we all just stand up and sing our lungs out. Especially my favorite, "In My Heart There Rings a Melody!" Boy! Singing that song makes me feel the best ever. Boy! Gets me real excited. Maybe it's that "There rings a melody of love" line that gets me again. That exciting line about love there keeps you wide awake!

And after church, all the old men go outside and are just talking and talking and talking.

"Maybe we should get a new preacher from the Bible school."

"This one's no good!"

"Have to get a new one!"

Boy! They love to talk back and around about that. It's like choosing up sides for baseball. Maybe they ought to use a bat for that. Whoops! Rhyming again! And like I said, I always chose little David although he'd just drag himself out to the field, because I wanted Roberta to like me. I didn't have to argue like these old men about it. Just did it! Actions speak louder than words again.

I know I'm talking a lot about church, but I need to tell you some-thing I've never told anybody else. This isn't going to be easy, but I been thinking about this a lot, and I really am becoming a sinner more and more now. The preacher keeps prayin' and talkin' about, "Is your name written in the book of love?" How do I know? Never seen or read it! Can't even find it! What in heaven's name is he talking about? I'm just confused!

I didn't even tell Bruce or Mom about this, but I've got to tell you all about it. I gotta tell somebody, and I know you won't squeal on me or blab it all around. In my Sunday school class, Mrs. Kiefer (remember I had pulled up Joanie's dress in first grade) was teaching us about all these different guys. Peter on a rock, Matthew, Mark, Harold, Bill and John, and the bad one with that girl's name, Judy, or something like that.

Well, that was all pretty boring, too, and I knew this awfully long sermon will be coming after Sunday school, and all I'm thinking about are those delicious Heath bars. They're really small and cost five cents more than Snickers, Baby Ruths, Butterfingers (the gooey butterscotch ones), and Hershey bars with nuts, but the Heath bars were all chocolate and toffee and crunchy. I can't stand it, but that's the only thing I'm thinking about all the time!

And wouldn't you know it! Because I got so good at numbers with Peggy's help when I went blind, Mrs. Kiefer made me the treasurer of the whole Sunday school class to keep all the collection money. She trusted me the most, so we didn't even vote for it! Some selfish kids only give a penny or two, but I gave a whole nickel! I'm a big giver! So I got to put all the pennies and nickels in my front pocket, so I could take them all home and hide them in a sock in the bottom of my bureau drawer. I'm wearing clean socks every week or two, now, so they don't smell! Now, you just can't leave money out in a piggy bank where people can steal it. There are some people who do that kind of thing! You have to hide it! I mean, think of this. People are singing that "Steal away to Jesus" hymn more and more. Gosh, stealing stuff for Jesus! I sure hope he isn't doing that, too!

Well! That sock of mine got so heavy after a while, I thought no one would ever know if I just borrowed two nickels for one Heath bar. Of course, I'd pay it back, because you're not supposed to steal. That's one of the church rules: "Thou shall not steal!" I think Mom was the mother who made up that church rule. She was so good at rules! But anyhow, I really did plan to put it all back. But when Sunday school was over that year, there were only thirty-seven cents in that sock and mostly pennies.

Dad says, "Pennies build up, though." I just didn't know what to do, and maybe nobody would see it. And for gosh sakes, with thirty-seven cents, the class would always have enough for some juice and cookies for our last snack. That's going to really be the kindest thing to get for our class! Good thing that class has me in it!

Now, I'm not getting those really fancy cookies with gooey frosting but just plain old little ones. That's good enough for these guys! They don't know the difference anyhow! Maybe nobody will even be there! Ouch! There was only thirty-seven cents! Nobody said anything, because they probably don't know how to count as well as I do, but I really was feeling like the biggest sinner of all now. And now I know I'll never get written in the preacher's book of love! But nobody can just stop eating Heath bars all of a sudden! That's not healthy! It's something, how those littlest, tiny Heath bars make you want to eat them the most.

Mom says, "The greatest things come in little packages." Boy! She knows what she's talking about there! Ain't nothin' like one of those pretty little Heath bars!

I didn't want to, but I was getting to thinking about candy bars all the time. It even got so bad that summer, that when nobody was looking, I went behind Reynolds Store where they put the empty pop bottles in wood boxes out back, and I pulled out two little, itty-bitty Coca-Cola bottles for two cents each and one bigger Pepsi bottle for a penny. Well, I took all three of these bottles around to the front and up to the old cash register, right next to the meat cooler and baloney slicer. And I got exactly one nickel back from Grandpa Reynolds, who said, "Thank you for the bottle redemption!" The preacher had just preached about sinning and signs of redemption, so that was something I was learning a lot more about. Yep! That redemption thing!

I think it's kind of strange you only get one little penny for bringing the lots bigger Pepsi bottle back and two cents for a little, tiny Coca Cola one. "Pepsi Cola hits the spot! Eight full ounces! That's a lot!" But that's the rules again, and you've got to follow them no matter what! Never break a rule! Anyhow, a nickel can buy you just any old plain candy bar. Nothin' too exciting! The only problem I have is, I just can't carry in too many bottles at one time to get that little Heath bar that cost a whole dime. I only have two hands, you know! Now there's where I could have used Andy's extra little sixth Amish finger. Could at least grab one more Coke bottle for two penny candies. So I just got a Baby Ruth, Snickers, or Powerhouse. Just plain old, boring bars like that!

Even though you try hard, sometimes you just can't do your best! I was a little upset with myself, because those bars weren't quite as tasty, but what can you do? You have to be kind of careful. You can't overdo it! Sometimes kids just don't know when to stop! They have to learn patience, like I'm teaching Bruce about. But I got so nervous, I couldn't even look old Grandpa Reynolds in the eye, and I thought I might even get myself caught. His neck was jumpin' up and down like he just ate a live fish or something wiggly and his eye was looking a little bigger and squinty that day! Right into me! Even the preacher can't pray enough for me now. I may be going straight to hell, and that's no fun at all! But you really gotta work hard and keep doing this redeeming stuff!

Doing all these bad things is really bothering me more. I even wet my bed a few times, and I'm way too old for that. And to show you how bad it got, one time Mom gave me a dollar, a whole buck, to go up to Bruce's house for a dozen eggs that cost fifty cents. I was supposed to bring her back the change. Because I was so good at arithmetic with Peggy's help when I was blind, I was going to say to Mom the eggs cost sixty cents (that's five cents an egg) and give Mom forty cents back for change, and then I'll have ten cents left over for two candy bars, by golly! One for Bruce and one for me. Or if I want to be a cheat, I can just get only me one Heath bar for a dime. Old Bruster should have stopped me right there! That means he's sinning here, too, I think, and he's a Catholic! Oh boy! What a mess!

His preacher's going to have to pray hard for me, too. Bruce says his preacher prays for you in a little box where you can't see his face, but even though he can't see you, he knows who you are by the way your voice squeaks. Anyway, I was getting pretty nervous doing this. I must have messed my arithmetic up or something or forgot about those phones and party lines or something. Somebody must have ratted on me. So, and this is the worst part ever, when I got home with the quarter, dime, and nickel for Mom, my mom did something she never did before. She lay down on that bed and just sobbed buckets of tears. She knew all along! I had broken her heart!

I know every month she gets a little teary-eyed about something. I never knew what, but that's how we all know it's a new month. We don't even need a calendar in our house! Sue's beginning to help with that monthly calendar thing, too, by making those little, tiny, red pencil checks on it every month. Those girls work together! And Sue talks to and smiles at Dad more than me now. Sue doesn't even pay any attention to me. And she's getting little bumps on her chest like that lady on our forks. She doesn't even want to play pitch and catch with me any more. I'm not having a lot of good days!

Dad says, "Someday, Tommy, you'll learn about girls!" I might someday, but I never saw Mom cry like this before. And she couldn't even talk, and I felt so bad, I went right to the hillside and sat and thought in my mind a lot. I can only think up on the hill or with my goats anymore. Sometimes if you're really good at something like arithmetic, it really isn't the best thing for you to be too smart at it after all. You might really want to think about that some more. You can be your own fooler, you know. No tomfoolery here! I mean, freedom's great, but you gotta be good at it. Of course you can pick lots of bad things if you want to. I mean, it's a free world!

Mom never exactly needs to say much, because she speaks to you mostly by looking straight at you. She looks right through your eyes into the back of your head. They call them Esther looks! She isn't the crybaby type and doesn't like people whining. And we have a saying in our family, too, that goes like, "Old honest Abe said, 'You can fool all the people all the time and some of the people some of the time, but you can't fool Mom!'" And boy! That there is the Truth!

So I sat there on my bottom up on the hillside up by the apple tree under the cemetery really quiet for a long time, and for the first time in my life, I didn't think at all about candy bars. Not even one! I got all teary eyed inside, like you're crying. Got some big, wet spots on my T-shirt. And just like Adam and Eve eating those apples, I knew something awfully terrible was going to happen to me. I just knew my cemetery stone right next to my hillside and thinking spot was not going to say, "Tommy T was such a nice boy." I think it was going to say, "Tommy T was a bad sinner!"

I wasn't doing so good with those commandments like Thou shalt not steal. Gosh, I was already doing that stealing thing. Then Thou shalt not commit adultery. I'm not sure what that is, but I might have done that, too. I think they're ten of these things, so I hope I get at least one of 'em right. And one of 'em says you're not supposed to bury false witnesses against your neighbor, whatever that means, and I really didn't love neighbor Grandpa Koblaha too much anyhow. On burying things, I just do the garbage for Mom and I'm a good boy doing that.

But even that that commandment thing didn't stop me from being even badder. I just didn't seem to care anymore about anything! Even found an old bow and arrow and started shooting it up straight up in the air so high you couldn't even see it. Then I'd try to find out where it comes back down. I know! I know! I should of worn Dad's navy helmet so my head wouldn't get hit. And I dared myself to put my tongue on that Flexible Flyer sled runner to see how cold it was and tore off all my skin so I couldn't taste candy for a whole month. Now that's just dumb! Then I started wearing my shirt out all sloppy, not tucking it in at all, and I threw that hairbrush away, too. Who needs it? I wasn't even polishing Shinola on my church shoes anymore. And I didn't even listen when Mom said, "Go get your toilet trees and clean up for church." I thought that's pretty dumb. I've heard about lots of trees, like apple trees and cherry trees, but toilet trees! What kind of stupid tree is that? Then, before church she said, "Did you forget to take your shoe trees out?" For heavens sakes! What's all this silly tree stuff? I just don't understand that one. What's going on around here anyhow? It's getting like I don't know anything anymore!

I even started galloping way too fast on our poor old Penny horse. Sue only trots and posts! But boy, I got her all foaming at the mouth and wheezing! I just wasn't behaving very well at all any more. I didn't even care if I pulled that bit harder on poor old Penny's mouth. I didn't even put her saddle on her much any more. Just rode her bareback all over the place, hanging onto her mane hair really tight. That pulling hurts, you know! Poor old Penny, over thirteen years old and a real strawberry roan! And sometimes I bounced right off and hit the ground. I just didn't care anymore!

And I've seen that Tom Mix and Hoot Gibson on the cowboy shows do that kind of stuff on Youngstrums' new Philco 7-inch TV with a bubble in front to make the picture bigger. You have to push the kids back, so you can see, and so Heine can see best, too. Told those kids they can get blind like I did, if they sit too close. I'm scaring 'em and becoming a little bit meaner, too. Just a really different kind of boy now!

And I started thinking more about girls than I did animals. And girls with no clothes on, especially Carol, because she's a grade ahead of me. Can you imagine if Mom catches me thinking that? I'd really be in trouble! And one time I peeked out of my door at night and saw Cathy, Sue's friend, from behind. I saw her bottom in the dark, but she didn't see me. I planned to do that for a long time. And her bottom didn't have any freckles like on her cheeks. Boy! I couldn't sleep all night. You know, if I had a bottom like hers, I could sit still all day, but mine's way too skinny.

And in that very same, big, potato-chip can I hid in the hayloft, I put three more *National Geographics* inside. One had pictures of girls from Alaska with big furry snowsuits on, and one had girls from the Belgian Congo with no shirts on at all. Wow! So you want to know what? I thought up this brand-new game I called Congo-Alaska. And I thought this one would really be exciting to play with Beverly, the miller's daughter, because she seems more grown-up than us.

So here's how you play, but please don't let anybody else know the rules. It's a private kind of game! Cross your heart! Well, either Bruce or I is going to be the boy holding up one or two fingers behind our backs, and then Beverly and either Bruce or I are going to have to guess one or two fingers up. Now, whoever can't guess right has to take off one of their clothes. We start with your shoes, of course. Well! Bruce and I always guess right, except for the shoes and socks part, and I won't tell you exactly how we knew how to guess it right all the time. Except for shoes and socks, old Bruster and I never missed. Of course, Beverly never got to be the finger hider, just Bruster and I! Well! One time Beverly took everything off but her unders, and then she just quit the game. Just stopped! We didn't have a quitter's rule then. And you know what? I really don't blame her because I was thinking more of those no clothes on thoughts now. Girls don't think that way! They're nicer!

I think Bruce just thought he was playing a silly game, so he wouldn't have to confess anything to Brother Jerome for doing that. His thoughts were probably really nice, clean ones. If I was Catholic, I'd probably be in that box a long time. I'm not sure they let you out of that confession booth after something like that. Boy! Those Catholics have more fun! Get a lot busier. They can stand up and kneel down and move all around, going in and out of the confession closets all the time. Forget one sin, and you can run back in and do it all over again. All we can do is sit real quiet and real still there, right in our pew with our stomachs grumbling and get really ready to jump up and down when that hymn singing starts. Boring! But even if you're a Community Church boy, you really have to put those dirty thoughts away!

And I won't even tell you about some dirty, old, beaten-up magazine from the Buckeye Health Society that Bruce and I found along the roadside once. I had never found anything so good thrown out like that before. But this one had lots of pictures of people playing volleyball and swimming and families all standing all together, holding hands. And guess what. Nobody had any clothes on at all! Not even the kids! I couldn't believe it! It took me a long time, but I wrote a real, grown-up letter to that society and put Bruce's name and address on it and didn't even tell Bruce about it. I wanted to surprise him! Well, not really! Then a few weeks later, Bruce was all excited because he got this letter back to Mr. Bruce Beckwith, inviting him down to Akron to visit and join the Buckeye Health Society. That society must have been able to read my cursive. All we ever joined before was 4-H. Old Bruster liked the fat lady lying on the diving board the best, and me, I liked the volleyball players jumping up and down the best, more action that way!

Boy! We got so excited, because in about six years, Bruce is getting his driver's license. Now, six years is a long time, so we have lots of time to plan and find out where this Akron place is and to see how Mr. Bruce Beckwith and I could peek in there from behind some trees. Boy! Bruster and I are going to drive all around the country and find lots of places to go, but six years seems like forever. But we got to practice on Bruce's McCormick Farmall Cub Tractor when we were twelve. What a great name! Got it hardly broke in. Of course Bruce drove it more, because remember, he's eight months older than me. This tractor's got a long steering wheel and a clutch. If you take your foot off that clutch really fast, you can make that tractor jump and buck and jiggle your bottom off. That's real fun! No mane hair to pull here, either. You just hold on to that wheel tight and don't buck off. Smelled some of that gas because it smelled sweet but made us dizzy, so we quit that! Somebody said it could blow you up and kill you!

We're sure this tractor will take us all the way to Akron, but it's going to take two weeks getting there that way. We'll just pack lots of food.

Mom won't know. But old Bruster and I were growing up, and there were lots of things to plan now. Life's fun! It's all good! Things were finally getting better at last!

◆

Spring is coming, and now I know talking about this next thing is really going to make you so sad! And this is the worst thing that's ever happened to our family in all our lives! In early February, the snow went away one time, and I let Penny out of her box stall to gallop all around the pasture. So this is all my own fault. I was thinking she didn't like to be all boxed up in her stall. Who does? And I tested the electric fence with the back of my hand for just one short shock and not the front, so my hand won't close up tight and keep shocking me, just like I'm supposed to and the way Dad taught me!

That's our most beautiful strawberry roan Penny right in the pasture.

Looks so sad, don't she? Bet she knows what's going to happen!

But old Penny was so excited, jumping all around, and then something horrible happened! I can't ever get this out of my mind! She fell right down and couldn't get back up. Her legs would kick, and she whinnied, and her big brown eyes seemed so sad, but she just couldn't get up, no matter how hard I pulled on her head or mane. Dad told me to run real fast to Grampa Koblaha's house and get some whiskey. I ran like Penny down there and even whinnied like her to run faster. There wasn't much left in his bottle, and the others were empty, but even that didn't work. Usually just a little bit of whiskey gets horses right up and trotting again. And then that afternoon, it started snowing again out in the pasture, so we covered up poor old Penny with blankets and burlap bags, and snow flakes fell all over her. And the sky got really snowy and really gray, and nothing moved, and we just had to wait all day long for the vet to come.

My mom kept saying, "Where in the world is the veterinarian?" It was getting so dark, and when the vet finally came, he said he was awfully sorry, but he just couldn't do anything for poor old Penny. I was sure he'd just give her some more whiskey or some pill to get her up and back to the barn. But then he said he'd take care of everything and told us, "Not to worry. I'll take care of her." Well now! That made me feel a lot better, but that's when poor old Dad got all teary eyed. I didn't know big men can cry. I've heard them laugh a lot, but I never saw one cry before! I wasn't sure what was happening! And I went down to sit with poor old Penny and cut off some little pieces of her hair, so I'd always have some of herself to think about forever. I tied them to a little piece of paper.

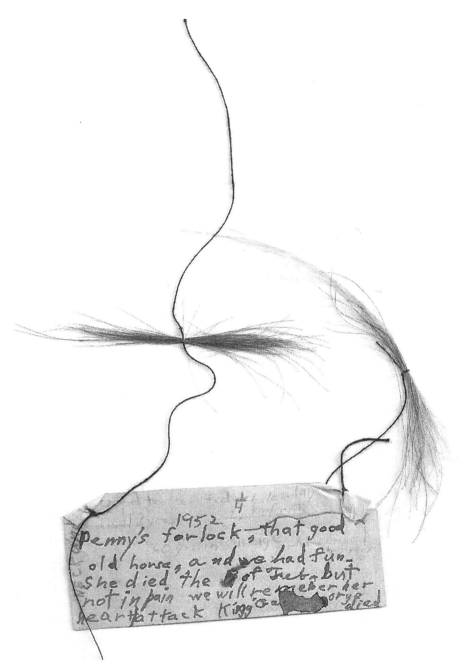

Penny's forelock, 1952.
I wanted to keep Penny as long as we could with a little bit of

**her hair forever. The left hair is under her neck, and right one
is part of her forelock. Look close and see how I wrote, "That
good old horse, and we had fun. She died the 5th of February
but not in pain. We will remember her heart attack. King
George died today too. A good trotter. Feed ¼ bail a day and 2
cups of oats. 60 years in our age. She served her perpose."**

And later when a big truck came, Dad put Sue's portable Crosley radio on real loud. He didn't want my sister Sue to hear anything bang, because Penny really belongs to her, and you already know, my goats were all mine. And I think you know what happened. I just covered my ears. It's too sad to talk about it. That was the saddest day our whole family has ever had. We just all hugged each other and cried all night after that.

It was so lonely going down to the barn in the dark to feed my little goats, Nellie and Millie, the one with horns. It was so sad because Penny wasn't there anymore. They just neighed a little bit and nuzzled their noses in my face. They really missed their big, beautiful Penny friend in the stall next door. I talked to them a lot all alone, and they really understood me. I could live my own way in the barn. My goats always wanted to talk and make me feel better when I opened the barn door. It was too sad to even keep Penny's bridle, saddle, or oat barrel in the barn anymore. Just too hard to look at! And I don't want to talk about it any more!

Did you know this? One of our rabbits and two baby chicks died once, but they really didn't count much. I mean, how can you really get to know a rabbit and baby chicks very much like Penny? It was so sad, I changed my goats' names to Carnation and Pet, like those two sweet milks in those little tin cans. Kind of a stupid name for goats! I thought that might help a little bit, but our beautiful strawberry roan Penny with the biggest mane and loudest whinny and the fastest gallop in the world was gone. Nothing helps you with that, so help me, God! I felt so bad for my sister Sue. We just all cried and cried that night, all night long. And now I know I really need to start being a lot better boy and to make things a lot better for all of them. I've just got to get my life going better!

Boy! I'm so sad again. I've got to find a different thinking place. Can't take it anymore! Maybe sittin' under a toomstone or something. All those colored lights in the sky sure got to me, too! You know, I can't even look in Penny's box stall now. Goaties can't, either! I shouldn't have gotten so mad and galloped her so hard. If I hadn't sinned so much maybe both Roberta and Penny would still be here. I feel sadder for Sue than me because Penny was really Sue's. I feel bad for our whole family. We all loved Penny, like we shared her! You'd think prayer words and church going would help, but sometimes one bad thing just goes on to another. Sometimes you just take the wrong trail. Sometimes you feel so bad, you just don't care and start lying and doing bad stuff more. But then that makes people like Mom feel sad, too, so you have to feel bad for them, too. It's not only me feeling sad! Think of my sad sister Sue!

CHAPTER 11

TOMMY'S GOATS

Well anyhow, I still have my precious goats! Somebody to listen to me. And I really need to spend some more time with you talking about my goats. They mean more to me than anything else in the world. You may be thinking they were just like any old pets I had, but I really didn't only just have them. They were really mine! And me, I was the only one they had in their whole lives. I had bought them in the second grade before Penny came to live with us on our farm. Dad drove the old Green Hornet up the hill to bring the cute little baby goats, or kids as we called them, back to our barn in the backseat of the Green Hornet. They dropped a few pellets in the back seat, but that's OK. They're hard and don't squoosh. And I gave Mrs. Partpart ten silver dollars I had saved from my Christmas stockings for many, many long years to pay for both those baby goats. I didn't need a holy saver, just myself. They were all mine only, and I was in charge, and that's the best way to learn farming. Be in charge!

Now, I know a whole lot about baby animals, and Dad had told me all about the birds and the bees. Birds and bees were some of the first animals to make babies together. You may have forgotten all that, but then there's so much to remember here. I had a brand-new baby sister in 1948, born three days after Bruce's little baby sister, and every day at school when I saw Bruce, we'd both say, "Did your baby come out of your mom's stomach yet?" So you know we both knew a lot about these babies being born and how that all happens. And one time I got to see my mom standing in the kitchen, laughing and giggling with water all over the floor and yelling, "Rex, I think my water's broken," and off they drove in the car really fast, laughing all the way. I didn't know our moms had water up there. I have some up there when I have to pee really bad but not that much. So I know making these babies and having them come out of your bottom is a lot of fun with lots of laughing and having a good time and all that stuff. And now that I'm a country boy, I've gotta know all about this kind of baby stuff, or I can't farm good. And one time I got to see Mom nursing little baby Kathleen, which really isn't a pretty thing to watch. Boy! Kathy loved it because she's a great grabber, and these are real BAZOOMS! She didn't take any breaths, and I thought she might smother. You've got to know this farming stuff, because you're going to have to hold those little baby calves up to a lot of big udders and bosoms.

And here's one more thing about that! One time out of our school window, all of us kids got to watch Sheila's dog and my dog Tippy get all stuck together by their behinds at the same time, and they couldn't let go for half an hour. We kids were shoving each other all around to make sure we could really see it really good. My Tippy's a good fighter, but she just wasn't fighting now. She wasn't even laughing, either. She was just looking kind of serious. And you can really learn a whole lot more about important things like this by just looking right out of the window which is better than just sitting down at some stupid desk with your head down. Unless, of course, you're carving your initials on it or something. It's all right there out the window in front of you!

So now you can tell I know a lot about making babies. You can be sleeping and make them, too. It just happens like that! And poor old Tippy! That sweet dog went along to school with me every day just to keep me company, and this embarrassing thing had to happen to her right there in front of all these dumb, stupid kids. Tippy could tell you more about that horrible time, but I don't think she ever got over it! After that happened to her, she did a whole lot more dog-fighting. She could take anybody! Boy! She was tough! Really proud of her! Sometimes she and I even had to take the long way around to school, way back behind the mill to keep her out of trouble. She was going through a lot of trouble things, too, just like me. Boy! We spent lots of time together. My hair doesn't look much better than hers, except no burrs. See, I still got that rhyming thing going good!

Then some of those mean kids all decided because this horrible thing happened, Sheila and I were supposed to sit right together beside ourselves in church all the time, like we were married or something. But because they were Catholic and we were Fowlers Mills Community Church people, that never happened. Thank God! I'm sure glad someone had that best idea to make up lots of different churches. I ain't marrying Sheila, and I'm not sure I understand what that's all about anyhow. But I will tell you it was embarrassing! She chose me for square-dancing partner one time, but that was it! Fast dance that was! Nearly tore my arm off—my baseball-pitching arm, too! Nobody gets away with that! Not even if they're girls.

The old phonograf called out, "Do-se-do your partner!" real loud. Hey! Wait just a minute here! No, sireee, not me! Then the square dancing began again, and this phonograf record with that caller, called out, "All a man left." Boy, I sure did! I left as fast as I could. This here "a man" left right out of there! No sticking around! No, sireee! Not even for half an hour and all the kids watching us. You saw what happened to poor old Tippy, didn't you?

Anyhow, a few months later, Tippy had eleven puppies under the barn, because Sheila's dog had wee-weed in her, and now you know that's how they make babies. I never saw my mom do this before, but she crawled right through the rhubarb patch and under the barn and pulled out each one of those little puppies to see if their eyes were open. And Mom had big bosoms (remember, we call them "bazooooms"), and I had just little ones. Us boys just called 'em little tits. So it really should have been me who crawled under that barn. But boy, that's a mom's job, and I'm tellin' ya! She could really crawl! And Mom really did the job, you bet! And then she handed 'em all to me, one by one, to put in a big box. I told Mom I'd pull her feet out if she got stuck, but she said really slowly, "That's not necessary, Tommy." Boy! Mom sure had a way with words!

And then my next job was to help Tippy keep all those yappy little puppies in that big box and make sure they all got enough to eat, all eleven of them. That's a real litter. We had to make sure the little runt didn't get pushed out of the way, so he could find a little teat to suck on. That teat word is one of those farm words I told you about before. Don't forget it! You're getting to know a lot of these words now. So I really know a whole lot about making these babies, more than any city kid ever knows. They don't know nothin' about that stuff.

Now I forgot all about this. I've been talking too much about babies and stuff, but like I said, what I really want to talk to you about, and it's something you need to know, is my precious goats. Just like Grandma, when I say that precious word, I really mean it! Everybody always called them Tommy's goats, even though they have their own names. And I told you already, taking care of goats is a very important and serious thing, and that's why I'm glad we got them away from the Partparts, because they couldn't even get their own family name right. Just think! Two Partparts! When you think about it, though, it makes a lot of sense. One part for each of them, and together that's two parts, like two Partparts—one for each of them—one Mr. and one Mrs. They just should have called themselves Two Parts. I could have called my goats Goatgoat. Doesn't sound good, though. Kind of stupid! That's why I make up names that make sense!

But anyhow, you just don't sit there on your butt all day and play with goats and make them your best friends. You do a lot more than that! You have to work with them and make them mind a lot. Millie has horns and can really butt your butt real hard, and her little sister Nellie is littler and sweeter, with big brown eyes and no horns. But she does have these two little pieces of skin they call waddles hanging down from her chin that can make her jump and kick if you squeeze them 'cuz it hurts, so I never did that again. We boys have some things a little like that hanging down below. Dad taught me about *down below*. That there is navy ship talk! There can be a fire *top deck* or down below. Sailors really know their navy stuff! Millie looks a little more like a boy goat, but she has one of those doggone little udders, too, so it's hard to figure out who she is. But I know she's all mine! I always called them Millie and Nellie, not Nellie and Millie, like dad and mom Rex and Eckie, not Eckie and Rex.

I thought twins were supposed to be the same. But I got one goat here that has horns and butts and acts kind of bad sometimes, and then I got her twin sister who's got no horns, but is really sweet and gentle and always nice. These twins are hard to figure out, but I got both goats right here at the same time now. Can't have just one twin, and I don't know which one I'd choose anyhow. At least they're not all mixed-up like Tippy. It's like two goats making one goat who has everything, and they're all mine! I think I'm a little more like Millie and not as sweet as I should be. But sometimes I'm a little like Nellie, too. It's hard to know! But these goaties here know I'll take good care of 'em all the time!

Dad got me two long chains that I hook to their collars and stake them out every day, so they can run around in a circle and eat all the juicy grass they want. And all you see is two big circles of grass all mowed down with a goat running around in it. Clover's the best to eat because it's sweet. They like sweet things just like me. We're a lot alike, my goats and me. Sometimes I'd sneak them a candy bar. And sometimes they get their chains all tangled up in a bush, and I untangle them before they strangle themselves. So like my dad says, "You have to be on the ball," and I sure was!

See how much the same me and Millie are. We're both strong. And that's our Tippy dog, our wood bridge and cemetery behind us.

Kathy's my second helper with the goats.

That's Millie keeping an eye on the new boy Eddie and his civil war hat that he never takes off. I showed him how to hold a goat the right way.

**You can see how much Millie wants to get
in the house 'cuz she misses me.**

I really want to learn how to milk these goats, so I can get a lot of money for my whole family, because, you know, Dad's a teacher. And teachers, you know, just teach awfully hard and make kids learn, and they don't make any money for that. And just so you'll know, goats have only two teats, not four like a cow, so you only get a quart out of 'em instead of a gallon like cows give you with four teats. But that's the kind of stuff you can learn in 4-H if you really want to. I went a few times, but it was more like going to school, so I didn't like it. I learned how to save an overheated hog, but we didn't even have one, so that was a waste of time.

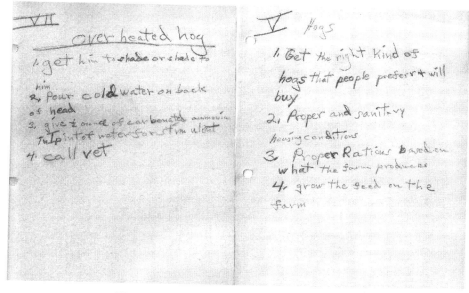

How you take care of overheated hogs.

See how I wrote that down for you. You really do learn a lot more being out of school. But if they do make you go to school, make sure you get a desk near the window where you can keep an eye on everything that's going on out there. You have to be on the ball!

But to get back to my goats again, I almost forgot! Dad says you have to look for little drops of blood that you see best in the snow. Then if you find some, you gotta take those goats to meet a billy goat or ram really fast. If you do that, then you can get them fresh, so you can get some milk from 'em. Well, I don't know where any of those rams are, and I never saw any drops of blood, so after a month or so, I finally gave up. No billy goat gruff here! I guess in the second grade you're just not supposed to be a milker!

Of course, you gotta start out as a tail holder like Pinky, and I was getting real good at that up at Farmer Carroll's barn. Anyhow, talking milk, we have Peggy's dad Pete, the milkman, who used to be Amish, bring us all the milk we ever need with lots of cream on top two times a week. He got to driving the Moss Farm Dairy truck all over Geauga County, so I guess he's not Amish anymore. He can even stand up to drive and not sit down, and he even jumps out of that truck before it stops moving. That's something Bruster and I want to do when we learn to drive. Those grown-ups can really teach you a lot of good stuff!

Because I'm in charge of the barn and Mom's in charge of the house, I spend a lot of time with my goats. I talk to them a lot down in the barn and change their names a lot, too, and then I change 'em back again. Remember! Bruster the Rooster used to be Bruce the Goose. You just have to keep changing things around a lot to keep everything going OK. Try lots of things, so you can't get bored. You gotta have lots of surprises! Lots of people don't know what's happening anyhow. They're always surprised. A lot of things just don't make sense like they used to anyhow. Not even all those stupid rules they have anymore. Sometimes you gotta make up your own. My God! I'm sounding like a teacher but sure not a preacher!

Gosh, I forgot again I'm telling you all about my goats. You know what, I can tell them secrets I never told anybody else and only they and I know. Like that *I've Got a Secret* show. Everything's only ours down there in the barn!

And another thing, when you open up that creaky barn door you can hear my little pet pigeon, who never even had any name, coo really softly. And all these little mice, or bigger ones with long tails, squeek and run around a lot, so you can hear 'em up close before they hide. You hear their little scratchy feet. And Mom always says, "Tommy! No supper until you feed your goats!" And she meant it. Just like she meant bread and water if you're not home when the dinner bell rings at six sharp! Animals come first!

That's a rule for a cowboy and his horses, too: feed 'em first! So even if it's a cold and chilly winter outside and our stream and pond are frozen over (once our pet blue heron got his feet stuck in the ice, too), you have to take an empty pail from the house, run lickety-split, pull up a plank on our little bridge, chop a hole in the ice with a hatchet, and pull up some fresh water with a rope and pail.

Our long pet snake Stanley, thank goodness, was always away for the winter. He goes down south, so he doesn't get in the way. I'd twist his tail if he did. Snakes don't fight with me! One time I twirled Stanley around by the tail and a little tip came off right in my hand, but old Stanley came back to lie on the bridge and sun himself again later. Old Stanley doesn't give up! I'm no snake, but we're not scared of each other. Really, we kind of like each other!

But back to goat feeding—then you put two cups of mill-ground goat feed in their bowl and leave the fresh pail of water for 'em and race back to the house with the frozen ice pail to melt it down for tomorrow. That all takes at least two minutes and some seconds, too. It was kind of spooky in that old, pitch-black barn out there, so it's not a job for a little scaredy kid. It works better if you have a flashlight that has real batteries that work, too. The easy part is, you don't have to change the salt block, because it's just always there. A block only cost twenty-five cents at the mill for the all-white kind or the brown kind with iodine. That's the only medicine goats need, not all that castor oil and stuff. They don't need more butts or runs! Those goat pebbles they put out are really hard anyhow. Don't smell much, either. They just roll around all over the floor like marbles, but you can mush 'em in your toes if they're fresh. So watch out in your bare feet!

To let you know how much I know all about this, let me tell you about the very best Christmas I ever had in my life. I'm all grown-up now in the fourth grade and don't really need all these little toys anymore, because there are so many more jobs you have to do on a farm. I have really outgrown toys. I mean, who really needs another Mr. Potato Head any more? They got kind of boring. Heck! Potatoes! We plant our own. Funny, because when I was little and looked at the Mom's toy stable and manger, all I wanted to be was the wise men with the big hats, because they carried all the presents in the dark. Gold, frankenstines, insects, and mirrors, and stupid stuff like that! I'm not sure they know what they're doing or carrying around there. Let me tell you, though, only Santa's bringing all my stuff! You know what I mean! But the baby Jesus doesn't really care about Santa stuff cuz he's just still in diapers. Now me, I just get these same old two flannel shirts and corduroy pants I get every year, though. I mean, you have to wear something! And I sure know a lot about money now and how much all those things cost, too. Made plenty of my share, didn't I!

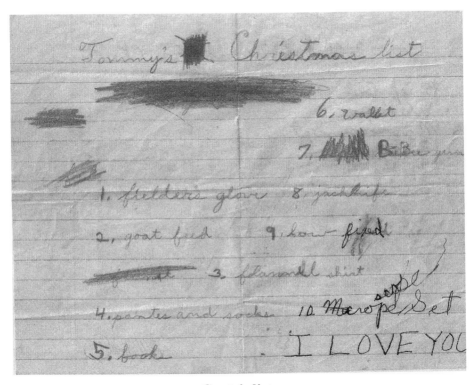

Santa's list.

I was hoping for a BB gun, too, but got my Rawlings fielder's glove. Had to write in pants, shirts, socks, and books, too, because you're supposed to. Santa thinks you're a better boy for that! It's better than if you just put in only a BB gun, jackknife, and bow and arrow getting fixed, because that all means danger. Anyhow, I got my first five things. He gives you what he wants to, no matter what you ask for. Actually, Grandpa and Grandma gave me my Rawlings glove.

So Santa came that year, and you know the Truth about Santa by now, don't you? Well, first we had to line up at the top of the stairs with the oldest at the back, so Dad was the caboose. Anyhow, Santa did come, and he brought me the shiniest new pail, which cost about a dollar in Carlsons Hardware on Main Street in Chardon; a big block of brown salt with that iodine in it, costing twenty-five cents; and twenty-five pounds of goat feed for fifty cents down at our mill. So that's a lot of costing right there. It was a lot more than my sister Sue got that year, I know.

That goat feed also has a little molasses in it, so it tastes pretty dog-gone good. Molasses is not a bad word and just something a little extra there! You know, I tasted all of Penny's oats, too, which were chewier, and some of that good old goat feed that isn't really too bad, depending on just how hungry you are. It makes a dandy snack before supper! That stuff was all brought by Santa, of course, and again, we sure know who that is! Don't we? Now kids, I just want to make sure before we go on, no tricks here!

It's funny now, but many, many years ago when I was only in first grade, I used to argue with Bruce a lot about Santa, because my mom told me so, and she always tells the Truth. Bruster and I don't wrestle any more; we just argue like grown-ups do. But by the second grade, I had this Santa thing all figured out and just how many miles he'd have to fly in one night, and you have to remember, of course, that the McGeoughs had all the fireplaces. We didn't have even one! And I don't believe that Santa coming in the front-door trick and all that cookies and milk stuff anyhow. I mean, the front door? Really! How do you come down with a bound through a front door? Come on, kids! I mean, just read that *The Night Before Christmas* thing. Read it yourself, because your mom might trick you by changing the words a little. But I never told Mom and Dad about that kind of fibbing and their tricks, either. They always like to see you look surprised sometimes, and we really pretend real good!

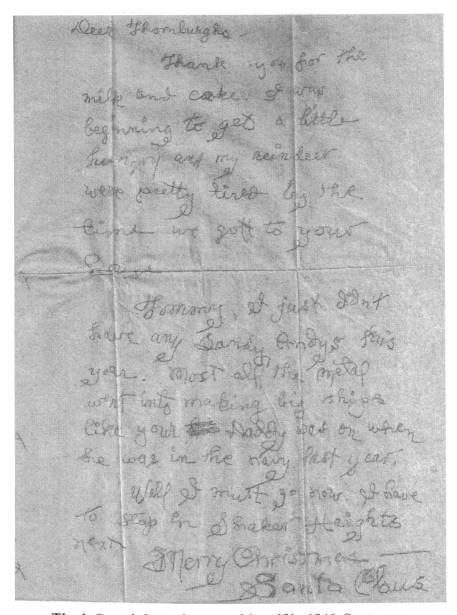

That's Santa's letter he wrote himself in 1946. Santa sure could write, too, and sure was a nice man. But I think my dad was doing those Santa Claus tricks back then, too.

**Here I'm tricking these little children, too. I learned it
from my dad and hid all the candy canes and good stuff
in the hayloft. Put all the stuff in a wastebasket behind the
potato chip can of bad pictures, so I wouldn't forget.**

But anyhow, the biggest surprise in my life was coming! That's
what Mom and Dad kept saying, so I was waiting all Christmas Day
until it got almost dark. And can you believe? Dad's best Amish
friend, Abe Weaver, had made a special, black, shiny, leather double-
goat harness, not store-bought, and I couldn't believe it. Wow! Was
it shiny and smelled like shoe polish! It would have come earlier on
Christmas Day, but Abe had seventeen children, so that's a whole
bunch of mouths to feed right there. Like a bunch of cows! What a
surprise, though! That Christmas was the best I ever had, and I know
all the people in Fowlers Mills must've known all about this surprise
before I did all the time.

My goat harness.

See what I mean. Just like "This Is Your Life," you never know when somebody like Ralph Edwards is going to surprise you and make you famous and what's going to happen, and that's the best part. Lots of secrets! Abe Weaver wasn't Ralph, but he sure did surprise me! Where did my dad get that extra ten dollars that cost? Maude, Della, Gladys, and Fern and everyone could keep the best secrets except when they talked in church about Dart and Pearl up in the cemetery, or when you listen in on those telephone party lines. Then you know the real Truth! We have telephone number 421.

Boy! This harness thing is exciting! Now I can make plans to drive my goats and goat cart all over Fowlers Mills, to the church, school, friends' houses, and all over the place. I probably won't be able to make it all the way to the Buckeye Health Society, though. Have to wait for Bruster's McCormick Farmall Cub Tractor and sneak enough food to get going there to sneak in.

Well! Holidays come and go, you know, and now I've got to get back to work here! Been off too long! First, I had some real harness breaking in to do, even though it was pretty cold, blowy, and wintery out. I put those little bits and bridles on and walked those goats all around the barn practicing. They didn't like the bits at first, but just like Penny, they got used to it. They don't have teeth in the back where the bits go, and that's why they nibble with their front teeth all the time. I led them around like that all winter. Round and round the barn!

Because my dad's a teacher, he has to have two jobs as church janitor, too. I help him a lot, especially with the wasp-swatting and bell-ringing, and I got pretty good at cleaning toilets, too. Remember for the girls, you gotta put those toilet seats down. Don't want 'em fallin' in and running to their mothers. You can lose your job that way!

Yep! Teachers don't make lots of money. They teach to help us kids. To show you what I mean, Mom and Dad had to write down every little thing they bought. They even borrowed from my sister Sue who gets paid for sitting. That's an easy job doing nothin'.

See what I mean. See they paid me ten cents for the coal job. Yep! I was makin' big money! Grandpa got three bucks for manure.

But my dad was the best ever at finding old things. And he keeps 'em all. He found this old, broken-down wheelchair with the back all gone, and that right there makes a great goat cart. So spring came, and I finally got this goat harness on both goats at the same time. That can take the whole day, so that's one day you just have to miss school! I don't know why they bucked so much, but I finally tied those goats to the wheelchair, and now we're going to ride all over Fowlers Mills. And we're going to see the whole countryside, because I'm not driving a car yet to drive those two twins, Millie and Nellie, all around. And I don't think these goaties can sit straight up enough in their seats yet to see out. These kids are still little, you know! And all the people seeing us are just not going to believe this!

So I got them up to the dirt road in front of the barn, and all of a sudden, Millie went one way, and Nellie went the other, and we fell over the bank, almost into our stream that went under the road. We ended up in a huge pile with the harness, the cart, and all the bushes wrapped all around us, kind of hanging there! Millie and Nellie were crying so loudly! All they ever said before was little neighs and whinnies. I felt so bad for them. I mean, what kind of good shepherd am I anyhow! Don't even have one of those crooked shepherd staff poles to pull them out. Poor Nellie, hanging there upside down! That's not a "Lost Sheep" there. That's almost a killed goat!

Well! We finally got loose, and nobody got hung, but I sure wish I had known more about those whiffletrees, traces, and all that wagon-and-harness stuff that Farmer Carroll knows about for Tom and Jerry. But I guess I didn't ask him much about that. I was just too busy driving those big Belgian draft horses all over, and Farmer Carroll didn't talk much anyhow, just "Yep" and "Giddyup." Well! That was the end of the biggest dream I ever had—to drive Millie and Nellie all over Fowlers Mills like I planned on. Even if I had driven them to school, us kids already tore up most of the schoolyard grass, so there wasn't much for them to nibble on up there anyhow.

I was sad but kind of glad, too. I was getting too excited about all this. Now I'll just have to walk to school like all the rest of these boring kids. And it isn't fair to Millie and Nellie just standing around all day at school talking to each other. It's not a goat school, you know, and they'd probably even hate 4-H, too.

That's why I took gardening in 4-H one year instead of goat husbandry. I was away on vacation one time, and that's why that poor garden didn't get any water. Surprise! And wouldn't you know it, that's the same time the 4-H garden inspector came. The only seeds he saw growing were gourds, and they went all over the place.

Reprinted JANUARY, 1951

4-H CIRCULAR 130

A+

Vegetable Gardening for Beginners

VICTOR E. KEIRNS AND E. C. WITTMEYER
Extension Specialists in Vegetable Gardening
The Ohio State University

Name _Tom Thornburgh_   Age _11_

Address _Route #2, Chardon, Ohio_   County _Geauga_

Name of Club _Munson Good Workers_

Name of Club Advisor _Robert Hodges_

Additional bulletins or information may be secured from your county extension agent

1-51/3M

THE OHIO STATE UNIVERSITY AND THE U. S. DEPARTMENT OF AGRICULTURE, COOPERATING
AGRICULTURAL EXTENSION SERVICE, C. M. FERGUSON, *Director*, Columbus, Ohio
Printed and distributed in furtherance of Acts of May 8 and June 30, 1914

See how much money and candy bars you can buy from 4-H if you garden just right. I didn't show the gourds that I hid in the cucumber patches, but they grew all over the place. And carrots don't stay shriveled up, but mine sure were. Threw that white ribbon right away. Should have called that 4-H club Munson <u>Bad</u> Workers!

Well, I took three crummy little carrots to the fair, but they got all shriveled up, even though I tied a nice bow on them. Should have called them *very special tiny carrots*. So I only got a third place white ribbon that year. Might have been the only white ribbon anybody ever got in the whole Geauga County Fair ever, but that didn't make me feel very special. It would have been better if I just store-bought some carrots and took them. I felt like a dummy and ripped my name tag off those carrots really fast! I hope nobody knows my name! I told everyone else I got a blue ribbon! I just pretended it! Sometimes you make these big plans, and they just don't work out. I should have taken my goats to the fair in 4-H and not those stupid teeny carrots! You can only plan so much! That's the hardest part of this growing-up stuff. As Mom says, "Things work out for the best!" Well, I don't know, Mom. We might think a little differently on that thing there, you and I! I'll tell you, nothing here is working out for me anymore!

There was one more thing that didn't work out. Like when Bruster and I were going to make the biggest underground fort ever. Fort's not a bad word there either. It was going to be a beauty! We were going to dig all underneath our farm, with lots of tunnels in the dirt and little rooms all over. Well! I snuck out a flashlight, and we saved up almost ten candy bars. There really were ten; I wouldn't lie to you here! And then we emptied out Mom's cookie jar and dug a few holes before we stopped and ate all the candy bars and cookies. You've got to get your energy way up high for this kind of work! Well! We never dug even one more hole in that stupid fort! We kept one little hole to hide candy bars in if we'd ever get any more. That was going to be the fort's hallway fridge. You know, we'd still be digging if we hadn't stopped! So sometimes you've got to just give in and say, "Uncle." Old Bruster and I were much better at making things up than we were at getting them done. We had lots of great ideas, so we were best at starting things.

It was the same way with our raft on the millpond. We chopped down two saplings and tied them with baling twine, but that's as far as we got. The hatchet wasn't sharp! We really weren't, either, there! George Washington cut a cherry tree down, but he must have had a sharp hatchet. This thing wasn't cutting anything! It wasn't going in my museum! I think old George lied a little bit about that cherry tree, too! Said he didn't do it. Yaahh! Right! I'm telling you, you can't fool moms or dads! George shoulda behaved better! You have to if you want to grow up! And I know my history!

We chopped down two more saplings and some chicken wire to make a baseball backstop, too. That hatchet couldn't chop more than two, it was so dull. But old Bruster and I didn't ask anybody or have to wait. We just made that backstop ourselves. We got Bruce's mom to drive their gray Dodge with no name up to the school, dragging the two saplings behind. Like always, we dug those holes deep and did it for our school, so the little kids wouldn't have to run all around chasing the balls when Bruce and I were up to bat! That's the kind of boys we were, always looking out for the little shrimps!

But we did borrow Klatkas' boat at the edge of his pasture by the mill pond, and I can't remember now if I told you about that or not, but I probably did. Doesn't matter anyhow! Nobody cares! There's too much going on here!

Maybe someday they'll make a little magic wood box that tells you what you're doing all the time, so everybody else everywhere knows everything all about it all, too. Then I'll know myself what's going on. Won't just carry pencils around inside it either! And then you won't have to remember anything at all! Just push a button or pick a card, and everybody knows everything! Kind of like Fern and Maude know it all on the party line. Mom says I push her buttons sometimes. Dad pokes my tummy button to make me stop. That's enough of that button talk! That box'll even tell you though what to do or who you have to play with. Or if you're playing civil war, do you bring up the rear or the front, and when and what marbles to shoot. Hey! Just shoot 'em freelike! Of course, right here now in Fowlers Mills, every single person knows exactly what's going on around here all the time anyhow! Gosh! They're nosy! That rhymes with Rosie! And that's real cozy!

But back to my goats again! Gosh darn, I almost forgot! I'm forgetting more and more now! I'm getting more like my old, wrinkled-up, great-grandma T. Every night she goes on a long train ride with some nice man, and she really likes that, but in the morning she gets 'em all mixed up and can't remember which man it was. Well, right here, there are just too many things happening! There are just so many things a kid can think about without getting all mixed up.

At the third Halloween party in that community house that didn't fall down after all, Nellie goat did team up with me there to win two Hershey bars for the Best Boys Costume in my age group by letting me lead her all around the floor with her bridle on. I got myself all dressed up like that real old cowboy Gabby Hayes on TV, just like an old gold prospector. Someone had a dog in his or her costume once, but this was the very first farm animal ever at this party, and it was about time! I chose Nellie, although I really liked Millie an awful lot, because Nellie was quieter and more gentle and wouldn't butt as much and didn't have sharp horns to butt anybody in the butt. That's some of my rhyming again! Rhyming is the best way to remember stuff. I even put a little diaper on her to catch those hard and tiny goat pebbles that shoot out the back. They're kind of like rabbit pebbles—tiny, hard, and can bounce if you pick 'em up and throw them up against the wall or just shoot 'em around like marbles. Don't chew 'em, though! They'll hurt your teeth! Nellie and I were really good that year. We were kind of like big movie stars! Everybody was looking at us!

At my first Halloween party, I didn't win anything being Aunt Jemima, like the Aunt Jemima Pancake Mix, and Bruce going as Uncle Mose. I thought it was wonderful that little black boys like Little Black Sambo liked so many pancakes, because I sure did, too. All us kids like 'em! And being them in the Halloween costumes, I wanted to do something special. Aunt Jemima has the most beautiful smile ever. I think I'm saying nicer things now and being nicer to people more. Well, old Bruster and I didn't win that year, and all we got was four really big Dixie Cups of cider and cookies that made us sick and throw up all over the floor. Bruce even said he got the runs, but we didn't know it. His runs aren't as fast as mine, so it's harder to tell. I wasn't sure how I could help his runs, anyhow, and I sure wasn't feeling too good myself! But we're still eating pancakes and lots of maple surp! Burp!

Now in the fall, if you really want to get the runs, here's another way. If you and Bruster pick up a bushel of old, rotten, wormy apples up off the ground in anybody's old apple orchard, you can take 'em up to Rhodes Cider Mill. Old Man Rhodes and his helper say "How 'bout them apples!" and throw 'em in a huge barrel and boil all them worms out. And they give you a free gallon of cider just for that. Boy, that gets you going and going right away! Keeps you running. Anytime! Anyplace! It tastes so good that old Bruster and I just lie back on a log and drink the whole gallon right out of the jug, taking turns, of course! But you've got to be on your toes fast if something happens! You get up with a tummy ache, but it's worth it! Wow! Cider! Giddyup and go!

I don't think you're going to like this, but the second year Bruce and I didn't win again, either. And this time, doggone it, I was sure we would! That's because we had never seen two of the same kind of kids all together inside the same exact animal costume at the exact same time. So old Bruster and I made lots of plans and dyed some long underwear and a bedsheet brown. That's a different kind of dying! Not like poor old Bunny Rabbit we buried dead in a box down by the garden. We're doing colors here! A lot of these words get mixed up, so be careful! Never say, "You hope to die" if you're just coloring some sheets and underwear. It's all different! So be careful and think about it! Now here, old Bruster and I even took a dare to run outside in our long underwear. Boy! You have to be fast before someone drives by! We took a chance here, but nobody saw us, thank God!

Well, Bruce became the head of the horse, and I was the rear, because I can really jump and kick hard. We went all out! No holding back! I kicked so much, and Bruce whinnied like a horse so hard, our legs really got tired and almost fell down. And all these stupid little kids were poking us and pulling on our horsetail, too, so I just kicked harder and held on tight to old Bruster's butt. Put my head right up in there, anything to hang on to, and I kicked harder! Old Bruster blew a big gas ball out! He was really pretending he was like one of those Belgian horses! Got me a little bit and stung my eyes, but I'm no quitter!

Well, doggone it! Wouldn't you know it! Two of those little, itty-bitty, sissy, third-grade shrimpies, Chucky and Carl, went and got their mommies to help them. And those mommies did all the work and sewed some dopey, fancy giraffe costume together. Sure looked store-bought to me! Wasn't even a farm animal, but one of those dumb zoo animals. Now, that's just not fair! Old Munson Township Constable Kieffer should make a law about that! He should take 'em to the Chardon Jail on Main Street for that! And there old Bruster and I are just sitting there on the floor in our dumb, brown-dyed, long underwear. Wish I had died! And now I don't mean that other making color kind of dyeing.

I don't know about Bruce, but I sure felt pretty silly and mad at losing to some stupid, little, third-grade twerps! Those mommie's boys. It just isn't fair! Kids are supposed to do all the work, not their mommies, for heaven's sakes! I had kicked my bottom off, and I think I even cried a little bit under that sheet when they picked the giraffe. But nobody saw me. I really thought we had it that year. I was awfully upset and wanted to tell the whole Munson Township how bad I felt. We'll get those mommie boys and put big fat seats on their mommies' brooms next Halloween and fly 'em right on out of here! Of course, you had Mom's rule, don't whine! I know—but Mom only has to say it once! But that township really should have done something right then and there about that terrible thing right on the spot! They have a job to do! I told some people but not everybody yet. You bet I will, though! We'll get even! And I really think old Bruster was a better loser than me. He just said, "Tommy! We lost!" Well, by golly, dadgumit! We sure did! And that will never happen again! You bet!

The next year Nellie and I took home those two big Hershey bars at the very next Halloween party. One big one for each of us, just like that! Having a real farm animal to team up with in this costume thing really helps out. Of course Nellie shared her Hershey bar with her twin Millie. But me, I don't share so much anymore because I worked so hard on this one all by myself. Of course, Nellie helped some, too.

Well! I told you some of the best things about my goats, but here's the saddest thing you'll ever hear in your life. I know! I know! Life is not easy! And I really feel bad about telling you all this, because I don't want to make your life any sadder. It's looking sad enough right now! But this was up there some time in the fourth grade at Easter, and Mrs. Kiefer was making our children's choir practice all our songs really hard for the Easter service. My sister Sue was an alto, and I don't even know what I am anymore, probably some of both. I really didn't care anymore about this dumb choir stuff anyhow, because Roberta was all gone now, and I'd rather just sit in the back row with my lips shut, because it was so boring anyhow. But finally we got out of there and came right home, and there was our mom standing in her apron with the biggest tears in her eyes I've ever seen. I've never ever seen her cry like that before! Never ever!

And Mom put her big arms around me, gave me a big mommie hug, and I just knew this was going to be the worst time ever. And I had really tried so hard to live better and be a better boy, but here it was! And I know you'll understand it all! This piece of paper's getting all wet drops on it just telling you about it. You'll be having tears in a minute, too! It's so sad! Mom hugged me and told me, "Millie's gone, and your dad is taking care of her!" She didn't have to say where. I knew!

Ohhh nooo! I sat down on the couch with Mom and cried like I never have before. Poor Millie! My Millie! She was the strongest and bravest twin ever and could stretch the tallest and put her head and beautiful horns up over the stall door whenever I cracked open the barn door. She loved to see me! You could just see her beautiful head sticking up over the stall door and only hear little Nellie's hooves down below. Millie was most like me! She butted the hardest and always protected her sweet little sister Nellie, her little twin kid with the tender waddles, and now she was gone!

Dad told us Millie got her horns caught jumping up on the stall door and broke her neck. He has some tears in his eyes, too. I never wanted to hear anything more. That's enough! I don't know how Dad did it, but he's so strong, and he took Millie all the way up the hill, past the cornfield and pines all by himself behind the cemetery, right to the edge of our woods and buried her right there. That's where she could always see us all the time, all over our whole farm. Then Dad patted a nice little pile of dirt over her and put a stone there, too. A real pretty, round one! I felt so bad for Mom, too, because she always has to take care of us when we bring our dying rabbits into the house, and poor old Penny died, and now this! I never knew this before, but rabbits cry out real loud, too, when they're dying. But now Mom has lost another best friend again.

I was so sad every day and just moped around. Every evening that spring and summer after feeding little lonely Nellie, I'd go up to Millie's grave behind the cemetery on the hill before the sun sets, where it was really quiet and just the leaves were blowing in the breeze, and I'd just sit there beside that beautiful stone and think about Millie.

I'd say lots of things like, "You've been my best friend. I miss you!" And I'd say prayers for her, too, and I'd think a lot more about this dying thing. To show you just how bad I felt, many years later in high school, I still couldn't get over it, and I was thinking way back and wrote this poem about Millie. I'll show you a little peak of that into the future!

A poem for my poor Millie.

No more her nibbling nose is warm
For stillness comes to shroud her form.
Some empty eyes replace her own
Our day of play-once here, now gone.
Her cry, I found, was like a song,
A call to romp through grasses long.
A narrow path where clover's found
will lead you to a tiny mound
Shaded round by maple trees
Often soothed by evening breeze.

You can tell Millie's a really tough and strong climber. Like a tomboy goat! I'll always miss her!

See my sad, sweet, little Nellie goatie. You can almost see the waddles under her nibbly nose and neck.

Lots of things made me sadder now. I got really sad when I saw a picture on the front page of the Cleveland *Plain Dealer* of the little

Rosenberg boys walking away and talking about their mom Ethel and dad Julius going to have to die in a chair because someone said they were spies, and they were saying good-bye. I'm sad because they're all alone now. I know how they feel. I couldn't sleep, thinking about that. All this dying stuff. I sure hope things get better around here!

I fed Nellie all alone tonight. I'm so sad for her. She's all I've got. I'm feeling pretty sad up here by Millie's grave, and I'm patting it all over with my hand like I'm really petting Millie. We can see everything over the whole valley. There are just too many sad things going on, and my whole family's sad again. It doesn't even matter that Nellie and I won the Halloween Hershey bars. Maybe Millie and I shouldn't have liked each other so much. Boy! I remember that Christmas when I was going to drive my goaties all around in their brand-new harness. Maybe it's better not to plan everything. I mean, look at Bruster's and my fort and that raft that never got built and my 4-H carrots! Lots of things don't work out so well if you plan too much. Maybe you just have to be lucky or not. Or maybe things just happen whether you like it or not. Oh man! I wish Millie was here! I really miss her! But at least I still have Tippy and Nellie!

Poor little Nellie. All alone now.

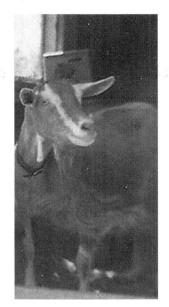

Nellie.

Well! I'm growing up and getting real old now and will be in the higher grades next year, and I'm getting kind of tired of writing about all this stuff anyhow, so I'll just hurry this thing up some!

CHAPTER 12

UPPER GRADES: FIFTH AND SIXTH

Yeah! Upper Grades! Yah! So what! Everybody's getting real old around here now anyhow. So what else is new! I mean, up here, we're talkin' and doing so many different things. I guess up here, you just try out all kinds of stuff. I can't even keep up; I can't keep anything straight!

It was tough, but I got over Millie. Almost! All the little shrimpers who are really dumb and don't know anything are down in the lower grades now, right where they belong, and we big guys are all moved up to Mrs. Zepp's big kids' room for fifth and sixth. We big kids are the smartest. We know everything! Even sometimes things we don't know! And this Mrs. Zepp really means business! She's in charge of the other two teachers. She's the boss! And boy! She sure can teach! She never knew herself how good she was, because she never knew if we learned anything. Sometimes it looked like we didn't learn a darn thing and I don't mean darning torn up socks here, but we did! She never got any report cards on herself. She just gave 'em! Boy! She was tough! Mrs. Zepp's not going to let you get away with any monkey business! No tomfoolery here! You've got to keep a close eye on these wild kids, you know!

That's me in sixth grade in 1952. No whole class pictures anymore, thank goodness! It's just us, kind of special, all alone now. Of course, my front tooth sticks out, and my ears point up like Tinkerbell.

We sure look the happiest with our new sister Kathy here. Just kidding! We look kinda scared, don't we?

Tippy makes sure Kathy stays put.

Kathy sure loved gabbing and giggling. She was a real job!

That's supposed to be us taking care of toddlers and not the barn.

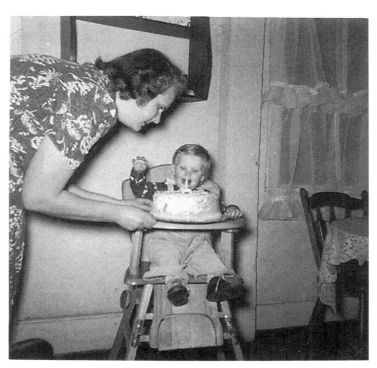

**See how Mom takes care of the little babies,
and we take care of everything else.**

We have no bathroom over in this town-hall school class, just a stove! We boys get to go to the bathroom lots over at the little kids' school bathrooms. It takes us boys a lot longer, and we go lots more times than the girls, so we take our good old time. We have to be away longer and have to miss lots of schoolwork because of that. And the girls always have to go in twos because they can get lost. So they get a break here to make sure they come back. They always give the girls a little extra help! But we guys know right where to go. Sometimes we go lots of other different places, too, and not just right to the boys' room. You know like we say, "Got to see a man about a horse!" That's really boys' bathroom talk there, not farm talk!

And Mrs. Zepp lives on a farm, too. And she doesn't care what she wears. It really doesn't matter! Sometimes her hair sits on top of her head in a little bushy ball, and sometimes her brassiere strap or slip is falling down, but she doesn't care. She keeps her hankie in there. She dresses more like me. I don't care, either! Boy! She's great! She can really teach and runs the best spelling bees. That's a different kind of runs there. You can tell I really know how to spell now. Yep! Those spelling bees! Bingo! One word and you're gone! Yup! Spelled hobby like hoppy once and bingo, I'm down! No last two standing that time! You gotta be smart in these things. I have lots of tricks, like, remember, there's a "one" in "pioneer", an "in it" in "definite" and a "me" at the back of "lonesome". You'll win every time!

Yup! Things are changing pretty fast up here in these upper grades. Some guys' voices are starting to sound kind of funny. Mine doesn't squeak yet, because I was only born in August. And kids are coming and going. We have to put up with a new scaredy kid from the city in our class every year. It just isn't us same old country boys anymore!

Summer isn't even the same anymore, either. All those things we thought we'd be doing our whole entire life, we just didn't care about anymore. Here's one to think about! We just don't jump around and chase those cows all over the pasture just to see 'em run funny like we used to. You know, stupid stuff! No, sireee! And I'm telling you the Truth like I always do. Like big kids, we actually jump on their backs like Johnny Mack Brown in the movies and ride 'em like buckin' broncos. You talk about bony backs. Boy, that hurts! We didn't have cow saddles, except you can stuff a towel in your pants if you want to, although it looks like you got a load on!

Dad says, "Grab the bull by the horns" when he wants you to get going, but I'm not ready to do that one yet. I have to learn how to handle these stupid cows first and get this thing all fixed up. But you know Dad by now! I bet he's pulling my leg on that one! Watch out! I'll pull his shorter West Virginny leg on him! That'll fix him!

See how Dad and I are just the same. Long arms and lots of muscles. And Dad's got his good old Lucky Strike with him.

Well, things aren't so sad anymore. We're getting it all behind us, and there're so many more things to do and new places to go. We're never done! I'm getting a lot older but not slowing down here a bit yet! And with these two-wheelers, you can ride all the way to Wilson's Mills

Road and back in a jiffy. It's really fun except when I got my dungaree leg caught in the bike chain and had to carry my bike all the way home. I didn't win that race! And then all of us—Eddie, Bruce, Jack, and I—got BB guns for Christmas in the fifth grade. Hey! We can shoot 'em up full of holes!

That's a very wonderful Christmas present to give, especially if you really want to give someone you really love so much something really nice and extra special. That's just a special gift suggestion for you! And you know they're powerful. I got a Daisy Pump gun. I hit a starling smack in the head. What a shot! It dropped over dead, and after that I really couldn't shoot anything live anymore. It hurts too much! I just hit tin soup cans all lined up after that and maybe an old barn lightning rod or two just to see 'em pop really nice. Once I got my palm and thumb pinged loading it up. Boy! That really stung. My hand shook all day long! It messed my cursive writing up! Teacher gave me a whole day off on that one. Nobody can read it both ways anyhow!

One time old Bruster came over to play, and I forgot Mom's underpants and girdle were hanging on the clothesline. Boy! That was embarassing! I got all red. I'd better clean that clothesline off before the guys come over! You know how wild they can get! They'd be running around the grass with a girdle over their heads. And that don't win you any prizes! Anyhow, Mom needs that stuff, so don't tear it up! You gotta watch these guys!

But Bruster and I did lots of things together. We were really good at making slingshots and catapults out of saplings to shoot stones and Osage oranges through the air like the Romans in the movies. That's probably more shooting than we really needed to do, but we sure hit things on the bull's-eye! And we were inventing everything we could. We just did a lot more daring things, like jumping from branch to branch like squirrels or climbing up cave walls like diggin' spiders. You name it!

And now Eddie, who has a Davy Crockett coonskin hat, also got a civil war hat, a blue Union one. He liked hats. So we'd sit down and make lots of battle plans and pretend we were a whole army trooping up the hillside to attack. We'd dig in, and then all at once we'd come racing down the hill again, screaming Rebel yells. Of course, we'd protect our flanks. We'd just attack every bush and what's hiding behind it and try to shoot those bushes and corn stalks like they were the generals. That's because they're the ones who made up the war. They'd meet under a tree, have lunch, and decide they'd better have a little battle, so their soldiers could have something to do and not get too bored just sitting around drinking coffee or you know what. Those generals weren't mean like pirates. They don't hurt anybody because only the soldiers do that. I mean, this was a civil kind of war! Lots of action! Shooting up the front! Bringing up the rear! This war thing was really exciting and lots of fun! We really got into it! We saw all this in that movie *Red Badge of Courage* with all the generals in their fancy uniforms with lots of medals standing around, talking and planning something exciting like, "Let's have a civil war! Yeah!"

You know something? We weren't sneaking around doing stupid little kid stuff anymore, like trying to hide those dirty little magazine pictures with the naked women in them. Nope! Bruce and I were out to do bigger things, like save the world! And that's good because that's the way you get yourself into the history books. If you remember, I had read *Mad Anthony Wayne, Boy Soldier*; *George Washington Carver, Boy Inventor*; and all those other orange books in the back bookcase, so I knew all about history. I didn't have any problem at all pretending to be those guys, except this boy here did have a little problem picturing myself to be Clara Barton, Girl Nurse or Jane Adams, Girl Whatever. And if you haven't forgotten already, my dad was a history teacher, and I had been to Concord, Mount Vernon, and Appomattax, so there wasn't much of that stuff I didn't know.

It was getting so Bruce and I had so many things to take care of now and so many more important jobs to do. If we were ever going to be in the history books, we had to make Munson Township a much better place! We figured it was about time for the two of us to clean up the school kids' bad language. No more swearing! It was time for the two of us to protect and be true to our school! Yep! No more fooling around! We had seen and had enough, old Bruster and me!

We just needed to protect our school as hard as we did before, during that Korean War police action, practicing all those dangerous atomic bomb drills. I guess it's over by now. Never saw a lot of cheering and ice cream going on. We did our job! Soldiers at home! I was so strong back then, I could carry lots of people on my back at one time and carry them all to Partparts' caves to hide them in the lemon squeezes and save them from atomic bombs. Although it had been lots of fun like little kids to rub up against Roberta, Peggy, Rosemary, and even Ruth Ann under the desks during those dangerous bomb drills, this was not kid stuff anymore! Not small potatoes! We had already seen Yucca Flats test in Nevada blown up all over the place on television. This wasn't just funny business here! This was serious! So Bruster and I needed to be better than all the rest and get serious about saving our school!

So Bruce and I got busy with our "No More Swearing" campaign! This wasn't just another one of those stupid little kids' campaigns like pulling up dresses to see unders. No, this was a lot different! We had to work fast, because these kids were getting older faster, and these horrible cuss words were coming out more and more. Now I know the exact plan, because when I was a little kid, my mom washed out my mouth with soap and water for swearing at Sue. And Mom was so smart and had warned me, so I know this exact kind of thing works every time. And Bruce and I always discuss lots of things about the world and how to make it better, so old Bruster and I were a good team!

So here was Johnny, only a fourth grader and Amish. He had a long, bowl haircut, and all of a sudden, he would twitch his hair to one side and say the *sh-- word* really fast and loud. Right out loud! Can you believe it! He'd even do it right there in the classroom, like a hot baseball grounder! You never knew when it was coming! Now, you can't have that kind of thing going on in a nice school like ours. Johnny said he couldn't help it, and it just seemed to happen really quickly without him even knowing it, a bunch of times in a row! But Bruce and I knew we had to do something fast right here and now. We couldn't wait a minute! We had to get right to work!

At first I thought what Johnny was doing was pretty cool and funny, and I tried to copycat him. I thought just being Amish was really cool. They don't have any zippers or buttons on their pants and don't wear dungarees, just a flap, so no girls can catch you with your barn door open. Amish don't say "Is your fly open?" because they're farmers and use those barn words. They just get to sit down and relax like a girl going wee-wee. They get better aim that way! And what's better, they get schooling fooling around behind the barn, if you know what I mean! Even though my hair was long and pretty shaggy like a haystack, I just couldn't make it like Johnny's. I also liked that little extra Amish sixth finger like Andy had sticking out the side of his hand, but only Amish have it. It can make you a better pitcher, squeezing that ball better. I thought about telling Johnny's mother, but that would be tattling like girls, and I can't speak any German yet. The only other word I knew was "boulish," and I don't think that's German. So Bruce and I had to take care of this! It just couldn't go on any longer! This world was just going to the dogs! We had to act fast!

So here's what we did. We grabbed Johnny at recess down in the basement and dragged him screaming all the way down to the boys' room. In there I washed his mouth out, while Bruce held him down. Bruce was strong as an ox, and I was better at doing the washing, because I knew what it felt like. Well! Johnny was like a wildcat! He was tough and scrappy, so we finally let go of him when the school bell rang. We went back inside, but no Johnny, though. I think he just left and went bye-bye! Even though Johnny kept on swearing more now every day, nobody else did.

So Bruce and I felt pretty good about the way things were going now. I mean, Bruster and I weren't bullies or anything like that. We weren't the fighting kind. We just beat up everybody who might even be thinking about bad words. Even if they just looked like they were! No bullies for us! We just beat 'em all to a pulp! We even did more than just getting that swearing thing gone. We also beat up some kids jumping on Bobbie's back underneath the cellar steps. We made their noses bleed! We meant business! We didn't have to have all the teachers sit around and talk about it and tell us what to do. You just gotta stop the bullies, so we just did it. Nobody had to tell us! I think all the kids began to know that everybody in the whole United States was going to have their eyes on Munson School from now on because of all the good work Bruce and I were doing. We didn't get paid for it, but we did it because we're really just the most caring kind! We did it for our school and to make our teachers proud!

Bruce and I were on top now! We kind of ran the school even though Mrs. Zepp was really the boss. Bruce and I knew exactly how to get our workbooks done lickity-split and get done early. And that's the way you get out of school real quick to help Mrs. Warner, the cook, set up all the tables for lunch. Mrs. Warner was married to Mr. Warner because they had the same name. They kind of looked alike because they were both short and fat and related, except his big mole was on his other cheek. And he didn't do anything but sit around down in the furnace room all day, smoking Camels, I think. He'd never "walk a mile for a Camel." Really, he'd just sit around all day and not even get out of his chair. If he had been in the navy like Dad, it sure would've been Lucky Strikes "make fine tobacco!" That's lots of the good stuff for you we learn on TV now. Mr. Warner also drove the bus and put his stocking feet up on a box most of the day. Now, because he sits around most the time is why he stays so short and fat. He's not so lucky there!

The best part of all this lunchroom-helping stuff though, was licking out the leftovers in the two big, steel dessert pans. It didn't matter if it was peach cobbler, butterscotch pudding, tapioca pudding, or whatever, Mrs. Warner gave us two huge serving spoons, and then Bruster and I just went for it. It was kinda like that hand to hand combat we saw in the movies, but Bruster and I didn't hurt each other keeping our spoons close to our belts! We weren't picky at all though. We scraped 'em clean! We didn't even have to wash the pans out after. We just took an old towel and wiped 'em all out clean and shiny like new, just so you could see your face in the bottom of the pan. That was good enough! Who cares! Didn't have to wash our hands either because only one hand was dirty and we weren't shakin' hands anyhow. Now, Mom says, "No dessert before supper," but not Mrs. Warner! Her rules weren't the same as Mom's. Dessert's right up there first for us fast-working kids!

Mrs. Warner was short and fat like a school cook's supposed to be. I've never seen a skinny one yet. I'm so full now, I can't think, and maybe I already told you that. She always had a hairnet in her hair and a big mole on her cheek that looked like a bunch of raisins, but she was the best cook ever. She said, "You have to season it just right!" And every time she said that, big drops of sweat dropped right off her chin into the big pot of soup or pudding bubbling away on the stove. I'm not sure what made it taste so good, but it was the best I ever had. Sometimes it was a little too salty, especially if it was a hot day and we were all sweatin' like pigs.

What a lunch for fifteen cents! And remember, if someone hit a deer, we got deer meat all week. It was a venison gift to the whole school! And old Bruster and I would help collect the lunch money, because we both had worked with lots of money and coins before, and we were really good at it. And boy, we could add fast! We could subtract it pretty well and quickly, too! And everybody knew we were the kinds of boys they could really trust, old Bruster and me! We had already proved ourselves!

Mrs. Warner was such a good cook that everybody ate seconds and thirds, and we sure learned a whole lot about cooking right from her. Old Bruster and I were Mrs. Warner's top pot cleaners. We were doing something really serious here! Better than those dumb kids blowing spaghetti noodles out their noses or shooting peas across the tables. Yah! We knew what we were doing!

And you probably know I was especially good at cooking junket with lots of food coloring and almond or vanilla in it, as well as chocolate chip cookies. The only problem with cookies is that most of the dough is gone before you get 'em on the cookie tin. That dough's so good. And this was something strange—only about five little, tiny cookies got left over for that cookie sheet. Anyhow, too many sweets are no good for ya! I mean, why cook dough if you like it raw?

Mom's kitchen was pots, I mean, lots of fun. It seems like that's where we were all the time, never anywhere else! If you had nothing else to do, just eat something! And because I had a sweet tooth that wasn't getting any better, I just had to work with it. The best thing for that bad tooth was syrup on snow. We had maple sugar bushes and camps all over the place, but the best syrup was our Amish friends', the Millers, pure amber Grade B for only four bucks a gallon. Thick as molasses! That's not a bad word again!

Sue and I would take this old washpan outside and pack it full of fresh snow while Mom boiled the syrup until it bubbled just right. And then this is how it was done! We'd take turns dripping syrup on the snow. Dad was the best and took his little ol' time making people and animals, but mine was more like glops or puddles, so I could gobble 'em up a whole lot faster. For this kind of eating, being quick was good. I'd dream about that all year and for that first fluffy snowfall when we could pull out that gallon of syrup. Sugaring season after the snow goes was great, and you could get a good smell out all over Fowlers Mills of Farmer Carroll's sap boiling in the sugarhouse evaporators up on the hill.

When Farmer Carroll was sugaring, they stayed up all night boiling that sap with wood fire. Your eyes and mouth sure got full of smoke in the sugarhouse. Best part wasn't just licking sap but putting a stick in the runoff barrel and scooping up that really thick, gooey stuff at the bottom. Lots better than sticking your finger in a pail for some of that not-so-sweet, watery sap!

Once my dad got a little baby piglet we called Josephine, but she died real soon from something they called cholera. And for that they gave us back a free gallon of Grade B maple syrup instead. We never got to know Josephine very well, and she was really never part of our family, but I'll tell you, that syrup was awfully good. So we forgot about Josephine pretty quick. It was really worth it when you think about it. Pigs aren't so snuggly, either, although she was awfully cute. I never wrote even one little poem about her, either! She just sort of came and went!

But back to Mom's kitchen—it was really all of ours. Not just Mom's! We were in there all the time! Kitchens belong to the whole family; they're not private like somebody's bedroom. Mom never said, "Go to the kitchen and think about what you did!"

We all had our special animals in the barn, but we also had pets all over the farm, like old Stanley, the black snake on the stream plank bridge, and the huge turtle I carved a *T* on the shell and found it every summer again. I even staked it out once, but Sue made me let it go. And of course, we even had our favorite big blue heron standing on its stick legs in the pond right in the middle of the water lilies. The best wild animal, though, by far, if you're looking for one, was Jose. Every chilly winter morning, we'd jump down barefoot on the cold floor and run down to the kitchen as fast as we could to warm up our freezing hands and feet. And right there was Jose, this cute little mouse just twitching his nose and sitting on the side of the sink. He had a nose that nibbled around like Grandma's. He was so cute! We fed him little scraps of food every single day. Mom would talk to him a lot. One day he left, and I'm never sure why, but when I hear some little feet running around in the walls, that's probably Jose. But that's enough about these little critters!

Bruce and I were doing lots of things in a secret way, kind of like that *I've Got a Secret* TV show. After all, you remember also, we were true blood brothers! So just like the brave Apache Cochise and all his brave friends in the movie, we took a little penknife Dad gave me and cut our wrists just a little so they bled and tied them up together tight with a grapevine we cut in the woods, the kind you swing on; you can't just use plain old string. Crimineees! Yikes! It stung a little, but big braves don't cry! And then Bruce and I whooped a big war cry and chanted away a little up on the hill and became blood brothers forever. I think something in Bruce's blood made my hair a little curlier, and I like weenies and beans just like him a lot more now. And you know, after we did that, old Bruster could run a little faster with some of me in him, and that's how blood brothers help each other out. It's like we're really each other now, kind of like Millie and Nellie. Of course, I'm still me. It didn't go that far! I mean, everybody could pick us apart. But then, you know, Bruce got to know what I was thinking all the time, and I got to know what he had on his mind. Sometimes I wished I didn't. We kept a lot of secrets! And it was more than me just sneezing, thinking dirty thoughts, and more than just sun in my eyes; it was lots of things that those other kids really didn't need to know about. Secrets and surprises—that was us! And I don't mean those silly little noises those little shrimpers sneak out their bottoms and giggle about 'em, either. No, sireee! We had really serious secrets!

Bruce had lots of White King pigeons in his barn that made these cute little squab eggs, but one pigeon was all different. He was black, gray, and white all over, and he was a real passenger pigeon who carried lots of secret messages in the war. Those other lazy, fat, White King pigeons just sat way up in the rafters, making these little, tiny eggs and just pooped and cooed all day about it. But this passenger pigeon would really fly all around the barn and only had to sleep at night. He never pooped! We named him Gray Arrow, because he could really fly through the air fast. And that's action for you! That's why you only need one of this kind of pigeon in the barn.

With all the nosy neighbors and party lines, Bruce and I really needed to keep our secrets hidden. This new telephone thing was really getting to us! It wasn't like saying really quickly in a second or so, "Hi, Grandma! I'm good! Here's Sue!" like we used to do years ago to save a dime. People were just talking too much now, except for Farmer Carroll. So no more calling number 421 on the telephone anymore! That's our number if you need us really quick, and that's if Maude and Fern ever let you get on the party line!

So one night Bruce climbed all the way up the ladder in his barn, or at least that's what he said, and carried Gray Arrow to school all wrapped up in his coat. Me, I brought in an old orange crate I found in the barn. We hoped Gray Arrow didn't have a broken wing with all this carrying around and could still fly, so we unwrapped him to take a look, and would you believe, that darn bird flew all over the classroom. And the kids all yelled and were jumping up and down! Which, by the way, is not the way you catch a bird again! Why don't those dummies know that? Kids just don't mind, and they get away with everything!

So he flew faster, got tired at last, and landed smack on the teacher's desk. Then he, but I don't mean Bruce, pooped right on that desk, all over our spelling papers. I don't know if Mrs. Zepp ever gave us a grade for those papers, but she sure liked that pigeon so much that she let Bruce and I pick that poor, tired, little pigeon right up and put him in the orange crate. Then she let us walk him all the way home from school to my barn, just like that. We got there and let Gray Arrow out of that crate, and right away, he flew right up to the rafters in my barn, so now you had to keep the barn door shut all the time. There was a little window up there with a hole in it he could peek out of. I know Mrs. Zepp loved us, but she must have really loved birds, too. On the way back to school for lunch, we stopped at the mill, and for only a dime, we got a bag of pigeon food specially mixed for pigeons. It even had the little hard peas and grit in it that pigeons really like. We were gone all morning, but first things first. Mrs. Zepp wasn't worried one bit. She sure trusted Bruce and me! After her, we were like in charge!

So Bruce and I had to make more secret plans. I was going to let Gray Arrow rest up for five days, but then I couldn't wait and was going to climb up one night while he was sleeping and tie a little message to his feet so he could fly it to Bruce's house. The message I wrote was, "Hi Bruce. I am fine. How are you?" It wasn't really very secret, but it was a good way to start, because that's how I start all my letters to my West Virginia grandma. It's just a friendly way to start writing something. People don't get all mushy with you.

Since Mrs. Zepp loved that pigeon, too, we planned to teach it to fly a message to her house, too. You can teach pigeons things like that because birds are really smart. That's how the soldiers sent secrets in the war. But you do have to be careful, because passenger pigeons can get mixed up sometimes if they have to do too much and fly to the wrong house. And that's exactly how wars get started. Can you imagine if Gray Arrow flew a message to Mrs. Zepp's house saying, "Bruce! I hate school, too!" Boy! Would we be in big trouble! We could never go to school again, and we'd just have to become robbers like that Jesse James guy in the movie or something bad like that, and then we'd just have to hide out and live in the woods eating berries all the time, which really isn't too bad.

But—and this is really going to upset you—before I could tie that secret message to Gray Arrow's foot while he was fast asleep at night, some of those city people from Cleveland drove all the way out to surprise us on a Sunday afternoon. It was one of those stupid Sunday drives again that can ruin your whole day. That's a surprise you don't need! Now, I forget exactly which Sunday, but it doesn't matter. And then their three kids, who weren't very smart or were sitting in their car or in church too long, got all excited and ran down to the barn before I could show them how this all farm stuff works. Then they opened that barn door wide up, and dadgumit, Gray Arrow flew right out that barn door like his fly was open. Then he flew way up in the air around in three big circles before taking off for Bruce's house. I tried really quick to break into the party line to call Bruce, but Maude and Fern were talking and talking and talking about somebody, and they wouldn't stop gabbing away. They kept saying, "Fern, I think somebody's on the line." Well, of course we are! What in heaven's name were those old biddies thinking of! This was really a bad emergency!

Would you believe it, though, the next day Bruce saw Gray Arrow sitting way up there on the top of his barn rafters, and we were so glad he had made it back. We were so worried he might get lost. That rascal! And that made us know that passenger pigeons can only fly one way. Right back to their homes! And that's the way it's supposed to be. One way!

Well! I guess our plans didn't work out very well, and it wasn't even our fault. City boys just don't know a lot. The only good thing about their crummy visit was we got doubles on cherry Kool-Aid. Boy! Was I glad to see them go! Boy, was I mad, but I didn't show it. Mom says, "Sometimes it's better to keep your feelings to yourself!" and "Don't blow a gasket if you don't need to." Well, for that, I think that's what I needed, to blow a gasket! That was a horrible thing those city kids did. It just ruined all our plans, and now nothin's secret anymore.

But if Bruce and I really are good blood brothers, we have to find better ways to keep our secrets just between us. We started hiding messages in trees and bushes, but then you can forget and have to run all over like some stupid treasure hunt to find 'em. And the other kids and all the moms snooped around and found 'em, too, so that was not going to work out. We really needed a getting-together meeting like those stupid civil war generals had to figure this thing out.

But we got a great idea! We found some cards in the Nabisco Shredded Wheat or Post Toasties box. And we liked both of 'em, because they both have lots of sugar. In there were Straight Arrow cards that told you all about Morse code. Rice Krispies with the Snap, Crackle and Pop guys in there was a lot more fun, but you don't get those Morse code cards in there like those prickly Shredded Wheat sticks have. Dad did lots of Morse code on his navy ship with big flashlights and signal flags. Remember, Dad brought those flags back home from the war in his blue navy chest. So we learned a lot about this Morse guy's code, and Bruster and I practiced talking only in "dits" and "dahs" for hours, even at school. Everybody thought we were learning some new weird kind of language. We talked regular American talk with everyone else, though. But Bruce and I did mostly dits and dahs for a long time, almost two weeks! We didn't say a whole lot because we always had to look back at those doggone cereal cards a lot to see what in heck we were saying. But we got so good at it, we made up this plan that Bruce would stand way up on his hill in his front yard at night, and I would stand up on our hillside in the dark, so I could see his flashlight, and he could see mine.

So one pitch-black night, we started blinking our flashlights with short and long dits and dahs. My first message to Bruce was, "I home where you?" And he flashes back, "Home." My second message was,

"What eat supper? I ate hominee and sausij." I was getting to be a pretty good speller, but I wasn't so good at spelling food. I probably got my dits and dahs mixed up a little bit, too. Easy to do when you got long messages. Anyhow, I couldn't understand Bruce's Morse code. It was different than that Morse guy's stuff. I sure wish Mom had bought one of those Captain Video Ranger Rocket Rings cereal boxes instead. Heck! Bruce and I are better at just reading each other's minds. Those decoder badges probably don't work, either. Moms buying those cereals is just a trick they do to get you to eat your cereal and stay healthy.

So thinking pretty quickly, I went right to the telephone but had to wait again until Maude and Fern got off the party line. They kept saying, "We're talking now, aren't we, Fern? I think somebody else is listening in!" No fooling! But the old biddies finally hung up so I could call 314 to find out why Bruce just couldn't figure out what I was saying on the flashlight. It's probably because he couldn't spell "hominee" and "sausij" like me yet. Then he told me he had weenies and beans, which I would have liked a whole lot better, anyhow, and they're so much better for you! And son of a gun, old Bruster got brownies for dessert. That bugger! I'm going to have to change his name again for that! But we straightened things out on the telephone before too many people clicked in.

Ahh! Excuse me, Maude! We're talking here! Well, then we tried the Morse code flashlights again. But you know, you can say an awful lot more on the telephone than flashlights, so we finally gave that Morse code stuff up and started speaking just plain old American again. That's what most people are talking around here now anyhow.

I might have hurt Dad's feelings, because flashlights and signal flags was the way they always talked in the navy. I mean, they didn't have to say a whole lot. I have no idea if those navy guys got tricked like us into eating that crappy cereal, too. Those doggone Shredded Wheat sticks prick your mouth unless you have a lot of milk and sugar on 'em. Best to always keep lots of sugar around! Sugar cubes was the way I got Penny's bit and bridle on. Of course, Penny had to see me eat four or five of 'em first to get the idea! You know what I mean!

Now you know, those flashlights began to look like a lot of twinkle stars, and that got pretty dumb anyhow. I really hated letting Dad down, a real navy man, but it really was a huge relief just talking plain old

American words again. I don't know how we ever won the war with that Morse code thing anyhow. I'm not even sure that's what won it. Bruster and I thought about stretching a string or wire straight as the crow flies between two tin cans. We had heard about that, but we just couldn't get a whole quarter mile of string or wire anywhere to stretch that far. We had plenty of cans, though! We never tried writing each other, because, you know, I got Ds in cursive, and block printing is for babies. Bruster brought up smoke signals, but heck, we'd burn the house down with that. And, you know, Bruster and I always had a whole lot of important stuff to talk about, anyway.

So when we stayed over at each other's house or camped out, we just talked and talked about everything. We talked about being Catholic or in Fowlers Mills Community Church or if you have to go to confession or not, like Bruce did. And what do you really have to tell the Father Maher in there, even if you couldn't see him? He'd probably see me peeking through, and he wouldn't even have to ask me any questions, because he knows I've been really good. I'd be out of that box in a minute. That would give all those real sinners more time confessing in that little closet. Do you have to tell him the Truth or not? Like all the bad stuff?

And we talked about stuff like taking trips on Bruce's McCormick Farmall Cub Tractor and how to make Roman catapults in the woods and all that stuff. Or how can you live with so many sisters. He and Bud have six sisters, and I have only three, and that's enough! Or stuff like, if you beep out gas, do you have to say who did it? Just how honest do you have to be? I mean, it's just like a burp but out the other end. We didn't giggle all the time like Eddie and me. We mostly talked about really important stuff, not dumb phone talk stuff like Della, Fern, and Maude do!

Bruce also has a brother at the Catholic Church in Chardon who teaches him a lot, Brother Jerome. I don't have any brothers, so I have to learn all this stuff by myself. Bruster talked about the burning smoke smelling like perfume and Catholic rules and words I didn't understand. He told me some word that sounds like "insects" burning and Father Maher swinging some smoke in a pot around. Bruce says they give you a High Mass with lots of candles when they bury you. For me, I think all I'll get is just a little picnic with lots of ice cream and cherry Kool-Aid if I ever die!

Heck! All we have in the Fowlers Mills Community Church is a couple of candles and a little white tablecloth to catch the drips. You can't do a whole lot with that, unless someone spills some grape juice or bread crumbs at Communion. Of course, we have Mrs. Rook, and believe me if you can, she takes up the whole back end of the church. Boy! She can make that piano go!

Anyhow, Bruster was better than me at following rules, although I think he's beginning to slip a little. But he's a lot better at Catholicking than me. That's why Bruce can talk so much about religion. Catholics just have a whole lot more to talk about. We gotta get more stuff in our church. I don't know about this, but Bruce's family has rosaries, so you can tell exactly who they are. You can hold them or just wear 'em around your neck like a lucky charm if you want. All I have is my Indians ball cap, so everyone knows what I'm going to be. I even wear it in winter in the house just to stay in shape. Good to practice this stuff whenever you can! Anyhow, I'll just have to learn a lot more of these religious things at the Fowlers Mills Community Church.

But all our preacher really says is you're supposed to be good and pure and love your fellow man, which sounds pretty silly to me, but I'm trying. I mean, like Dad is my real fellow man, and I really love him! Who wouldn't? And my grandpas, too! I can't say that about Grandpa Koblaha. And, of course, I love Bruce some, too, but it's sure not like loving Roberta. You know, things like that really sound simple, but they sure haven't been for me so far. I've had a tough life! Maybe if I read the Bible more, it would help. But there're so many words in there! Have you ever seen that book? If you just count the chapters, you'll see just how many people it takes to write all those words. I think they're just making up more of those commandments so you'll never know if you got 'em all. I don't think I was doing so good with 'em because that BB gun had already shot that Starling. Guess I really goofed up on that Thou shalt not kill one. Gosh! I hope they make up some more and I don't run out of 'em.

And now, too many Bible words again can hurt your eyes. I'm warning you! Remember that big eye trouble I had in the first grade. Lordy, I don't want to go through that again! And you don't, either! And Peggy sure saved me! She was the Holy saver there on that one. I may even have told you that twice, but I just want to make you sure you got it! And if I start repeating all these things too much, just go right to the end of all this for the big surprise. There are just too many things I've gone through. And I'm telling you, I'm through! And you know what Mom says by now, "Actions speak louder than words!" Anyhow, I just can't sit still long enough to read all those doggone verses!

But back to stayovers at Bruce's. I did get to kiss Rosie again, and I sure liked that. That kissing is something you do growing up after you learn how to kiss Mom and Dad, grandmas, and all the aunts and uncles and cousins in West Virginia. It's kind of like getting to practice it more again, so I can do it better when I grow up! Rosie can even kiss Bruce, too, if she wants to, but for gosh sakes, he's her brother! When I sleep over, we think of lots of stuff and make up all these plays. And Rosie would be the wife in the farmhouse, and I'd pretend being her hard-working husband out in the fields all day long. Then when I got home from the fields all tired out, I'd get to kiss her and all that mushy stuff. Now, that makes farm work really worth it! Those were the greatest plays, and all his little sisters would clap so loud and mostly fall sound asleep, because some of those plays never ended. But anyhow, that's just some of the stuff you'll know over at Bruce's house because I don't think you ever got the chance to sleep over there.

I thought I was done with being a sneak, but I still have a little sneakiness left inside me. You just can't get it out all at once! One time I actually stole an Amish man's trap on the bank of the millpond just behind the cattails. I think they can shoot you for that. Eddie Spagetti, another friend, and I were working around the edge of the millpond trying to gig bullfrogs, which isn't a very friendly thing to do. We were using one of those three-sided hooks, throwing 'em out and pulling 'em in. And then we almost stepped on this doggone trap. I don't think I'd ever seen one of these traps before, but we sprung it with a big stick, because nothin' was in it. Man, that thing snapped shut! Wow!

Eddie had his Davy Crockett coonskin hat with a real tail on the back, and I had my Indians baseball cap on tight, so you can tell right there we were awfully serious about what we were doing. Eddie came into school about fourth grade, so he still hadn't gotten the city stuff out of him yet. But he was trying to look more woodsy and show off with his coonskin cap with that real tail hanging on it. I wasn't exactly sure if it was the real thing like my buffalo coat, or not, but so what! He sure pretended like it! It had to make him feel good. I mean, he was never going to make it to be like Daniel Boone and, like in the movies, hide under the pond from the Indians sucking air through an Indian stovepipe straw to stay alive and brave things like that. Man, he couldn't even scale a bluegill fish. He could only burp it like a baby. That's as far as he got! But Eddie did have a little runt of a pony that we could jump right over, up onto his rear like Hopalong Cassidy, and that takes good jumping legs, and we sure had them. I did anyhow!

Anyhow, we just couldn't believe it! There was this shiny metal trap right there in the cattails on the bank of the millpond. The kind you see in the Sears and Roebuck catalog for at least three bucks. It was completely empty. Nothing in it! Must have been put in the wrong place! So I got to figuring, and I knew more about catching things and working in the woods than Eddie, because he had just moved out from the city. All they had in there was just a big front yard. No farm or barn! Here he just had a little shed where you couldn't do much but keep that teenie-weenie runt of a pony all shut up in there. It ate like a horse, and that pony really was tiny, but not a little hinie. It had a big rump that looked like a bump! I don't even think Eddie gave it a name!

So first of all, you don't put a trap down where nobody can see it. Everybody knows you can't catch anything that way! You've got to set it someplace where the animals go. You've got to be thinking like animals sometimes, and we know they're really smart. If they want to hide, they just look for a hole. And they know where every hole is. It's like going to their rooms! Like Mom says, "Have a little privacy!" So I thought we could help this Amish man out and put his trap where it could really catch something big.

I knew just the place up the riverbank running into the millpond with a deep hole piled up with leaves on the far bank under a big beech tree, really close to the right-of-way. Even Eddie knew that! So I let Eddie, because he's my guest, carry all the big buckets, frying pan, and all the frog stuff. I said "Follow me", but I let Eddie go first because of that guest thing again. Since I knew more about woods and rivers and stuff like that, I carried only that trap all by myself behind him with no help at all and stuck it in that hole just right. That's so we could still see it really well!

First, I did the hardest part and stepped down really hard on the handle to open the two sharp jaws. Then I let Eddie put his little fingers in there and do the easy work, putting the little hook in place with his skinny fingertips on the spring between the two sharp jaws to keep it wide open, so it wouldn't snap shut on him and take off his fingers. I thought he might be brave at first, but he wouldn't stop shaking. The coonskin cap got in his eyes, or he just didn't know much about all this trapping stuff.

It wasn't his fault, because he still had a lot of that city in him. And you know what? They don't teach trapping in the city! If Eddie was trying to be brave, it was the bravest thing he'd ever done! I mean, he looked like a frontier man with his coonskin cap and fluffy tail hanging down, but inside he was a scaredy. He was going to have to get a lot more courage, and you're just going to see what I mean about that later.

Eddie's dad did tell him that some old man up in Chardon living in a shack down by the track (Did you get that rhyme again? You probably got it on your own by now.) would give you three dollars for a skinned fur and five dollars if it was a fox one. And I got to thinking about candy bars again, because I was getting more wisdom teeth and getting taller with my pants going up two inches over my shoe tops every year. So you can just see I needed lots of candy bars and sugar to keep on growing. All I could think about awhile was just how many candy bars we could get for three dollars, and you know what, this here fur wasn't costing us a cent! Every now and then, I thought about that poor old Amish man out there, but not for long, because, you know, I had lots of things to get done, and time was growing short! Well, Eddie with his coonskin cap and I got to playing civil war stuff again, ordering our troops all around the field and like always, covering our flanks, covering our rears, and, doggone it, we almost forgot about that trap we borrowed!

But anyhow, we got our memory back again after a few days and hiked on back there to that old riverbank and found that old hole again but no trap anywhere. My heart sunk! I was sure that Amish man had found us out and snuck his trap back. Where in Sam Hill did it go? I just prayed he couldn't talk any English and tell Mom I had stolen his trap. I only hoped he'd keep his trap shut! Maybe he'd get Johnny to talk German talk, and then Johnny would tell his mom, because that boy never got over having his mouth washed out in that "No More Swearing" campaign. But Bruster and I really did it for the school, so it would be good and kind again just like the preacher says. We really cared! Kind of like missionaries! We did it for all the little suffering children in school and the whole world, too! We were pretty important now, but Johnny was still swearing and blinking up a storm and twitching his hair around more now than ever before. Well, like Mom says, "Just do the best you can!"

Now about this trapping, you aren't going to believe this one. But since Eddie and I can see far out just like Indian scouts in the woods, we can see this little chain still tied to the root by the hole and nothing else! So what did we do? We just pulled and pulled on it. Now, this is where you're probably not going to believe me again. We pulled that thing so hard, we finally saw that trap coming out of there. And right in that trap was a big, hairy foot, and on the end of that foot was some huge animal that looked like some big, hairy monster you don't ever really want to see.

We are talking about big and scary now! It was huge and hissing like it wasn't happy at all to see us. I mean, we didn't look so great ourselves and looked a little raggedy, too, but this thing was scarier than the worst movies you'll ever see. His teeth were all squished up and snarling, and his nose holes were wide open and huge. You could put your whole foot in one.

We were so surprised, we just let 'er go and almost fell head over tea kettle or something like that right down into the river. And Eddie, dadgumit, almost ran away like a sissy! He kept yelling, "Let's go! Let's go!" Like go where? Old Daniel Boone, here, just couldn't cut it! City boys whine, but we country boys just shake it off!

I knew this monster wasn't a skunk, but it could have been a beaver or a bear or maybe even a muskrat for three bucks or even a fox for a five-dollar skin. But we had a big job to do, and that's where you really have to keep it going! So I'd better not quit, and I got right at it. And doggone it, I just couldn't quit thinking about those darn candy bars again. Whenever I'm moping around and need to feel better about something, I always think about candy bars, especially after all my sweet teeth keep coming in more. Those darn things can ruin you. I'm getting about ten of those sweet teeth. Never got my wisdoms, though, just the sweet ones!

I don't know if I was born with it, or just worked hard to get it, or what, but sometimes if you think about something over and over and over again, you know you can make it happen, like falling in love with Roberta! Anyway, when I was small, I used to think about Mom when I got hurt or something, then like I told you later, I started to think about Jesus and God helping me but couldn't get a clear picture of 'em in my mind. There's only one picture of Jesus in our church, but there's not even one picture of God at all. I think you're supposed to just dream up what He looks like. Bruster thinks God has big hands. Not me! I have small hands but long arms. But then, when that God-dreaming thing doesn't work and I'm sittin' there awful bored in that church pew (gosh, what a smelly word!), just dreaming about all those wonderful candy bars always seems to really make me feel a lot better. So that's what was inside my mind lots.

I got awfully worried if somebody asked, "What's on your mind?" or "A penny for your thoughts." And I'd just have to tell them, "Heath bars and Baby Ruths!" That's if I really wanted to tell them the Truth, and I'm not sure how important that Truth thing really is anymore. Why don't they just ask them own selfs? Boy! That's stupid! I don't know what's happening to me now!

But anyhow, getting back to the trapping job we had here and thinking about all those Heath bars we'd get for this fur, I knew we had to work fast. So I ran back home, got my Daisy Pump gun and ran all the way back up the hill, with the barrel pointing down, of course, like they tell you to. Then I ran off down the right-of-way and through the woods back to where Eddie was still just standing there, doing nothing at all. Got a monkey on my back and maybe a fox in the hole. He was just standing there, looking straight up at the trees! This five-dollar fur could have got away from us! Sometimes you just can't take your eyes off anybody.

So I just shut my eyes and started pumping BBs into that hole. You can see there what a brave guy I was. I wasn't afraid, not me! And what a sharp shot I was up close! Boy! We tugged so hard, and he hissed (don't mean Eddie here) so much, it seemed like hours before we finally pulled that critter out. I hate to say this, but he was actually stone dead by the time we got him out. He came out feetfirst. This wasn't like a plain old sunfish or something like that just flopping around. This was one of those really wild animals. You never know how many of those wild animals come running out. You can't take 'em alive unless you have like Tarzan or Superman blood in you.

This was the first time, and only time, I ever killed something really big and wild alive. Little Starling birdies don't count. Boy! Seeing that poor animal there on the bank, not moving, and blood coming out of his nose and mouth just didn't make me feel very proud anymore. I didn't feel like brave Cochise anymore. There was no fight left, just one dead animal! He was just real alive a minute ago and fighting us off real good, and now he wasn't even moving anymore, like stillborn and not even thinking about us! It was just a dead bunch of messed-up meat and fur.

It really didn't make me feel very good about myself, and, just before, I thought this was really going to be the biggest excitement of all. And wouldn't you know it, old Eddie was down there puking in the river, making those fish gag, too. That river smelled like sour spagetti. That must have been all Eddie Spagetti ate. Uugghhh! I didn't even know what he was thinking about. Probably something weird! Like where's my mommie? Boo hoo!

This boy needed help! What a mommie's boy! You could see I wasn't one of those kinds. I don't have a mommie; mine's a real mom! The Truth is, I'm my mom's only boy, and I take extra good care of her when Dad's not home. Eddie's sure not like Bruce and me who always know what each other is thinking. Bruce and I are just that way, and Eddie and I are just a different way. They're both good eggs, though! And sometimes Bruce and I get things mixed up, too.

But the thought of candy bars, especially Heath bars, those little, yummy, teenie-weenie ones that cost ten cents came into my mind again, so now I really knew we had a big job to do. And now I think I'm going to share more candy bars with Bruce than Eddie anyhow. But to get 'em, we had to get to skinning this animal. So look at me! I got this big hay rake from the barn, and we wrapped that dang old trap chain all around it, and Eddie finally stopped vomiting and shaking long enough to grab his end and carry this thing on this rake handle, with that dead thing dangling between us all the way down to the shed right next to our barn. Of course Eddie being a guest got to go first again. That's how old Daniel and Davy carry 'em in the movies. Of course, guess which one of us strong guys carried the heavy end?

Now you may remember, I had my special hunting knife I used for knife-throwing into trees and mumblety-peg and knife games like that. I never could hit a tree trunk, though, like Jim Bowie in the Davy Crockett movies. I'm still learning, though. I got that knife as a grand prize for selling Burpee's Vegetable Garden Seeds to anybody in Fowlers Mills who needed some. They were the best! I told people, "You don't want to buy any seeds, do you?" But they bought 'em anyway. I was really good at selling. Just say Burpee's, and they bought 'em. Mrs. Partpart bought two packs of gourd seeds, which you can't eat anyhow. She probably mashed 'em up and made old Bert eat 'em all for dinner. She was that kind of person! Of the Partparts, he was the good part, and she was a little different. I'm trying to say a lot of nicer things about everybody now. Don't want to hurt your feelings!

Right-of-way spikes and the special muskrat-skinning hunting knife.

**There's the whetstone we should have used more on
that knife and Grandpa's lion on his desk.**

But this was my very first chance to really use this hunting knife like a Bowie knife for something big. It was duller than the hatchet. But now, I was feeling a little bit more like a real hunter and frontier man. I even swapped my Indians ball cap for Eddie's coonskin cap just to get the feeling of all that tail fur on my face and get even more frontiersie here. And since I was just starting to become an animal skinner, when I'd get to be a big kid in high school, then I could get three days out of school with a special hunters' high school excuse they give you for deer season. Yippee! Fantastic! Top of the world!

But now we really had to get right down to the skinning part. I wished we had a book or something telling us where to cut on this thing. This wasn't any cuttin' paper dolls, you know! We figured out that this had to be a muskrat because it had a smaller tail than a beaver. So we're gonna only get three bucks for this here skin anyhow.

Well, since I had done most of the hard work so far, and Eddie was still a house guest on my farm, and I wanted to be really polite and kind, I tossed him the knife and let him go at it first again. Well! You won't believe this, but maybe you just will by now. Eddie went and pricked just a little tip of that knife in, and a little blood squirted out. It wasn't a lot but just enough to run all the blood out of Eddie's face, and my Indians ball cap hat fell off his head. And then he started this throwing up thing again. How much spagetti is this guy eating? Gosh! It went all over my ball cap and nice new leather knife sheath. I should have thrown his coonskin cap in it, too! What a mess! He must have had his eyes closed, 'cuz he sure didn't look very frontiersie. Things like this can ruin your life! I couldn't believe it!

What a horrible way to start, and what a baby! I mean, who are we going to tell all this stuff to? I mean, they're gonna laugh their pants off! Hey! Maybe that's OK if they're girls! Wow! No pants! Just kidding! I don't think that kind of dirty stuff anymore. I wish Bruce had been there, and Davy Crockett here could just pick up his dumb coonskin cap with that fluffy tail hanging between his legs and run on home. You know what—and please don't tell anybody this—I think I saw a few tears in Eddie's eyes. And you know in your heart, he was really trying. He was just a city kid, and it was all new for him. He couldn't do any better! Now me, I've been doing this stuff all the years of my life. It's going to take him some time to catch on.

It reminds me of the time Bruce and I ran over Eddie's toe in Bruce's McCormick Farmall Cub Tractor, and he yelled and cried the whole day. We sure broke that tractor in. All Eddie got was a little broken toe! Don't tell him, but I actually wanted to stomp his other toe for that. Really! I've got to stop talking like this, pray a lot more, and get a little bit more kind and caring. Eddie really is a good guy, but he just wasn't made like us country boys. Roberta kind of liked him, though. They all thought he was kind of cute.

I really think I chose the wrong boy, though, for this job. It should have been Bruster, the Rooster! He was a lot tougher, and both us know all about woods and Indian trails and stuff like Indian scouts do. We're woodsie kinds! But this thing just happened like a surprise. When something like this happens, you've got to be really kind to the guy you're with. You can't just go running all around looking for a bunch of other people to help you out, no matter what! You've got to stick together! Right there's the law of the woods!

Sometimes what happens just happens! That's just the way it is! You can't plan for it! Even Tom and Jerry don't know what's coming down the road when you're driving 'em. You've got to make a mistake or two.

Take a chance! That's how you get to know stuff. And Eddie was with me when we stole that trap, so we're both stealers anyhow. Can't leave him out of it! Sometimes you don't know what's happenin' anyhow! Boy! We sure go for surprises! So go ahead and work on it! Gosh! I'm sounding just like Mom and her doggone rules here! And you know what, Bruce might not have been as sneaky as me about that trap, even though I planned to put it right back where I found it, and that's the Truth! Bruce just might have gone off and let somebody in on it. He's not a big fibber!

Well! After a day or two, it started to blow and snow hard. And that poor muskrat critter was getting frozen solid, and my knife was really dull now. Even our old scythe whetstone couldn't sharpen it. And I wasn't even sure what part of the furry skin made it a pelt. I mean, did the pelt guy down by the railroad tracks want his feet and toenails, too, or was that something a little extra? Maybe they could be like feet for making things for little key chains and stuff. Maybe we'd get a Mounds bar out of those feet. Pelts! That's what we heard fur trappers call 'em. So I wasn't even sure what part to skin anymore, and that pelt was sure getting pretty messed up and full of holes and looked terrible. Smelled like rotten hamburger! And I wasn't sure that pelt man would even give us twenty-five cents for this mess!

So I sawed away awhile, and old Eddie couldn't even look at it. And he didn't look so good and wasn't saying much, either. No Rebel yells here! This was just going on too long! So we finally gave this whole thing up and buried that muskrat behind the barn, so Eddie would quit gagging and throwing up, for goodness' sakes!

Then we took that trap and hid it in the hayloft, right near my dirty pictures in the potato chip can and never used it again. But we didn't put it too close to the can, because you can't trust anybody smelling around for potato chips. If you have a good nose, you can smell that stuff all over. That poor Amish man is probably still looking for it and maybe us, too, if somebody rats on us.

Thank God, the Amish don't believe in party lines, just a secret line or a fun party for themselves. And they don't even believe in shooting off BB guns like us, so we're safe there. But they do keep their knives good and sharp, not dull like us. Just had bad luck here and some bad help on this job! I was sure we'd get 'er done, because in my head I had already spent all three bucks on you know what, with, of course, a cut for Eddie Spagetti. It was like candy bars just dropping away! I never ever got over that one!

But you know what, Roberta had already moved away and left us behind, and Eddie had already made it up to two or three on her list of favorite boys at the time, so I really didn't have anybody to spend money on anyhow. And maybe it was better she moved away, because I just couldn't keep my mind on my workbooks when she was sitting so pretty at her desk there. And back then, I kept wanting to sharpen pencils all the time. So I kept jumping up to that wall sharpener a lot, so I could walk by her desk every chance I got. This sounds stupid, but I got to be the best pencil sharpener in the class. You know, that's not something guys really brag about. It's kind of dopey! I'd sharpen everybody's pencils. But I don't think that's what makes you famous.

I don't plan on falling in love again, because you're just not yourself when you're doing that! You just don't think right, either! And after all, Farmer Carroll didn't need a wife. All he needed was his mother. I still had mine, too, so I don't need to get married anyhow. I mean, I really like Bruster, but I don't think he and I will ever get this married thing. I went to a wedding once, and they had lots of ice cream, peanuts, and candy mints, but that's not what we're talking about here!

And I knew things were going to be a lot safer now, because I knew Roberta had to get braces, and I knew I needed them, too, because I had this big front tooth that stuck way out like one buck tooth, and they called me Ollie, like in the *Kukla, Fran, and Ollie Show* on TV. And everyone knows when two people both get braces and kiss, those braces can really get stuck together tightly, so you have to choose a girlfriend really carefully. Then all the kids try to pull you apart and laugh when that happens. And they have to pull all your teeth out when you can't get unstuck. It's just not fun to go through life like that!

And there's something else, too. Remember those exciting atomic-bomb drills? Well! They just weren't any fun anymore, because I couldn't rub up against Roberta under the desk anymore. Boy! Way back, I couldn't wait for those bomb drills, always hoping we'd get snowed in up to the roof like back in 1950 and have to spend all night with Roberta at school. Now, that's my kind of school! I just don't even care any more if I stand right there in the middle of all those atomic bomb red stickers on the wall where you're not supposed to stand instead of between the green tapes like you're supposed to. Green tapes mean you won't get blown up! I think that's how it goes. I kind of forget! It really just doesn't matter anymore anyhow! Nothing does! I don't even care if I blow up anyhow, just like the Yucca Flats bomb tests on TV.

So now the only person I have to buy any candy bars for is just only me, and of course I'll share 'em all with Bruce, even Steven! Whoops! I mean, even Bruce, my best friend. I don't even know any Steven and probably never will. And working Sugar Bush for two dollars a day, picking up sap pails, is big money for candy bars! The days of working for just ginger ale and watermelon are over!

Well! Things aren't all bad! Bruce and I go camping all the time out back in the woods behind his house, and one time I took ten candy bars, only the five-cent Snickers bars because you really get a lot bigger bagful that way. Again, and I know you shouldn't borrow without asking, but I found that March of Dimes card again and borrowed just five more dimes. That's all! It's right out there in the living room, so it's easy to slip little thin dimes in or out like you want to. They're the tiniest ones. Never knew why the nickels were fatter, but I'm glad for it. But you know, I began to feel sad about all those crippled children on the crutches on that card looking right straight back at your eyes, and I planned right then and there to give every one of those dimes back, one dime at a time! (Sorry, there's that rhyming again. I can't help it). But one dime at a time is just like it's supposed to be! That's the best way to fill up that whole dime card!

Wow! That night camping away in the tent, it really rained, and lightning cracked away out all night long, making you jump and twitch all over, just like our most exciting guy Jackie. So many trees came down on Bruster and me in that pup tent, we couldn't even sleep a wink. No Winken, Blinken, and Nod for us that night! No, sireee! So we stood watch all night just like Dad did in the navy. Dad's got a great eye, and this'll keep them open all night long. We took turns, or really both of us kind of peeked out the tent flap all night long just to keep a sharp eye out on any falling trees. That way we could jump out of the way quickly if one squashed us. I'd get squashed for Bruce. That's the way blood brothers do it. Heck, then I'd finally be a real hero! Boy! We were so happy when morning came, and we saw a little light out the flap. If you wait long enough, it'll happen! Then we could pack up and get out of there home. I don't think we slept an inch, and our eyes looked like newborn puppies the next morning, like almost shut! No Mom there to pull us out, though!

You probably already know this, but my luck really wasn't getting any better at all! Maybe it was because I didn't really pray enough in church anymore, or maybe not in the right way. Sometimes I peeked when you're supposed to have your head down. I like to see what other people are doing. Sometimes you catch an old nose picker that way! Maybe they'll kick me out of this church. Whatever happens, like Mom says, "It's for the best!"

The best thing about church, though, is Wednesday night family suppers and Fern's baked beans with lots of molasses. Remember, that last word there is not a dirty one! Hey! Fern's beans could blow you out and keep you coming back for more. They would keep you beeping away all week or more if you ate extra and really big if you get thirds and fourths! No secrets or hiding there! Everybody knows everybody there! There are lots of different names for that beeping thing. That last one's got a good sound to it! But they all mean the same thing. Hey! Call it anything you want! It's being free! Let the wind blow free! And now, you really don't have to yell out, "Hey! Who beeped?" Yep! No secrets around here anymore!

I never really knew what to say around Fowlers Mills Church anymore except the same old thing, "Jesus loves me this I know, for the Bible tells me so." At least somebody around here does! Of course, I didn't hear the Bible telling things and talking right to me at all, and I wasn't sure what Jesus even looked like anymore, except for that picture in the church. I didn't even know what grade he was in or when he got that beard or anything like that. I just wasn't a Jesus-type baby. I mean, people do change, you know. Look at Bruster, getting fuzz down by his dingdong, and I don't mean church bells ringing here! That's boy talk! Don't say that around the girls, please! Of course, I was changing, too. My socks smelled a lot more now and getting a little more stink in 'em! I couldn't wear 'em all week anymore like Farmer Carroll did. His socks were stronger. They stood right up on their own!

I just wasn't keeping track of Jesus and all that religious stuff as much anymore. I was having my own troubles right here! I know Jesus liked guys who went fishin' in the Sea of Galley. They say he was a fisher of men. Wow! That's fishin' for men is somethin' really strange and different! Can't imagine 'em grabbing that hook. No idea what kind of pole you use for that. Here Brucie. Nibble on that! I don't mean to be silly, but I wasn't even fishin' for plain old fish much anymore. And I sure have no idea how to ride my bike to that Galley Sea place anyhow. I did hear one time he was talkin' to some grown-ups in a temple when he was only twelve. Heck! I'm twelve already, and I haven't even seen a temple yet. I've just been seein' this same old church, sittin' in the pews and not saying much at all! Boy, I'm really not doing so good at all! But I did get tired of stealing Mom's margarine. I was just turning out all wrong more all the time! I've got to be better! And this story shows it. You've got to keep working on things all the time.

I know Roberta didn't love me anymore, and I wasn't at all sure about Jesus, either, now. I mean, I memorized all those Bible book names in Sunday school, like Genesis, Exodus, Leviticus, Numbers, and Deuteronomy (I just get tickled out of that last name, but I don't know what it means except doodie on me, maybe. Just guessin' here!). But I don't remember any verses except about that first day in Genesis when everything got made and God took a day off on the seventh day. Good for him. He worked hard! Then all that stuff about Adam and Eve and eating that apple. I mean, old Bruster and I like to steal apples, but we didn't eat any rotten ones. They're for cider anyhow.

I don't know if you realize it or not, but that Eden garden thing didn't really turn out too good, either, so I don't know. Probably better than my first day at school, maybe; I don't know. I mean, who are these guys writing all these books anyhow? I mean, if Adam and Eve have the only two boys in the whole wide world, how, for heaven's sakes, do those boys beget some other kids? I am not stupid about all that begatting stuff, you know! Boys don't make the babies by themselves, so how did they *beget* all those other people. I mean, nothing really makes sense around here, anymore! Does it? First you get tricked about that Santa Claus thing and now this! I might have to put some more thinking on it. Maybe I should learn some more Bible verses or join that dumb children's choir again, because I can still sing up there like a soprano. Bruce can't sing that high anymore, because his voice started to squeak all funny. And like I said, he started to have all those funny little hairs in lots of different places!

And when it comes to all that church stuff, I always start thinking about lots of other things I shouldn't. What if Reverend Kheenel calls on me, brother Tommy, when I'm sitting in that pew? I won't be like poor old Dad. Nope, darn 'em, and I don't mean socks again! I'd be wide-awake, and I still won't even know what to say. All I'd say is, "This pew is really hard!" and "When the heck are we getting out of here?" The whole church would laugh. I don't even think they call kids like me brother somebody anymore because these ministers are a bunch of old white-headed guys who just stick to themselves. So I probably don't have to worry too much about that. But knowin' me, I'll probably worry anyhow, just for kicks!

I worried when they passed that collection plate around too much. I was thinkin' I just might not think right and just stick my hand in there and grab some of that money before I knew it. I'd go for the paper ones, because you can crunch 'em up and hide 'em in your palm easy. But watch out there, Buster. I mean, Mom likes a clean plate at supper, but the clean collection plate stuff is going way too far! Have to get those Heath bars out of my head right now! That money all has to go to the missionaries!

But I really began to think a lot about me stealing and hiding things too much. I'm just not sure about it. I mean, I'm thinking about that hymn again, "Steal away to Jesus." I mean, you're really not supposed to do that. Can you imagine stealing for Jesus! He probably doesn't need a whole lot of stuff anyhow. In the books he's just wearing little cloths, doesn't shave, and goes barefoot and stuff. He doesn't need a lot of dimes.

But at least I didn't dream about those three bucks for that muskrat pelt anymore. But I did worry that Amish man would find me sooner or later. The Amish always get their man! Just like Sky King, that Mountie out West! And I just hope that Doc Edmonds, the county health commissioner, who lines us boys all up against the wall and gives us health exams every year at school, will check me out and find a big fat hernia in me. Then I can stay out of school for the whole year! I don't know if girls ever get hernias or not, but the county school nurse always took them off somewhere secret, and they always came back, giggling away. Now I know you sure don't giggle getting checked for hernias. It's not funny! It hurts, getting that big finger stuck up you know what. Ouch! Boy! Doc's got sharp nails! Next year I'm bringing him my nail clippers. But these silly girls just kept giggling and talking away about something coming every monthly. That nurse probably has sharp nails, too. I guess that nurse is going to be coming every month or, like they say, monthly, from now on. But I'm sure hoping for Doc's hernia check only just once a year. And that's way too much right there! Makes you sweat and pass out! I'll just check my own self, thank you!

But the best part I liked was when the county school nurse helped us make all that toothpaste out of baking soda and gave it to Jimmie, who only had a mom and a sister and was too poor to buy any store-bought. They lived in an old falling-down shack down by Butternut Road Caves. He never got to brush his teeth at all. We all know he couldn't, but we didn't tell on him. Giving him that toothpaste made us feel really good. Boy! Maybe I'm getting to be a better person after all. I really like poor old Jimmie! And his poor little sister could never swing on the swings like the other girls, because they were too poor to buy her underpants. That's just not fair! She should be able to swing sky-high, and because we are growing up to be really nice boys, we won't even look underneath. That's just how we are now! Thinking of the other person all the time!

Now, we're thinking more about our health! We heard a lot about a girl in the next township, Chesterland, who got polio and died. They said, "She went up yonder." That sounds better wherever that is. Gosh! That girl's like my sister Sue. Not some old, wrinkled-up man like Grandpa T. I never liked that "died" word ever since my little Easter chick I called Purple Peep only lived three days, because Dad said they dyed him purple too much. That "dye" word just makes me sad! I was sadder about Purple Peep dying than I was about Grandpa T, because I only knew Grandpa T for one day. I took care of Purple Peep by giving him eyedropper drops of water and patting his little head all day for three days. I loved Purple Peep! He was my first thing alive that died. He tried, but he just couldn't make it!

And there was another boy who got polio, and his leg got shorter. Nobody better ever call him Shorty, or they got Brooster and me to beat him up and worry about! And in the newspaper you see pictures of lots of kids in iron lungs that do all the breaths for them. I got the fever and Mom and Dad didn't sleep all night. That must have gotten my mom and dad really scared, because I remember Doc actually came out to our house and gave Sue and me gamma gobulin shots. Boy! Those shots hurt us bad! But Mom and Dad were just so happy about that. They both had the biggest smiles on their faces. They just thanked Doc again and again. Boy! I sure didn't! That Doc sure knows how to hurt a kid! Can't figure those moms and dads out sometimes! What's the matter with them!

But because we're on a farm now, they don't stick you under a blanket with the Vicks Vaporizer when you get all stuffed up. That's because on a farm, you just don't get sick like city kids do. Mom says the air's a lot better out here. Sometimes in the spring, it smells everywhere like fresh manure, but it's still the very best air out here in the country. That fresh manure air smell up your nose is actually really good for you. So, stay healthy! And again, you can tell by smelling that air if the cows are eating fresh alfalfa or Timothy hay. Both kinds are good for you! And to stay even more healthy, I'm sure all that castor oil we get sure helps, too. Mom says, "It keeps you all cleaned out." Of course, we still get all cleaned, taking those hot soapy baths every Saturday night, getting ready for church. We're so healthy it hurts!

But talking about being healthy here, you can still get a lot of nasty cuts and gashes on a farm. Wouldn't you know it, I got one trying to sharpen a scythe going the wrong way once. Doggone it, going the wrong way again! But that's how you learn! You have to make one mistake every now and then. I got another gash on my wrist going over the bank for a foul ball and lots more than that. Every single gash, Dr. Hayashi over in Chesterland would stitch me right up like a zipper. He was from Hawaii and fought in the United States Air Force with other American Japanese in the war. Then he married an American nurse in the war. Dad says he was a really brave flier. He made sure we won the war and was a real hero! Anyhow, every time he stitched me up, Dad would say, "Now, how much do I owe you for Tommy?" And he'd say, "Tree dolla! Tommy brave boy! No cry!" Gosh! Dr. Hayashi really knew how to make you feel good. He could say things without fooling around. Not like old Doc.

With my arithmetic, I figured he got about twenty-four dollars for all the stitches he sewed in me all those years. Five more and he could buy that Sears boat I wanted. I have lots of stitches! More than any other kid I know of! Proud of every single one of 'em! I like to count them all out loud in front of all the other kids, one by one. And it's not like trying to remember those boring Bible books and verses. Somehow, I can remember every single stitch I ever got. One was like a half-moon on my wrist and another like a bullet hole in my knee. Some looked like different animals, too. I just have a lot better memory for that kind of thing!

**Looks like my same shirt again. Check out the
stitches wrapped up on my left wrist.**

Well! This is the honest Truth! Now I'm getting older and can stay up really late for Christmas Eve service like all the other grown-ups. Now, everybody sits here like exactly the same big group of people—from the grades all the way to old wrinkled people. All us people are getting older and a lot more alike now. No little squirts around. I think I'm getting a lot more religious, too. And getting ready for church, I remember Mom always says, "Don't forget to take your shoe trees out of your shoes!" That's that funny tree thing again.

Christmas Eve, Mom makes us a real fancy dinner of meatloaf or something really good, and we do all that hanging stockings stuff, letters to Santa, cookies and milk, and "The Night Before Christmas" for my little sister Kathy. Mom and Dad, you big trickers! My baby sister Mary Beth is too tiny to know what's going on, so they can't fool her, just Kathy with the big blue eyes! Mary Beth just poops and smells really good. That makes her extra cuddly. Funny how the old ladies love to touch her all the time. Boy! She giggles and grabs everything, too. All my sisters go through that! Kathy gets to pull open the last little window on the advent calendar to see what picture's behind it. I already knew because I had already pulled 'em all open and peeked behind 'em every day and closed them up tight again for twenty-five days. Nobody knows that, though. So, hey! Blame it on the baby!

Anyhow, we get to open just one package, usually some shirt or book or something like that. Nothing really fun or very exciting—Mom's rule again! But I really get excited about going to Christmas Eve service at midnight with all us grown-ups. The church always has live candles all around and no electric lights at all. It's usually snowing, too. We all get a little white wax candle to hold during the service, so we can light it afterward and find our way back home in the dark. I love those candles and the Christmas carols, but I still get a little bored during the sermon part. I don't hear a word the preacher says, and our church in Fowlers Mills isn't a Holy Roller church where you can get up and shout and move around a lot like the one I heard they have in Chardon. Maybe I could go there. Sounds a lot more fun! It's probably my kind of church. So here, I just gotta sit real still in this pew. Peewww! That's the funniest word I ever heard of, but it sounds good for that thing!

The preacher shouts real loud, "He's coming! He's coming tonight!" Gosh! I thought he was talking about Santa Claus, even though I know that Santa trick. Sue says, "You dummy! He's talking about the baby Jesus!" Well, the baby Jesus isn't coming down any chimney with any sled and presents at our house, I'm telling you. We don't have a chimney, so that won't be keeping me up all night.

Then to really feel Christmassy, I started rubbing this candle between my hands, and the wax must've melted or something, because after a while, it got really soft and kind of drooped over my hand. Looked pretty silly! And our whole family started laughing when they saw that. The whole pew shook! That's all they were good for anyhow. Well! That was a real laugher, and a lot of shakin' was going on. Christmas is great! And you know, I think the preacher made the sermon really short that Christmas Eve because of that. I think all those really serious people in the front pews were probably pretty happy about that short one, too!

Now, lots of people are really serious about church. Gladys sings "How Great Thou Art" and "Just a Closer Walk with Thee" so loudly, I think she's going to pass out. But I know she is so serious and full of joy singing every word. My favorite is "Little Brown Church in the Vale," whatever that is. But I love it and can remember the low part best: "Oh, come, come, come, come; come to the church by the wildwood, oh, come to the church in the vale." That's the part I sing as loud as I can, no matter who hears me. It makes me want to jump up, shout, and march around. I can't wait for that "Mighty Fortress Is Our God," too. That's one you can really roar out and make the pulpit shake. Makes you want to march right on out of that church door. Now, that's those actions speaking louder than words right there! I also liked my sister's song about in the garden she sang like an alto on the Cleveland radio once. "He walks with me, and he talks with me, and he tells me I am his own." Boy! They could make harmony! Cathy was soprano like me. Well! I never hear him talking to me at all. That's the Truth! And I'm not sure what I'd even say back to him. I don't know him that well yet and don't think I'm only his own!

Mrs. Rook was my favorite though. And she showed all over she was the best Christian ever! She'd get so excited! She would move and shake her big bottom all around that skinny little piano bench and play that piano so fast and loud, I thought she'd fall off or shake her bottom off. Hey people! Don't worry! We can catch her bare-handed! And she's not very skinny, either. If it was a game of who could sing or play the loudest, I think she'd win. She was the best Christian every day, because you all remember what she did, don't you? She made her husband Jim eat that prune pie every morning for breakfast to make him healthy. I haven't talked about breakfast much, but all we ever got from Mom was this dry, gaggy cereal and a fried egg once a week for protein. Mom can crack an egg open without breaking it. I don't see how. But I don't think

I was doing very well with this church thing, because I loved to look at all the people in a funny way. And all I could think about was funny things happening here. And I'm not sure you get to heaven that way anyhow. So what! I'm not going there anyhow!

Now, I've told you about a lot of stuff like animals dying and all that, but I'm going to tell you about a real person dying. My grandpa! I mean, we all do it. I've already told all of you people a little bit about him, so you really don't have to know a lot more. And I get pretty sad and teary eyed now when I talk about him, so this will be really short before I get that way again. Boy! Do I ever miss him! You probably do, too! It's hard to know if I miss him or Millie the most. But it's Grandpa the most!

That's my funny grandpa. You can tell he was a good eater. He jumps right out of his chair for food.

It's funny! He was my grandpa, but when I was with him, it was like he was like my age. Like Bruce, Jackie, Eddie and Dickie, Grandpa and I were like kids together, too! He taught me all the good stuff, like how to yodel, pinch your nose, talk funny, and take a pee on the side of the road if you can't hold it when you're driving. Grandpa could make great bird noises, but I couldn't because I had a big space in my teeth. I worked really extra hard on whistling. We'd practice driving his car, and he'd ask me all sorts of funny stuff. Like when you draw something. Do you see what you're trying to draw already on the paper, or does it just come out of your head? I have no idea! But we'd giggle a lot and stuff and pretend to be lots of different funny people. He was the funniest guy and like the best friend I ever had.

Now, here it comes! Grandpa came to visit us one day but lay down on the couch sleeping most of the day. Usually he liked to scythe, burn brush, and work around our farm. But Bruce was over, and we guys were just running around doing lots of dumb stuff, not real serious like we usually are. Well! We walked past Grandpa on the couch, and I met him to Bruce, saying, "This is my funny grandpa!" Grandpa had the biggest smile for that, and that's the very last time I ever saw Grandpa. Mom said Grandpa drove himself off to St. Luke's Hospital where Kathy was born and knew he was going to die because he had a bad heart. He never even pushed the button for the nurse to help. He just didn't want to live with his bad heart anymore. He didn't even telephone me! I know he was sad when we had to leave his house after the war. Grandpa didn't like saying good-bye. That's Grandpa for you! Grandpa and I always wanted to do everything our own selves! We didn't ask for any help. Grandpa didn't like saying good-bye now because we already did that once after the war. And even though we got Dad home, that was kind of sad saying good-bye to Grandpa! And I never forgave myself for not spending that whole day right there beside Grandpa! I could have just been right there with him all day, yodeling together or something instead of doing all that silly stuff with Bruce. I could have tried out some new birdcalls like a double-throated warbler with him.

I still don't know why Grandpa didn't push that doggone button. Heck! They say I push Mom and Dad's all the time! That was the very first grandpa or grandma who ever died, except for some great-grandpas. But they don't live too long anyhow, and don't count as much. I'll never forget Grandpa! And I can't talk about it anymore!

I sat and thought about my funny grandpa a lot. If I was eating apples, I'd pretend like he was there with me, cutting those Rome or Golden Delicious apples into quarters and sticking them on the end of his penknife. Or if I was eating oatmeal, I'd pretend he was right next to me, eating his special oatmeal with sackrin in it. And if I was sickling grass, I'd pretend he was right there, swinging his scythe right beside me and sweating and smiling. And sometimes if I was out alone in the field, I pretended we were yodeling or doing birdcalls together, because he taught me how. I don't think anybody heard me out there, though. I pretended we were together a lot, and I cried a little about him at night in bed when I couldn't get to sleep. But that's kind of private stuff. Boy! I miss Grandpa!

Well now! In all my life I've never seen so much change going on in Fowlers Mills. Someone even put a big road sign up saying, Enter Fowlers Mills, Unincorporated, whatever that means. Nothing's like it's supposed to be! Just not the same! So much was happening around here, you just couldn't keep up with it. It's not going to be much fun around here anymore if this keeps up!

Of course, you know Roberta was gone, and now Grandpa didn't come out anymore. And more people were moving out from Cleveland, like Eddie Spagetti. And I'm not really sure if these kinds of people ever really belonged out here anyhow, although he was a pretty nice guy. It just doesn't seem the same now! We even have a new miller. Tommy's family moved away, and Beverly's dad became the new miller. You remember seeing lots of Beverly in that Congo-Alaska game, don't you? You shouldn't have looked, but we did that kind of bad stuff way back before we became good. Anyhow, her dad did the best corn grinding and didn't even have to use the waterwheel. He just turned that electric switch on. Can you imagine all that new stuff? But that's a lot quieter for all us older people now! Don't want to get deaf. Why not just get rid of the mill pond, millrace and mill shoot, for goodness' sakes? Who needs 'em now? Everything's getting fancier. Some people are just born to live in the country, and some just aren't. They can try and pretend a lot, but that's not who they really are! Things were really changing so much now, except for Bruce, and he always stayed exactly the same. He never changed except for that squeaky voice and those funny hairs he was growing down below.

And can you believe this? One morning Mrs. Zepp told the whole fifth and sixth grade we were going to have a new boy from Germany in our class. Can you believe it? All the way from the other side of the world in Germany. They called them DPs or displaced persons, because they didn't have a house after the war. So the next day, Detlef comes to school all dressed up in a white shirt and leather shorts and leather shoes and suspenders. I've never seen anybody dress like that before. Now me! I like unfancy clothes and things like my old smelly tennis shoes. Some of us made fun of him, but the next day he wore long pants, dungarees just like us, so he's pretty American now, like one of us. And I started changing my socks more like every four days now.

Sixth grade boys all dressed up to go to an Indians ballgame. No Bruce there because he's behind the camera, but from the left there's Dick, Eddie, Jack, little fifth grade Dickie, big Billy in jr. high, me and Detlef on the right.

Detlef was going to live in a little house behind Mr. and Mrs. Summers up off Auburn Road in Munson Township. I had Detlef over to my house to play, and he taught me lots of things they do in Germany, like hiking and things like that and singing a hiking song, which I didn't know the words of. They were different words I never heard before. Heck! I never even hiked before! I mean, I ran all over the pastures and through the woods, but that's not like hiking when you actually go in one direction, walk behind the other guy and just walk along slowly. And you go to one place and not a whole bunch of different ones at the same time. He taught me an important thing about when you have to go to the bathroom. You just go on the side of the road. That's what they do in Europe and Germany! They just do both kinds of things on the side of the road and not behind a tree.

Talking about going to the bathroom, Detlef got mad at me once when we were standing inside the boy's bathroom. He said he had to "go to the bathroom," and I said, "No, you don't! You're already right here inside the bathroom! You don't have to go anywhere!" He didn't know English very well, and that probably wasn't the nicest thing to say. He didn't think that was very funny, though. I felt kind of bad for that, so I never gave him one of those funny nicknames!

I also asked him about General Eisenhower, and he didn't like him at all. Boy! I never heard of anybody not liking Ike before. Everybody was saying, "I like Ike!" I mean, Dad likes Ike, so I guess maybe I do, too. He has a big and pretty smile just like Aunt Jemima. It's funny! Detlef's dad and my dad were fighting really hard against each other in the war, and now Detlef and I were friends. Funny how things turn out! You just can't tell whatever's going to happen any more!

Once when I went to play at Detlef's, his father was really quiet and went off to another room. Of course, his dad couldn't speak English, and he seemed a little shy, like me. Detlef's dad had been a soldier in the army in Germany, and he had to ride a bike to work over here before the sun came up, so nobody would see him. I guess nobody but Mr. Summers wanted to be his friend. That's funny, because now the war is all over. That's the very first thing I ever told you in the beginning! And I thought you got the idea really well back then!

It wasn't supposed to, but everything else around here was getting different, too. The Byler twins and Yoders moved out. I think they wanted to be more Amish. I don't blame 'em at all. They probably told their moms and dads they just wanted to work in the barn harder, not go to school, and have more fun. And they can quit school way before we can. Those lucky bums! I didn't even know who was going to be in our school or not anymore. I wish all of us could just be our same old class again, because I really knew what everybody was like back then. Sometimes Bruce and I would even plan to wear the same shirt on the same day because we were so much the same. But no hairs down below for me yet! Don't worry. We'll keep checking!

But things are changing quite a bit. I did start to get a couple hairs under my arms, and Bruce started to smell a little funny, too, like he needed perfume or pine needles or some mint to smell better, or something. I guess nothing is the same anymore! And like I said, I wasn't wearing the same old socks all week anymore. I remember old Pinky saying, "Enjoy your boyhood" before he went away, and they flew the school flag at half-mast. I wasn't sure what that boyhood thing was. I had never heard *boyhood* before, but I'm trying harder anyhow. So I better get busy again! Like the TV show says, *Life Begins at Eighty*, but I can't wait that long! I'm getting there too fast already!

But this is pretty weird! One night, feeding Nellie, I was lonely, with just one little goatie and me. My life wasn't getting too good, and I got sad a lot more! And this is the weird part! I got this idea in the back of my mind of getting my legs cut off on a train track, kind of like Uncle Hickie sawing his finger off. I was thinking people would really feel sorry for me then! I never did that, by the way! And I'm not thinking that way anymore. But I wanted to show people how tough and how much fight I had with only one leg and being a real hero. I was gonna cut only one off. Not two! And then everybody would know all about me and really like me a lot. They'd think I was really a big hero! They would all say, "Look at that Tommy! Can you believe it? He's really something! Wow! He's fighting like a one-claw crawfish stuck in a pail!" Boy! That really sounds pretty cuckoo! Boy! You know, you really start thinking some strange stuff like that when you have too much time on your hands. You really shouldn't try to be somebody you're not! That's just going too far! Mom says, "Just be happy the way God made you!" Well! I'm just not so sure he did the greatest job on some of us kids. Like Mrs. Zepp says, "There's room for improvement!" Mom also says, "Idle hands make a workshop" or something like that, so I'd better get really busy again, because time is just flying by! Not much of it left anymore!

———◆———

I'm up here thinking again. With so much going on, I can't keep up with it. I'm thinking blue about Grandpa again. Too much dying is going on! It really happens, so get used to it like me. Gotta get thinking life's fun and it's all good! You really gotta know what all the other guys are thinking, too. Bruce and I know all about talking to each other and sending messages, but I don't know about anybody else. There are lots of tricks people play out there, so you have to think fast. Use your wits! I mean, look at that Santa Claus thing. You can't trust 'em unless it's Bruce or Mrs. Zepp. She speaks her mind like Mom, so you know what's what. You don't have to guess with them, and that saves you a lot of time.

You know, it wasn't really nice of me to make so much fun of Eddie. He knows some things I don't, like civil war hats and city stuff. I was thinking going to church and talking religion stuff makes you better, but I think the best part of that is not what you sing or pray. It's about eating and seeing all those people at church suppers that are good for you. I mean, you really can't believe all those church words you hear or read. Just think about poor old Adam and Eve. Boy! Nothing's the same anymore. I mean, Bruce getting those new hairs and stuff. You know, I really should think more about poor old Jimmy and get him some more toothpaste and clothes. Boy! I'm thinking a whole lot more and have lots more imagination. Can you believe I was going to chop my leg off just to be a real hero? That's really weird! But at least this new friend from Germany who used to hate me likes me now. You never really know who you're going to see or what's going on every day! It's a bunch of surprises!

CHAPTER 13

MOVING ON TO CHARDON JR. HIGH SCHOOL

N ow, up here I'm starting to grow a couple hairs on my chest, too. I know exactly what they are, because I looked at 'em a long time in the bathroom mirror with Mom's looking glass. I was going to pull one out to show the Brooster, but I couldn't find one long enough. But doggone, if he wasn't getting a couple more down below by his ding-dong and some more on his chest, too. But you have to remember, the Brooster's eight months older than me, so don't you go worrying about me! I'm going to be OK! And my arms are starting to smell a little different underneath, too. That's from being around goats too much. Have that special smell like one! They smell a lot more than horses do. I didn't sniff under Bruce's arms, but I know my time will come. But things around here are changing every day! I'm finally out of that stupid children's choir. Thank God! I can't sing that high anymore anyhow, and I don't feel like sitting right up front anymore, especially with all those creepy old people staring at me with their hands all folded up and some soupy smiles on their faces. That's just not my cup of tea, as Grandma says. I'm tired of singing like a girl!

Years are moving on, and that means I'd really better get going and at least start collecting some of my old toys and things from the barn for a museum for whenever I get famous. Hey! But none of those dirty pictures now! You know better than that! And we're saving those anyhow. May need 'em later! I can get my old pencil box, if I can find it again, and an old toothbrush that I've really used and touched my teeth on for that museum. There are lots of things. Heck! Look at Bob Feller! He was more than just a fastball pitcher. I bet he'll have all kinds of things in his museum. He was a farmer out west in Iowa, so you can do lots of different farm and baseball things all at the same time. Don't have to be just one way! There are lots of things out there for people to see what you're like!

Maybe I was thinking too much about when I get grown and go way up the grades to Chardon Junior High School up on the square. I was just thinking about all those new kids and how it was going to be for me and Bruster and the other kids in my class. I mean, I was getting really nervous about that and had to get my life together before it's too late. I mean, Munson Township was mostly farms, and Chardon's a lot different. It has the courthouse on the square and the county jail right there on Main Street over the sheriff's office where a prisoner can peek right out of the window and wave. Sometimes you know exactly who it is. He might even ask you for a piece of candy because I think they only get bread and water up there. And that's why they put bars on the window—so kids don't pass 'em up candy. And those bars don't let 'em get any good look at the parades on Main Street. But it's probably better than being stuck behind some school desk. At least you can get up and walk around up there and look out the window.

And there are lots of other stores on Main Street, like Chapmans Shoes where you can see your toe bones all lighted up green and wiggling in some flourscope machine there, Cook's Drugs where you get those assburns, and Whettstein's Bakery with fry cakes. And that's also the place, right on the square, where they have the World Famous Chardon Maple Festival every year. They also have the Geauga Movie Theater at the end of Main Street and Isley's ice cream cones for a nickel. Not the store-bought kind. The skyscraper cones are super tall and good if you get butterscotch. But the scooper guy with ice cream dripping down his elbow and a dirty white hat on was kind of creepy and looked at the girls all funny like. And The Greek's place on the other corner has a popcorn machine in the window with lots of buttery popcorn and a big calico cat always walking on top of it. And you can get all the popcorn you want there for a nickel. That cat guards the popcorn, so you don't steal it. You've got to watch those little kids! That cat lies there right on top of that popcorn and rolls around in it a little, too. Boy! It smells a little funnier than what you pop at home. Now, if you're a grown-up, big man, The Greek pours you a little glass of something smelly to wash it down. But it's the only place you can get any any kind of meal on Main Street.

Chardon Square Main Street with some stores and the sheriff's house and part of the jail on the left.

That's the great Chardon marching parade. You sure won't see me in there with no Cupie doll.

And since Grandpa can't cut my hair anymore, I go to a real barbershop now with a pool hall behind it. If you're a kid you can't go inside, because they're afraid you might get hit in the head with a hard 8-ball. Then you won't need any hair cut off at all. But they didn't know there's no ball I can't catch, and I have a Rawlings glove. You can just hear the balls knocking around back there while they stick you out front in that high chair and tell you not to move. That way everybody walking by can wave and smile at you. I feel like a dope! I just sit real still looking at those greasy old Vitalis bottles in the glass case. I'd rather use Brylcreem myself! "Just a little dab'll do ya!" I just let old Leduc clip away and gab on about Wallie fishing up in Canada. Boy, he has a lot of fish stories!

Now, Chardon is a whole lot bigger than Fowlers Mills, and the people all walk up and down, coming and going a whole lot faster right walking uptown on Main Street and all that. They also have these iron rings to tie up horses, but that would have killed poor old Penny right there. She wasn't one to stand still. She, the beautiful strawberry roan, might be still alive if she could of. Those Amish horses were a whole lot better at standing still and never moved. But boy, could they ever race up and down those dirt roads! Wow!

You're not going to believe this, but the Saturday matinee was only nine cents for us kids. I mean, we actually paid money for 'em without sneaking in. Bruster and I saw all the best movies, like the *Mole Men* and some movie with slime oozing all over some big city. Which, by the way, is just one more reason you get out of those cities as fast as you can! But those movies made you not get to sleep at night, so you had to see other kinds of movies, too. The scariest one had some old-fashioned girl named Ophelia floating down the stream on her back in a dress but no bathing suit! I think she was singing and drowning at the same time, and then some other guy was looking really serious and holding this skull up and talking dopey things to it, like saying, "To be or not to be! That is the question!"

Don't know anymore what I want to be anyhow! What a dumb question! I mean, we're already here, right? Can't you see us, dodo? Where did that guy come from anyhow? Who the heck thinks these dumb things up, because you're already born. And you can't sing and drown at the same time anyhow. Silly girl! Try it! That's spooky! Don't tell any one, but I wet the bed really big that night, and at my age that's horrible. It was like I was dreaming I was in that stream, floating, too. Water was all around me. And that Pip guy in *Great Expectations* scared the pee right out of me, too. And then that Hamlet guy says, "To thine own self be true!" What's he thinking? That I'm going to lie to myself or somethin'? Come on! They need to flunk that guy! Don't think you should lie, but it doesn't mean you can't fib a little if you want to. I mean, it's a free world now! That's what Dad fought for!

The movies we like most are real rib-ticklers like *Laurel and Hardy* and Dean Martin and Jerry Lewis and all the cartoons. The kids all scream when those come on! Boy! You can split your sides on those! They're a lot funnier movies than the *The Fighting Sullivans*, about five brothers who all died in the war when their navy ship sunk. Now, that war wasn't much of a fun thing for them! Their mom really cried in that one. And every now and then, they have some movie about some famous man like I'm going to be, like Glenn Miller, Eddie Cantor, Lou Gehrig, Davy Crockett, Babe Ruth, or Jackie Robinson. Jackie Robinson was actually himself in his very own movie all about himself. That's the same thing I'm going to do, too. Be myself! Don't want anybody else being me! They can't do it as well. And I don't want to sit in the back of the bus like Jackie and his wife had to. Doesn't make any sense! If all the kids have to sit in some bumpy back seat, they'd be better off walking to school up the hill both ways like me. I'll show 'em how.

Those movies were good, but you know, they just pushed us a lot harder to hurry up and get our life going faster. Now we gotta get in a hurry to collect more museum things if we were ever going to get a movie made about the Bruster and me. And I'll tell you something. You can learn a lot more at a nine-cent matinee then you can sitting around in school. Sometimes just playin' around is the way you learn stuff. They even had newsreels about a man flying to the moon sometime. Yaahh, right! Come on! Can you believe that stuff?

See, here's something to know. *The Glenn Miller Story* shows you can get killed if you leave home and go on an airplane somewhere to play some music, and *The Babe Ruth Story* tells you if you eat too much ice cream and pie and don't take life seriously, you can die from cancer. The cowboy and Indian movies about Tom Mix, Hoot Gibson, Lash Larew, and Johnny Mack Brown make you worry a whole lot less. In those movies, you just ride horses really fast in circles all day and run around the hills chasing each other and end up back in the same place looking around for each other again. The cowboys always win except for good old Geronimo. Man, that Apache could really get 'em. He could really fight tough, and we almost stood up and cheered, except old Mr. Movie Meanie would shut the movie off if we dared to.

Of course, the best part is before the show—before that newsreel starts. You have to buy your Ju-Ju's and box of real, red Goober Peas first. Boy, they're tasty! But the best part is they make you pee red, which is pretty cool. They have a hard, red, shiny candy outside and a peanut inside. Crunch! Those are hard to share, but I give Bruce a couple. But you know what? He never pees red. We always look around to see who does. If you're a taller boy, you can look over and get a better look. You know, we had all these different names like tinkle, splash, number one, and all that. We don't use "wee-wee" much any more. That's for the little kids who don't know all these big guy names! But for coming out that other end, names are a lot harder to think up!

Anyhow, Bruster likes Ju-Ju's the best. Some kids like little choco-late circles with little white things on top called Pariells, like you see in your grandma's house in those pretty little glass candy bowls in the living room that break if you touch 'em. It's more of an old people and a girl's kind of candy. If you peek really closely at all the boys in the boys' bathroom, you can see who really likes Goober Peas the best. I don't know for sure, but with all those white things on top of the girls' candy, they probably just pee white. Except we aren't allowed in the girls' bath-room to know for sure! But that's enough toilet talk!

But here's something you might want to know. This mean old Mr. Brinkman would stop that movie right in the middle, wind and groan it right down, put the lights on, even if right in the middle of *Davy Crockett* or *Song of the South*, stand right up out in front of the stage, and talk to us like we're just little kids. He'd be telling us he was going to stop that movie right there and send us all right home if we didn't shut up and be quiet and quit throwing Ju-Ju's and Goobers all around the movie house! Now, who in the world does he think he's talking to?

That same old cranky Mr. Brinkman has these big wire glasses sit-ting on his bumpy old nose and his long white hair all combed up. He always dresses up really fancy in that same old gray suit. He's the only man who wears a suit on Main Street. He doesn't even seem to know that all us kids had worked so very hard all week long. Fingers to the bone! He ought to know, after all, that we really need a little bit of rest and need to have a little fun once in a while. All work and no play is just not smart when you're a kid! And don't forget this. All work and no play makes Jack a dull boy! Well, old Jackie sure ain't dull. We sure go for Jackie and really like that guy, but he doesn't get all his work done, either. So maybe Mr. Brinkman's right, after all!

When those lights go back on, you can turn around and see all the bigger kids in the back row, all sitting on top of each other, some kissing and dumb stuff like that. Really disgusting! One eighth-grade guy told us that they just put a big clock up behind their seats on the back wall especially just for them. The only reason for it is so you can ask your girlfriend, "Girlfriend! What time is it?" And, of course, you have to keep your arm on the back of her chair on her shoulder. That's the way you watch the movie! Helps keep her from flying out of her seat if she gets scared. And that's why sometimes they both sit on top of each other in exactly the same seat. You know girls! Guys really help a lot like that!

Now, the guys can't turn around in their seats themselves. I mean, that's a good thing to know. And girls are a lot better at keeping track of time than us boys. We boys just work too hard! We don't care about whatever time it is and don't keep our mind on it. We almost always get home late for supper. We just work away all day! And girls just don't seem to mind giving us guys the time of day at all, even every few minutes or so. They don't even squint their eyes. They just turn right around in their seats and look straight back behind them at the clock.

And when a girl turns around, her bosom goes smack in your hand on the back of her chair. And which hand it is depends on which side you're sittin' on and if you're a righty or a leftie. You can't hang on to both of 'em at the same time. Hey! Hold on there, guy! That's going too far!

Just so you'll know, we actually started calling 'em tits. It's lots easier to say! Short for teats! And now you can remember that farm word again, can't you? I'm not doing things like that, but man, with this new clock thing, junior high's going to be a blast! This thing looks a whole lot more fun than that dumb Congo-Alaska game, and no cheatin' here, either! You have to play by the rules! You don't even have to lie about how many fingers you got up behind your back anymore. A lot more honest, don't you think? And the girls never seem to mind telling you the time of day at all. They kind of like it! They seem so grown-up! I'm sure they're going to have lots of clocks in junior high. Wow! And Billy said one kid even puts a mirror on his shoe for when the girls walk by! That's strange!

You know what? Nobody ever got thrown out of the movies. They always went back on, and we'd all giggle about old Mr. Brinkman in the dark. We figured he could never throw us out because our moms and dads wouldn't be outside there to pick us up. We'd all be standing outside just throwing candy and popcorn around all alone in the cold waitin' for a ride. I mean, you'd think he'd know Bruce and I don't drive to the movie the whole five miles in his McCormick Farmall Cub Tractor yet. Heck! I'm beginning to think we're never going to make it to that Buckeye Health Society in Akron. And I don't want Bruster to lose his membership! We worked hard to get it for him!

Now, old Bruster was getting old fast! I know the old ticket lady Mrs. Brinkman couldn't see any fuzz on his face or see any hairs down below, but she was the ticket seller and was as cranky as Mr. Brinkman. I don't know if they ever had any kids or not, but being cranky must have run in their family. Or maybe they should have taken some nice walks together up on Main Street on the square instead of sitting in that old, stuffy movie house all day long. You take just one walk up there, and you'll know everybody else walking up and down on Main Street!

But one time that old, white-haired, prune-face with little wire glasses stuck on her nose made Bruce call up his mom to get him his birth certificate, so he could get in for only nine cents. That's important because all we had was fifteen cents. One nickel for candy and nine cents for the movie, which meant only one penny left over. The only thing you can get with a penny is two fishing hooks, or one penny candy, or save up five times to get an extra candy bar if you can wait that long. Remember! They weren't paying us much for all our hard work back then! We were going to have to get 'em to up that pay!

But again with that arithmetic figuring I do well, you could see old Bruster was really in trouble here. But I wasn't leaving a good friend like Bruce all alone. He was my Apache blood brother, you know. So we waited a long time, but we finally got in. I think Mrs. Brinkman finally called his mother. And you know Bruce doesn't lie! That's the one thing that he didn't learn from me. Bruce was honest, and that's exactly what I told old lady Brinkman. But she didn't want to listen to me, because there I was, telling the honest whole Truth again! She just wanted to get that extra six cents, so she could get some candy of her own and gobble it up. That's robbery! Heck! I'll find the money somehow and just give it to her. And I'm really good at sharing! Heck! Take six big pop bottles from behind Reynolds Store, and that would do it right there. Money's something I know how to share. Been at it for a time! I'll just give it all to that old prune ticket taker. Grandpa Reynolds inside Reynolds Store won't know a thing about it. He's all for redeeming stuff! I was really beginning to like doing good and sharing lots of things more and not being so selfish. I really was becoming a better person!

Bruce and I are getting to know a whole lot more about Chardon now. It's a big place! It has the courthouse and all those stores on Main Street, plus Chardon Junior High and all the upper grades and basketball and football games on Friday night. Friday night basketball games up in Chardon High School gym are really exciting. Everyone in the town is there! Thousands and thousands of 'em are cheering away! We grade-schoolers get to sit up on the stage where everyone can get a good look at us. And they have lots of cheerleaders who do cartwheels and show their unders. They always see who can do the biggest one and show the most to get the biggest cheer. The boys cheer the most for that. Boy! Some can do two at a time! Worth staying in your seat and holding off on the popcorn and candy just to see 'em and cheer 'em on. I know someday soon these cheerleaders are going to be yelling, "Tommy, Tommy, he's our man! If he can't do it, nobody can!" They'll probably get that right. And, of course, there's lots of candy for sale! Don't miss it! Then they also have this real basketball game in between that you can watch between going to the bathroom and the refreshment stand.

One time it got pretty exciting when they picked a bunch of us little shrimp to shoot some baskets at half time, because all we have at home is this stupid bushel basket nailed up on our barn door with the bottom kicked out. Well! Some clumsy kid stepped on my foot, so I got a foul shot. That's when they stop the game, so all the players can rest up, and everyone gets really quiet and stares right at you. You get a little nervous, and you wish those girls would stop jumping around and showing their unders, so you can look at the basket better. I mean, give a guy a break here!

So I stood on the foul line and tried to keep my eyes on that basket way up there. And I crossed myself, like lots of players do. That's the best way to make those foul shots go in. Well, Billy, an eighth-grader in junior high, shouts really loudly, "You dummy! That's only for Catholics!" Boy! Do I feel stupid! How was I supposed to know? And I didn't even hit the rim. I missed everything! Boy! Was I embarrassed! Maybe I should go to confessional with Bruce and stay in that closet box longer and not go running out so fast thinking I'm so good. And I was thinking with all my church going, I knew everything about church things. But I guess I'm not so smart after all. Besides that, I sure have a lot more to learn about this basketball stuff!

Boy, though! Chardon had everything! This was a lot more serious, busy, and bigger place. It wasn't a big city like Cleveland, but Dad said it had a stoplight and three thousand people in it, and that's a lot right there. They were not all in school, though. Some did other things. I mean, some made cakes, sold shirts, pumped gas, and all that stuff. Then when that siren over the library went off, all the store people and gas-station men came running out of Chapman's and Cook's and all those places with their helmets. They would run you over to get to that firehouse! Except the fire chief, and he was too fat to run, anyhow. The firetruck had to pick him up on the way out and help him into the truck out in front of Hummel's Drygoods. Boy! Those old-fashioned fire bells were lots better; they didn't make you deaf! And I almost forgot. You never ever saw those old Geauga Theater prune faces running off to the firehouse, either! Too busy counting money!

But with everything going on up there in Chardon, you just knew just being a kid was almost over! Things were going to count a lot more up there! And my sister Sue says the teachers really make you work hard up there and give you lots of homework. Can you believe it? Never heard that one before! I already have enough of that homework stuff here at my own home, like feeding my goats, burying the garbage, cleaning the stalls, shoveling the coal, making my bed, having to take care of my cute and pesty little sisters, and waxing the floors! So what's all this homework stuff about? Who needs it anyhow! Who made that silly stuff up anyhow? We had plenty of homework to do right here at home! Anyhow, I'm saving all my muscles for farm work, not hauling around schoolbooks like bales of hay. I mean, like that name school work is why you go to school, for gosh sakes! You can't stay at home for that. You do it right there! What do they think we are? Stupid?

Time's getting short, and you really do need more time as a kid to watch stuff on our new Philco 15-incher TV. I mean, you have to watch the best shows like *Howdy Doody*, *Uncle Jake's House*, the *Army-McCarthy Hearings*, and really good stuff like that. And don't forget the *Gillette Friday Night Fights* with the Gillette girl with those long legs walking around ringside in her bathing suit, carrying the numbers sign for all the boxing rounds over her head. That's if you can keep your eyes open that late. It gets late, but of course you wouldn't want to miss Jersey Joe, Charles Ezzard or Ezzard Charles, Sugar Ray, and Rocky. They could really deck 'em with a left hook. And that song, "To Look Sharp, Every Time You Shave! To Feel Sharp." Don't get me going on that one! I could sing it all night. I don't shave yet, but I sure felt sharp! Of course after that, there's just this funny TV screen with nothing to see but a cross and a bunch of lines and buzzing on it. That means there's no more TV to see tonight!

I'm asking you! Who has any time for homework? Where do you fit that stuff in? It just makes my big sister Sue more snarky, so I sure don't see no point in it at all! Maybe they should ask us kids about all this stuff first, instead of just making us do all that crummy schoolwork at home. Maybe the teachers themselves should do more of that crummy homework in their own school room anyhow. After all, they started it. Heck! Spread that stuff around like manure! Get it done right there! Mrs. Zepp never makes us do homework in the fifth and sixth grade. She's so nice and so smart. She knows we're way too busy for that kind of stuff! She knows we got lots of holiday stuff to do.

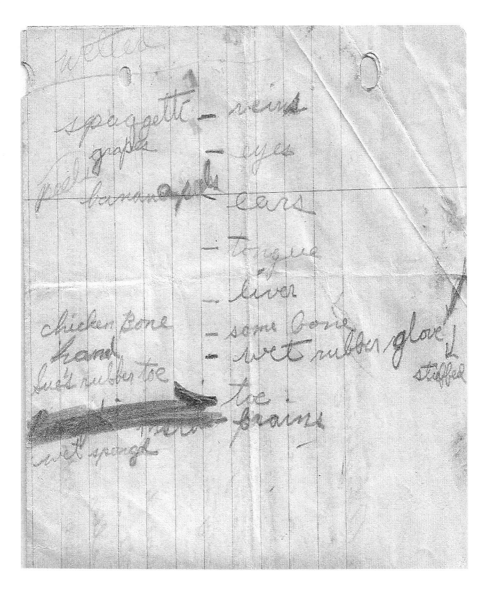

Scary things for Halloween.

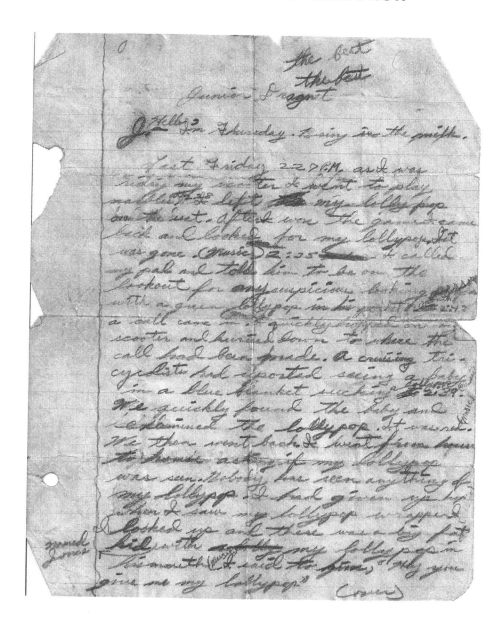

**Junior Dragnet—we spent more time making up
silly stories than doing our schoolwork. Here's
a stupid one, but I can't write it all in.**

Hello, I'm Thursday. Bring in the milk. Last Friday 2:27 PM as I was riding my scooter I went to play marbles. 2:28 I left my lollypop on the seat. After I won the game I came back and looked for my lollypop. It was gone. (Music) 2:35 I called my pal - - - - - A cruising tricyclist had reported seeing a baby in a blue blanket sucking a lollypop. - - - - then I punched him right in the nose and grabbed my lollypop. - - - - (Music) The story you have just heard is true - - - - only the flavors have been changed to protect the lollypop. This has been a STUPID production. Directed by Ed Wingenbach Writen by Tom Thornburgh

Anyhow, Bruce and I did a lot of thinking about all this silly stuff, and we knew it was about time to get really serious in our lives. No more just all fun all the time anymore, and no more stupid mistakes like this one I'm going to tell you about. One time when Bruce and I went up to the Maple Festival, it was the very first time by our own selves. Both of us got fifty cents to spend on the festival. And would you believe it? We spent it all in five minutes. You just can't do that kind of thing!

Some guy with a funny clown hat and long cane and a weighing scale was right on the corner of the square where Mom let us off. He was guessing ages and weights for twenty-five cents a guess. One whole quarter! And Bruce was so excited about winning that plaster of paris, painted bulldog. Since he was eight months older, he went first, of course. Sure enough, that clown guy guessed wrong and missed his age by two years. Bruce got a painted bulldog made of real plaster. Then he missed his weight by a lot. Yep! Another bulldog again! Boy! Was Bruce ever proud, the lucky bum! I was next and got really excited and ready to carry my two bulldogs around with me. Old Bruster and I were both going to be two bulldog boys. Sure enough, he got my weight wrong on the scale, because I was lookin' skinny. But dadgumit, he guessed my age right! Eleven— right on the nose! Well, I'll punch his nose! So all I got was this one stupid plaster Cupid doll with red cheeks. Bruce got the very last bulldog there. Boy! Did I feel like a fool, and I know everyone was looking right at me all the time. All that whole day long, I just had to walk around that stupid Maple Festival with that proud old Brooster the Rooster carrying two bulldogs and me with only one dumb Cupie doll hanging onto my arm.

Everybody looking at me thinks I'm really weird now. All I could do was watch the Rube Band blow their horns all the way to Water Street or smell that sap bubble in that fake Sugar House evaporator and stupid stuff like that. Got tired of hearing the same old thing, "It takes a thousand gallons of sap to make a cup of syrup." Burp! Who the heck cares! I got tired of people oohing and aahing over those delicious maple stirs and yummy pancakes dripping with maple syrup. I'm through eating pancakes anyway! Little Sambo can eat 'em all. And if my hatchet wasn't dull, I'd chop down every doggone maple tree I'd ever see. I'll kick those stupid sap buckets all over and pull those sap spiles right out of the tree! What a sap I am! I don't care if the big peerade ever starts and the Rube Band wagon runs right over me! Then I won't ever have to worry about anybody seeing me again with this dumb Cupie doll anymore.

I've got to get ahold of myself here! I'm going too far here! But I've had it, and this stupid Maple Festival is a waste of time, and my time is running out! Getting short! I didn't have a lot of it anymore! It burned me up when everyone came running up to Bruce and asked him, "Where did you get those cool dogs?" Boy! I felt like saying, "In the trash, you dummies! Why don't you jump in there, too, and pull some out!" It would have made me feel better! And Bruce said, "Nothin' to it! It's easy! That guy just guesses how many pounds and years you are!"

Boy! I felt like washing old Brooster's mouth out. But you've got to remember, he already beat me up once. Now I don't have even one dime to spend! We could have even gotten one maple stir for only ten cents and with those two gone quarters, at least five of 'em. At least I still had arithmetic in my head! Sure wasn't much of a Maple Festival for me that year! Not even a couple hairs of cotton candy. This might be my last one ever!

Boy! Was I angry! I figured out that guy probably knew my age because he already found out Bruce's, and then he asked if Bruce and I were in the same grade. We sure were! What a dummie! It's not fair! I just can't make any more stupid mistakes like that. But at least that guy with the cane didn't make Bruce bring his birth certificate. That guy looked really happy, though—he had a big, fat smile on his face. I could wash that right off, too! But old Brooster and I really stuck together.

Changed the spelling a little here, but same old Brooster! Hard times make you a better man!

Now I'll have to tell you this! I was getting a whole lot more serious with my life. That Maple Festival might have been the biggest change in my life. And I was getting more religiousy, too. Instead of just wanting to be Bob Feller, I thought more about being more like Jesus. I even gave all that money I saved in my Christmas stocking into the collection plate for missionaries in Africa. And I even peaked at Mom's *Guideposts* beside her bed. They taught you how to be humble (that's one of those religious words), and I needed some more of that humble stuff! Old Bruster can stay in that old confessional booth all day, but not me!

I know one of Mom's rules was, "Don't think you're better than anybody else!" But I really was becoming more religious and a lot more important now, too. I looked a lot more like Jesus but had no beard yet—well, a little bit, maybe, but I didn't use any Burma Shave yet. Now, I really had to get a whole lot busier and get all those museum things about me collected up. But you know, I'm forgetting where I hid everything and don't know where it all is. But this is just too much! I could've just hidden everything in the hayloft, but I just didn't want those dirty pictures in that potato chip can getting into that museum. That can be a real problem!

But at least I'm doing better now, not having to make myself touch every single one of those same exact trees in the same exact spot on the same exact way to school anymore. I'm not steppin' on every crack like those city kids do. Thank goodness we don't have any sidewalks! I don't have to sing "Row, Row, Row Your Boat" in my head all the time, too. Now I "can walk by a stone just sittin' there; don't have to kick it through the air; and knock the dusty milkweed off; don't have to gag and sneeze and cough!"

And you can really see, I'm rhyming everything a lot better now, too. Sounds silly, but you have to try lots of stuff. Playin' around's the way you learn stuff. Surprises are good for you, because nothing makes much sense anymore anyhow. I don't care what's going to happen. I won't know anyhow! You have to make a mistake every now and then. I mean, look what I learned from that Cupie doll thing. That Cupie doll's going in the museum, too. I'll name it "My First Mistake!" That's the way you get places! So, for goodness' sake, work on it!

And I can see old Chris Bogaski telling all those runnin' around, shrimpy little kids to put those red geranium pots right on my gravestone, and he'll be saying wonderful things about me and Fowlers Mills where I grew up.

And in the fifth grade I wrote this beautiful poem about my mother. I was really getting more churchy, although I never could stand all those old windy sermons; Bible readings; and long, boring prayers. I'll take the shorties, thank you!

You know something special? My Mom was so surprised when she found this poem. I'll tell you, she almost fell over! I hardly ever saw her cry, but this time she had some big, sad, wet tears in her eyes. So many of 'em! She was giggling, too, and couldn't talk at all. Thank God! Boy! Did she ever hug me tight! That's a lot better than anything she says in those words. Parents try to tell you everything so much! Sometimes they just don't know how to do it! You can tell most of it, or all you need to know anyhow, just by the way they look at you! I mean, just look at me here! I'm getting to talking a lot more about God and stuff, too!

Now I'm going to let you see that poem I wrote for Mom, the one I was telling you about. It's a doozy, ain't it! You can tell it really made Mom feel like a real special person.

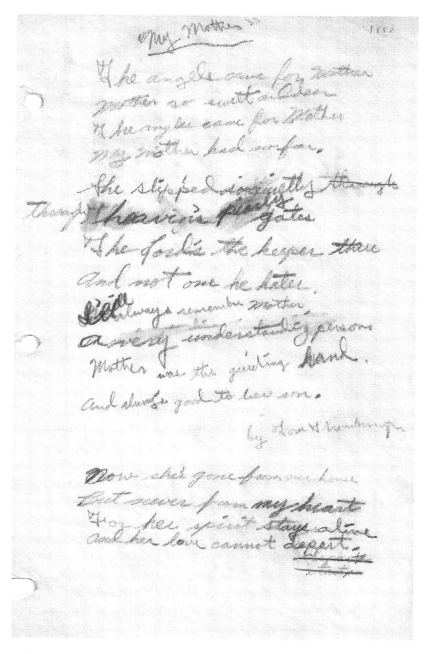

Surprise poem for Mom in fifth grade. Look close because I got the "angels" and "angles" spelling mixed up. Sounds a little soupy now when I read it, but I was thinking lots about Mom.

No Tomfoolery

My Mother   1952

The angels came for Mother
Mother so sweet and dear
The angles came for Mother
My Mother had no fear.

She slipped so quietly
through heaven's piarly gates
The Lord's the keeper there
And not one he hates.

I'll always remember Mother,
A very understanding person
Mother was the guiding hand,
And always good to her son.

Now she's gone from our house
But never from my heart
For her spirit stays alive
And her love cannot depart.
by Tom Thornburgh

Apparently enjoying their job of dishing out refreshments are Mrs. Ed Wingenbach (left), and Mrs. Rex. Thornburgh.

That's Mom, all right! No angels really came from Mom after all. She's the hard-working one! Runs in our family, all right, while other people just stand around and watch.

You can tell I had a little trouble with that "angles" word. I'd get dumped right out of that spelling bee for that!

Well! I've got to finish this thing! That Mom thing really gets to me! And I've told you so much about farming, going to school, farms, wild animals, making babies, and all that stuff you need to know. And now you can just go out and do all that stuff yourself. You don't need any teacher on that!

And I'm getting tired of all this anyhow, and I've told you everything I know. I've got lots of other things to do. And I really am becoming a better boy, or person, really, even though I'm getting a little nervous about it. At least I won't have to join the army after the sixth grade like Tommy S. You know, I think I'm a little different than him. I'm just not breaking Mom's rules as much any more. I'm kind of making up my own rules more now, because Brooster and I still talk a lot about what rules to follow and which ones to just pretend to. We still talk a lot about serious stuff like, does your brain grow as fast as your legs, and stuff like that.

Well! That's it! I've told you all about everything now! All the important stuff, anyway! All the stuff that's ever happened to anybody, including me! And, you know, all this stuff really happened! Cross my heart and hope to die! And if you don't believe me, just ask the Brooster. He knows a lot and always tells the Truth! He knew all about this stuff in the book before I even wrote it and he won't blab it all over the place! And if he does, just ask my mom! Mom isn't here right now, but she'll let you know exactly like it is! That's Mom for you!

So I'm going to slow down a little bit now, because if you try to hurry everything up too much, you can't keep your mind on your work. And I'm getting kind of tired of writing all this stuff anyhow. Boy! I'll never do this thing again! And you've got to be pretty tired of hearing about all this stuff!

If you ever finish this thing up, or are just looking at the pictures, I'll let you read a couple poems I wrote later on. They're doozies, too! And ever since Sue told me how those doggone Chardon teachers make you work so hard, I'm just going to take this here summer off and work really hard on just resting up, because I'm still not a sitting-still kind of guy. I'm a little more like a wild kind of guy. And then we can really all get back to working again when I get up to the seventh grade. Who knows? If you ever pass and get to the seventh grade, too, Bruce and I'll probably see you there! You'll be able to pick old Brooster and me out really easily, because we're the nice ones!

You know something? It's really awful! Just when everybody knows me around here in Fowlers Mills and I get real important, I've got to go meet a whole bunch of new stupid kids again! Just like back in first grade! That's really crappy, Pappy! What a drag! So why don't all of you just take some precious time off now yourselves. Rest up a little bit! Forget about all this stuff and try to relax and have some fun for a change!

Yeah! It's a nice sunny day up here on the hillside. Garden's all gone, and there's grass over Millie's grave now. I'm just thinking again about everything's that happened around here and what moving up to Chardon Jr. High will be like. Fowlers Mills just isn't the same old place anymore. Too many city kids are moving in. What do they think this is, their backyard? The Millers are moving away to get more Amishy after sister Saloma got a little wild and married an English guy. Pinkie's gone, and Grampa Koblaha doesn't fish much. And Grandma Koblaha still hasn't moved at all. Guess she's still alive, but she sure looks dead in the window. They put that new fancy Fowlers Mills road sign I was telling you about up there on Mayfield Road sticking right out that says Unincorporated, whatever that is. They're even talking about putting in a street light down by the mill. Not only sixty-four people around here anymore. With words and signs like that around, might be getting too city-like and time to move on! Another Carol's dad even built a tiny cement-block Hill's Hardware across from Reynolds Store where you can buy fishing hooks and bobbers right there that cost lots more money. Bobbers run you ten cents now! That's real Mayfield Road highway robbery!

I don't see old Grandpa Reynolds much anymore. I don't think his glasses work much for him. Heck! Stealing pop bottles for redemption isn't much fun now, and I'm coming up with a whole bunch of new rules anyhow! You have to follow the rules closely to play basketball for the Chardon Jr. High Hilltoppers. No Erin Brew or Luckie Strikes there, or they throw you off the team. Time to toe the line and get it right! I can't go around making stupid mistakes anymore. It's good to try stuff out, but you gotta get ahead and go up the grades.

It's time to be cool! I can't worry as much. I have to fit in! I can't be shy. No place to hide up there! There are too many folks! You won't see me hiding around some old coatroom unless it's chasin' girls. This Chardon thing isn't so simple anymore, and the whole world's getting bigger now! You can't plan it all out like you want it. You never know what's going to happen. Hey! That's how it goes! You can't figure it all out. Like old Hamlet says, "To be or not to be!" I still don't know where that guy came from, but he sure asks lots of questions! I didn't know anything about Fowlers Mills before, and look how much I know now. I bet thousands of other kids know their towns pretty well, too. We're not the only ones, you know1

Hey! Chardon looks kind of exciting up there. Imagine gambling with that guy guessin' your weight and necking in the movie seats. And imagine hittin' those basketball shots so those cute cheerleaders flip upside down to see their unders. Hey! We're starting to keep score here! I mean, with all those surprises and dares, what's not to like up there! You even get your own football helmet! It's going to be OK! And if you have any doubts or are shy about those new kids, old Bruster and I'll be there for ya! We had to do a lot ourselves, of course, but look at all the help we got along the way! Hey! Cheer up! It isn't all bad! Old Bruster and I will be there and see you next year!

Wee fly that treads on hymnal page
For freedom there, my life I'd wage

While chained I am to wooden pew
To window ledge and back you flew.

I envy you my fearless fly
To buzz the organ loft so high,

And snuggle in the preacher's robe,
And tweak the tenor's left ear lobe.

So dear fly!— While you carry on and roam
I suffer under pulpit drone

But you're a fly and I'm a man;
And both do only what we can.

Here are some of the poems I already told you about.
Here's the one I wrote later on about trying to sit still
in the church pew hearing those boring sermons.

Wee fly that treads on hymnal page
For freedom thus, my life I'd wage
While chained I am to wooden pew
To window ledge and back you flew.
I envy you my fearless fly
To buzz the organ loft so high,
And snuggle in the preacher's robe,
And tweak the tenor's left ear lobe.
So dear fly! — While you carry on and roam
I suffer under pulpit drone
But you're a fly and I'm a man:
We both do only what we can.

It's Skeerd Like Anything

Once when I was in a cave,
I was skeerd out a me wits.
I saw a darnright scary thing,
It just 'bout licked my mitts.

That there had greenish eyes,
And six or seven tails.
It had a great big yeller tongue,
And the claws done look like nails.

Boy, that thing was scary,
It was the scariest thing I see.
It kept coming closer,
And boy ye shoulda seed my knee.

It was just about on top of me,
I was shakin to the bone.
And chills went down from head to toe,
But I done ran for home.

Tom Thornburgh

This poemy thing was really getting going! Mom read too much of that James Whitcomb Riley stuff. Here's one of 'em in the sixth grade. Writing this silly stuff's better than doing workbooks!

I Is Skeered Like Anything

Once when I was in a cave,
I was skeered outa me wits.
I saw a downright scary thing,
It just 'bout licked my mitts.
That there had greenish eyes,
And six or seven tails.
It had a great big yeller tongue,
And the claws done look like nails.
Boy, that thing was scary.
It was the scariest thing I see.
It kept coming closer,
And boy ya shoulda seed my knee.
It was just about on top of me,
I was shakin to the bone.
And chills went down from head to toe,
And I done ran for home.
Tom Thornburgh

CHAPTER 14

THE LAST CHAPTER

Looking back seventy years ago now, it all seems a little like a mixed-up childhood. But it was all serious business for a small kid back then, just as it's supposed to be! It was a kid's world. So let's bring this story home today. The world's grown with millions of little swarms of activity having gone far beyond little old Fowlers Mills. However, for me, much is still centered there. It's as though that little piece of summer has worn itself out, but who of us couldn't use just a little more freed-up time of playful innocence and at least a little more playing, insightful exploring, and trying out this or that? We could all reach back for that uncluttered core of rich simplicity. Sure do miss that!

So when summer faded, where did everybody go? Mom and Dad never really let go of us, but we finally let go of them. We felt we had grown up and out enough to have rearranged all Mom's rules a little bit. Mistakes don't seem so disastrous this time around, and we go on making more. Of course, now we're the judges. Rural-and small-community living may appear simple to some folks looking back to the late '40s and early '50s, but for a kid, it wasn't. It was lots of country freedom for trying everything out long ago, but life was full of weighty decisions and jumping over lots of holes confronting chances, choices and changes. We came to some basic beliefs and a unique sense of things early on, followed by years of mulling over and double thinking. Many of those early grown-ups had their own strenuous, complex lives back then; however, as kids, that didn't light up our Captain Video Decoder Badges.

Out in the country, we strived to be independent and sure felt we were. We got lots of things done on our own without heavy scheduling or overinstruction. And helicopter parenting hadn't even been invented yet! We probably wouldn't have stopped to listen to all the details, anyway. It was quite a strange but ever-present mutation, evolving from childhood to adulthood. And, of course, everyone's way is his own! We probably could have used another one of those pioneer scouts to take us through the tall grass and thickets, but we weren't so much in a following mood back then. Yep! We had the answers! Life seventy years ago looked a long way out there, but now it's fully arrived.

It seems like fewer people around to have to please now. We sure wanted to belong, but we wanted our own spirited individual kid selves, too. What a teeter-totter of ups and downs! Possibly, if we had all been blood brothers, we might have all been more alike and things might have been easier but that would have been pretty monotonous. We're still looking for that unique special sense but feel a little more familiar with ourselves now.

Being famous with our own museum has lost its luster. The only collectible junk I have now is a cardboard box with that goat harness cracking its leather up in the hot attic. We have a number of celebrities out there. I'm not sure if we have enough yet or not. What we really need however is more of those real folks out there to get the real jobs done, like those amazing teachers who made us sit still just long enough to make it through the grades. Schooling was probably worth it! Anyhow, I tend to follow my own set of rules now.

So, let's see! What happened to everybody? Mom was Mom all the way through—never fancy or chatty but always on top of her game. One pearl necklace and a set of earrings for evenings out, and that was it. Taking it all in, she figured things out, keeping it all in balance, and her rules stayed solid. She was a totally committed, diligent, and loving shepherd all the way. Nobody better mess with her rules or her family, or she'd take 'em down with a quick word or that eyeball. One of those Esther looks and you knew she meant it. Made you think really hard, no matter what your age was. She affectionately steered stubborn and playful old Dad, all her kids, then our kids, and their kids all the time, well up into her '90s when we finally thought we were grown-up and sufficiently independent enough to let her go. Dad had saved her a special place right beside him there in West Virginia.

And Dad, with those long and comforting thirty-four-inch arms, helped take care of Chardon High School as principal through many changing years and then the township, the county, or whoever might be standing around. He had many close friends all over the place and was more popular among my high school classmates than I ever was. He always said he came through the golden age of teaching. Dad was born with that special people sense and feeling for others. He knew how to work all those subtleties and nuances, letting others believe they actually came up with the answers. He'd find a way to paddle the guys going nowhere and get them raging mad, storming right uptown to his friendly army and navy recruiter. Then Dad would hop on the phone and let 'em know they had another one coming up. When the boys came back all uniformed to thank him, he'd proudly show them off to all the classrooms, showing the rest of the kids what they had accomplished. I have their thank you letters to Dad to prove it! Dad even got his picture in the *Plain Dealer* holding his paddle titled the Board of Education.

That sixth sense of his always helped folks keep on wondering. It was hard to pin him down. Dad had all the tricks of easing folks up and always pulling for the little guy. His jokes got cornier, but his wit got better all the time. He was always curious and always the dreamer! He'd probably still be artfully carving that Thanksgiving turkey on into next Christmas if he had more time, and the hungry horde didn't cheer and clamor for more.

Dad and Mom kept camping out and dancing those big band sounds up close together, well into their '80s, until Mom sent that sweet old man on his way. But not until he took his puppy out one day on a long, meandering trail walk and plunked down, worn out, into his favorite old campsite easy chair and let go. Mom always said, "Jobs come first before you get to take it easy." Lots of us of all ages and all over miss him now!

Well! You probably already know about Grandpa Wright. You probably read the story. And Grandpa's Baldwin Wallace College student friend Harrison Dillard went on to win both the hurdles in the 1952 Olympics. And his second best friend next to me, Rabbi Abba Hillel Silver with the four names went on to become a strong voice for the creation of the state of Israel. And my West Virginia grandma kept calling us precious and stuffing us full of goodie bites until she quit at 102. She didn't really quit! She just plain stopped! We haven't eaten so well since! My other grandpa and grandma doted on us so much that when we had had enough, we let them go, too. Aunt Nina and Uncle Hickie went back to take care of Grandma's family farm in Tioga, West Virginia. He was very careful all the way and never lost his big finger stump. I took a snapshot of them doing their job while I was hitchhiking down there in the 60's. You probably saw it earlier.

Sister Sue taught high school for a number of years and is still taking care of family and everybody else in the world whether they need it or not. It must be in her blood! And she has yet to find one single person she doesn't like. And number one little sister Kathy still has her strong will and heart of gold. She made a lot of people scamper around in the business world, so you still have to watch her grabbing you with her amazing imagination, surprises, and humor. She's as quick as ever and everyone loves the fun she brings! And my cutest, littlest baby sister of all, Mary Beth, became the best giver in the world. Moving up to Chardon town in 1953 she never had the chance for enough of that country-life getting into her, but more as a small-town girl she grew to counsel and guide hundreds of kids through public schooling and now showers us all with loads of love and gifts.

We left old Farmer Carroll, Merle, Grandpa Reynolds, all three remarkable teachers, Pearl and Dart, Mr. and Mrs. Warner, the glorious Fowlers Mills church choir, Preacher Kheenel, Grandpa Koblaha, Heine, and all the rest of those illustrious grown-ups just staying behind, building the future of Fowlers Mills. Of course, old Pinkie's coffin lies somewhere below a shiny, pink granite stone in the neighboring Fowlers Mills Cemetery. Pearl's finally up there right beside him now, the two of them looking pretty peaceful now. Have no idea where that rascal Dart went. Bruce and I revisited them recently in Fowlers Mills Cemetery while checking out resting places. Along with our close friend Ron, we paid our special respects and bid final good-byes to some of those older folks. The only time we stopped chattering the entire trip back.

Old Pinkie and Pearl together again.

The party line's finally stopped ringing. Thank God! I can still hear Maude and Fern, though! It's wireless now! Bruce and I thought that wireless thing was a good idea but of course we never got it accomplished. I'm not sure if it was just me, because I developed tinnitus in my right ear, but both ears still ring today with Hazel Rook's bottom-bouncing and rousing piano playing "In My Heart There Rings a Melody." Still have thoughts of Gladys's singing straight at me, but I can take it now! I hate to say it, but I think Mrs. Rook got poor old Jim so full of prunes and did him in with too many fruit pies.

A brand-new, fancy Munson Elementary School got built to perfect specifications at some point. It is zoned for homework, of course! New words have been created now, that Johnnie, Nancy, and Jackie might really appreciate—diagnostic labels such as Tourette's syndrome, dyslexia, and attention deficit hyperactivity disorder. I'm not sure the schooling's any better, but I'm sure those poor kids kept in there today still suffer some. Computers pretty well now tell the kids when to go, where to be, and what to do including when to go to the bathroom. Older teachers have to download their own personalized algorithms for their allotted bathroom breaks. Hey! If that keeps up, they may just have to close another school, and the kids can all stay home online! Now, there's what we call real homework!

The Grange Hall disappeared and with it, the cake walks. I haven't heard any of those types of walking words in a long time. There is a lot less shoving and fewer bruises that way. Fewer personal injury lawsuits, too! Do people even make cakes from scratch anymore? The farms around just faded, and the community house finally collapsed, just as the mothers club had accurately predicted. The Fowlers Mills Community Church now has an authentic, shiny, brass historic plaque in front with a whole flock of new, up-to-date faithfuls in the pews. Passing the collection plate and offerings have probably gone digital now. Those coins always were a security problem for sneaky fingers! Reynolds General Store has not one bit of goods for sale! Wet or dry! Instead, a small company for kitchen remodeling keeps the name complete with Merle's can-catching tweezers hanging enshrined on the wall. The Town Hall has been actually relocated by a monster flatbed truck to some historic village in nearby Burton Township. The Chardon Maple Festival's gone modern and put in some amusement rides to thrill the kids and that cheatin' guess-your-age guy is probably charging two bucks now. Don't know if the Rube Band wagon can even find Water Street now.

Old Fowlers Mills is fairly antiquie now, with an abundance of historic markers. However, none mark Kingfish, the Congo-Alaskan game site, nor the hayloft hiding that famous potato chip can. Our barn collapsed, but the old home has its very own Hiram Fowler historic plaque and is all remodeled up nicely. The old mill overshoot waterwheel caved in, and the millrace got filled up with dirt. No kids are trying to drown now, which also cuts down on frivolous lawsuits!

**Fowlers Mills historic marker for the aged
with long ago memories of the past.**

That mill will be working there forever!

Now this! From the mill, superb nutritious and wholesome organic, stone-ground baking flour and pancake mix with essential antioxidants and abundance of fiber are all available by catalog and website now, thanks to a very mindful and heritage-sensitive wonderful younger couple, Billie and Rick Erickson! But there's no more goat, pigeon, or cattle feed for sale. You have to eBay for that! Dresses arrive from Chicos, Macy's, overseas and other fashionable places now and no longer get pattern-cut out of those elegant calico feed bags. The old dirt road has been smoothly paved over with no rough patches, so every single kid is completely safe from harm, being diligently driven around now to each and every activity extensively highlighted on their refrigerator door schedules. The cemetery still has a plot or two available if you need one but no more old Chris Bogaski handing out the Memorial Day geraniums with customary flair. You have to provide your own now!

Farmer Carroll's fields have an assortment of modern houses artfully arranged about with distinctive porticos. Complete also with enormous flat wall TV's that kids with earphones can watch in solitude without the intrusive noise of any other children gathering. All the dwellings sport immaculately trimmed yards strictly off-limits now for manure spreaders—none of that stuff! His sugar bush and hill became the popular Alpine Valley Ski Resort, and the cow barn got all spruced up, becoming The Brown Barn, selling fancy furniture to the Cleveland suburbanites awhile. The cow's very own personal manure trough right behind 'em got all scrubbed up and cemented over with only a stanchion or two left behind for displaying a few fashionable scarves, artificial flowers, and skillfully crafted holiday wreathes. I'm sure by now, every one of our dear family of cows and those big Belgians are all resting peacefully somewhere!

Now, old Bruster's finally hit seventy-three but still not too old to cut the mustard. He still has me there by eight months, but I'm catching up. He finally got his driver's license, of course, when I was still only fifteen and let me drive on the Indiana Turnpike once while he fell asleep. Since it wasn't a tractor, I didn't know the difference between the clutch and brake, so I pressed both of 'em for a few rough stops. Old Bruster woke up asking are we there yet. Heck no! We're still going. Thank goodness they took the clutch away on most these cars, so it's only hitting the brake now. By the way, we never made it to the Buckeye Health Society in Akron. Went on to bigger things. Bruce bashed and bruised up some tough interior linemen at his Cathedral Latin School in Cleveland and then on to more football and study at the Naval Academy. He followed that by flying jets through the skies of Vietnam and then overseas milk runs, as he called 'em, with Delta Air Lines. He just felt better up in the air! He finally came back down, and now, as always, he's still making things, going from project to project, building kit planes and a few houses here and there, which almost get completed on occasion. He still asks the serious questions and checks 'em all out talkin' up a storm. If you got an extra hour or two he can tell you about twenty-five different kinds of cement and propellers as well as how to get geothermal and solar energy pumped up your bedpost. He's still the same but regards himself as a legitimate grown-up now. What a guy! Thank goodness he's still got those six gorgeous sisters, plus his great wife, Joyce, to keep him as well grounded as possible.

Curious Jack, everyone's favorite, got some big Cleveland business even busier and has given up digging in dirt piles but still does some serious play with grandkids and cars—big ones now! I just can't forget what a fun and exciting guy he was. He was so smart and so kind that he knew exactly how to distract that teacher's attention so the rest of us could get into more trouble totally unnoticed. What a great friend! Now he drives a grand old antique car, one every year in the local parade, with his dear wife Karen of fifty years at his side. Now, that fifty years' event right there is getting more rare these days. Grandkids can't keep up with Jack's energy, either. He still eats up loads of oxygen and totally dodged this later era of being thoroughly Ritalinized.

Good old Dickie went on to the by-and-by after quite a run at Wharton, followed by some heavy banking and other thoughtful charitable financial doings. This guy knew his numbers so well! I keep thinking about his slide rule. His dear wife Sue and his family and all of us really miss him. There wasn't much not to love about old Dickie! He was for real! Some other lucky guy got his cute little sister Janet.

Eddie's also greatly missed and looking down from a higher place after becoming a decorated marine in Vietnam. He was extremely proud of raising a couple of outstanding boys and being an avid salesman for about everything all over the Midwest. He never lost that amazing smile. What a guy!

It was kind of unusual for that '40s –'50s time and country place, but all five of us boys in our little class all went on to college. We actually behaved and sat still long enough to make it to the next grades. Although we all as individuals might have been a little quirky at times, that just shows you what can be done when you all pull strong together. Our little group must have seen the value! I'm not sure how many ahead or behind us did the college thing. I'm not keeping score anymore anyhow!

And Roberta's still gone! She's out there in Ohio somewhere! She left us for another number one! I'm sure glad Bruster and I didn't have to beat him up, too. It's kind of a relief now not having to remind ourselves who's number one, nor any other number, for that matter! I heard just like her mom, Roberta became a fine nurse. But she was never one for Bruster, Eddie, or me, doggone it! I heard her little brother David got all muscled up and stretched out to eventually becoming one of the first picks in choosing up sides for sports. I hear he became a psychologist at one of those Ivies.

And Ruth Ann got rid of her last cootie in the seventh grade and blossomed so beautifully and perfectly built. It wasn't necessary for her to hang around high school 'til the end to marry a standout upperclassman and raise a nice family.

And Johnnie may still be cussing up a storm, lucky bum! State law didn't force the Amish to go on to high school. The law sure was on that boy's side! I saw him last in the summer of 1957 behind the Geauga County Fair cow barn, smoking a big old fat cigar and happily beaming away. I think he forgave old Bruster and me for washing his mouth out and was surely aware we were just dutifully doing our job back then of protecting our school! Being yanked over to Amish never sounded bad to me, but I'm sure the bishop would take note of my hair being a little thin now for a good Amish bowl cut.

Well, that comes down to me. I never joined 4-H again but still crave ice cream and candy bars whenever I can sneak 'em. I went on to join my dad and sister Sue at Chardon High School. Dad liked school so much, he became principal there, and I became "the principal's son." Wasn't bad at all, but the girls liked him better than me. I'd frequent the office every now and then just to check on him and make sure he was doing his job. Never took a book home but managed to get that homework done in nineth-period study hall, ducking spitballs. Still have no idea who thought up that homework notion. Then I went over the Alleghenies East to little Amherst College, which most of my teachers had never heard of, to fulfill their admissions need for diversity. They were looking for one or two Midwest, rural and public-school types back then.

Now, that college thing was another mistake. But that's how you learn. With all my mistakes, I should have been brilliant and gotten my quota filled up back in Fowlers Mills. Anyhow! That poor old muskrat we trapped felt less skinned than I did that first semester. Mistakenly I thought a blue book was something you were supposed to read, not full of blank pages. I was accustomed to checking true or false or multiple choice for exams, not writing actual sentences. Thought it was going to be a comfy collection of professors and their students sitting around in friendly and engaging discussions in that little fairest college on the hill. Sure! You bet! And to top it all off, just all guys there. No girls at all yet! What kind of place was this! Tommy S. had it better in his army bootcamp than mine! Times have mercifully changed and a woman is now president of the college.

But then I moved on to Ohio's own and only medical school back then. I couldn't turn down that home state $800 state semester tuition deal; I was still thrifty and counting coins, harking back to my thrifty Sunday school days. Med school put that cramming and memorizing chunk of my brain clunking to work in a much different kind of gear. But hey, at least four women were in the class there! We were making some progress! However I seemed to enjoy reading people more than anatomy books and muscle insertions, so I told the good Dean Williams I'd rather memorize spots on the wall than all these bones and muscles and might be in the wrong trade school. Needless to say, I really didn't get to know my cadaver very well either. Well! Then I went off to India, as Mom used to say, "to think about it". My Indian friends there were so kind to me, but I came back, finished up and went on to working psychiatry. Getting retreaded a little bit, but not retired yet. In fact I recently puffed up my resume with a Costco membership in good standing. I still really enjoy walking and talking with so many good folks in some busy inner city clinics today. It may sound like a peculiar fit for a guy who was thinking about being a farmer, or at least a country doctor-type and who was now married to a real New York City girl. But in the clinics those good folks sure inspire me, I'll tell you! They are a whole lot of really sharp, good-hearted, brave people, dealing with a whole lot through no fault of their own, not many breaks to start with, and only a few bucks to spare now. I'm still not so patient myself, though, but I'm working on it.

I have this great family group surrounding me, a wonderful psychologist wife Gail who fights tough and truthful for kids stuck in custody battles and four kids, all a little weird, healthily skeptical, and a bit irreverent but with the biggest hearts. They teach me more than I'll ever know! I have five exceptional and fun grandkids, to boot! I'm also hanging on to some great friends, but I'm always on the lookout for more.

Well! That hilly Fowlers Mills Road's all perfectly paved now, nice and smooth, and even has an official county route number now, but it still keeps on rolling up and down. And thank goodness I'm still on it, back home again, just taking all the back roads!

There are all the good old Munson boys: Jack, Bruce, Eddie, and me in the eighth grade, except Dickie, whose mom wouldn't let him go. That germ thing again. We're all dressed up for our eighth-grade bus trip to Greenfield Village. Proof we actually survived junior high.

That's really older Bruster and me now,
years later. Haven't changed a bit!

That's actually our old fifth and sixth grade Munson
Town Hall School, now relocated by flatbed to the Burton
Historical Village for fabulous tourist viewing.

**Our school and church, side by side, but they hauled
the Town Hall School all the way to Burton.**

**The Fowlers Mills Community Church and old
Reynolds Store across the Mayfield Road.**

Our Fowlers Mills house today, all dressed up.
See the historic plaque on the left.

Old Reynolds Store and a little bit of Farmer Carroll's
barn and that snazzy ski resort, Alpine Valley, on his old
hillside pasture. His big white house burned down. Someone
forgot how to play with matches the right way.

That's the old mill dressed up a bit. Hitching post still right there ready to be climbed again. Porch fell off and waterwheel caved in.

Rush hour in modern Chardon Main Street. That traffic jam is uptown modern progress, all right!

That's my last bit of Tomfoolery right there with grandson Gabe cheering me on while snapping that shot. No more showing off for me! Of course, see how extra careful I am teaching him how to keep perfect balance by holding both arms straight out to the side. No more of this free spirited, no hands hitching post jumping for me. Playing it straight from here on out!

Old Munson original Troop 91: Ronnie, Jack, Eddie, me way in back, Bruce, Roger, Dick, and Billy. In strict Boy Scout formation, left to right there.

My goodness! That's one last shot of those of those good old Munson boys again. Some of 'em were still showing off and and should be ashamed at their age. Way back in 1953 we started our own Munson Troop 91 before heading up to the big consolidated Chardon Jr. High. Just to keep us no nonsense Munson boys all together. This picture came about five years ago at a reunion with our old scoutmaster and marching driller Roger Emmons. And everybody still had hair.

Of course, with our usual Munson generosity, we had invited Ronnie Hamilton on the left, but really one of those uptown Chardon grade schoolers, to join up with us because he was living smack on the edge of the township line. Now that boy and his dad Olie fit in like charms and brought a little civility to the group. Of course, you got old Bruster, front and center there, throwing out that right shoulder showing off while they got me all stuck off by my lonesome self in the back row. Bruster, you gotta shape up if it's not too late! I mean look at what a perfect gentleman that Jackie is standing up real still, straight and tall, second from left. He's still as exciting and curious as ever despite his head having shrunk a little now compared to the rest of him. And Eddie third from left still has that famous grin even though he's covering up a little bit with that mustache. He stayed a lefty all the way, but don't tell him. And would you believe it? Dickie second from right got all rebellious and hippie like growing a beard on us, maybe though just to cover up that bouncing adam's apple. Classy 'til the end! Hair still combed just right. And then you got that two year older Billy on the far right where I think he still is. Always the calmer and wiser upperclassman and still every girl's heartthrob. Then you see old solid scoutmaster Rog hanging in there who had one full solid and generous life sticking fast to what he always believed.

So now you know 'em all again! Had to let you see 'em one more time! Better to see 'em up close than write 'em up. Well now! Mom say's I'm all done with this job now and can stop. So that's it! See you around!

Made in the USA
Middletown, DE
08 June 2016